English Convers

DESCRIBING ENGLISH LANGUAGE

SERIES EDITORS
John Sinclair · Ronald Carter

English Conversation

Amy B. M. Tsui

Oxford University Press 1994

Oxford University Press
Walton Street, Oxford OX2 6DP

Oxford New York Toronto
Delhi Bombay Calcutta Madras Karachi
Petaling Jaya Singapore Hong Kong Tokyo
Nairobi Dar es Salaam Cape Town
Melbourne Auckland

and associated companies in Berlin Ibadan

Oxford English and the *Oxford English* logo are trade marks of Oxford University Press

ISBN 0 19 437143 3

© Amy B. M. Tsui 1994

Typeset by Wyvern Typesetting Ltd, Bristol
Printed in Hong Hong

In memory of my father, Tsui Wai Ning,
and my mother, Wong Sau Ping.

Contents

PART THREE
Characterization of discourse acts: initiating acts

4 Elicitations

Contents

PART FOUR
Characterization of discourse acts: neglected aspects

8 Responses

9 Follow-up acts

PART FIVE
Further aspects of conversational description

10 Conversational processes and patterning

I CONVERSATIONAL PROCESSES

II CONVERSATIONAL PATTERNING

Acknowledgements

I owe my deepest gratitude to my mentor and friend, John Sinclair, who introduced me to discourse analysis and helped me to understand language. If not for his guidance and encouragement, this book would not have materialized. I thank him for being very critical and demanding and yet very caring and supportive.

I also owe a deep gratitude to Ron Carter who patiently went over the various drafts of this manuscript and has been most understanding and supportive. I wish to thank him for his kindness and for his professionalism in editing this volume.

To Malcolm Coulthard I am immensely grateful for his interest in my work and for being very generous with his time. He was a constant source of inspiration when I was formulating the theoretical framework and helped me sharpen my questions with his astute observations of conversational data. To David Brazil I wish to express a deep appreciation for helping me to come to grips with discourse intonation.

Several friends and colleagues have read the various drafts of the manuscript, particularly the first few chapters, and have helped to set the tone of the book. They have given me very useful comments and suggestions to make it more readable and the arguments more watertight. I wish to thank Desmond Allison and Arthur McNeill for going through the first two chapters. I wish to thank Graham Lock not only for reading the drafts I produced but also for spending hours on the telephone debating one piece of discourse data with me, even on Sundays.

My husband, Chi Kin, has been an unfailing source of support and encouragement, especially in times of difficulty and frustration. I wish to thank him for his love, his insights, and for helping me see things in perspective.

I would also like to thank the English Department at the University of Birmingham for allowing me to use the Birmingham Collection of English Texts, held at Cobuild at the University of Birmingham.

Finally, I wish to dedicate this book to the memory of my father, Tsui Wai Ning, and my mother, Wong Sau Ping, who both died while I was still writing it. I thank them for working very hard to give me a good education and for standing behind me whenever I needed them.

The author and publishers would like to thank the following for permission to reproduce material that falls within their copyright:

Acknowledgements

Routledge for extracts from 'A functional description of questions' by Amy B. M. Tsui, in *Advances in Spoken Discourse Analysis* (1992) edited by M. Coulthard.

Cambridge University Press for extracts from 'Beyond the adjacency pair' by Amy B. M. Tsui, in *Language in Society* 18/4 (1989).

Every effort has been made to trace the owners of copyright material in this book, but we should be pleased to hear from any copyright holder whom we have been unable to contact.

The author
and series editors

Dr. Amy B. M. Tsui is a Senior Lecturer in the Department of Curriculum Studies at the University of Hong Kong. She obtained her first and second degrees at the University of Hong Kong, and her doctorate in linguistics at the University of Birmingham. She has taught at the Chinese University of Hong Kong, the Hong Kong Polytechnic, the National University of Singapore, and as a visiting lecturer at the University of Birmingham. Her research and publications cover conversation analysis, classroom discourse analysis, speech act theory, systemic linguistics, pragmatics, and language teacher education.

John Sinclair has been Professor of Modern English Language at the University of Birmingham since 1965. His main areas of research are discourse (both spoken and written) and computational linguistics—with particular emphasis on the study of very long texts. He has been consultant/adviser to a number of groups, including, among others, the Bullock Committee, The British Council, and the National Congress for Languages in Education. He holds the title of Adjunct Professor in Jiao Tong University, Shanghai. Professor Sinclair has published extensively, and is currently Editor-in-Chief of the Cobuild project at Birmingham University.

Ronald Carter is Professor of Modern English Language in the Department of English Studies at the University of Nottingham where he has taught since 1979. He is Chairman of the Poetics and Linguistics Association of Great Britain, a member of CNAA panels for Humanities, and a member of the Literature Advisory Committee of The British Council. Dr Carter has published widely in the areas of language and education, applied linguistics, and literary linguistics. He is Director of the Centre for English Language Education at the University of Nottingham and from 1989 to 1992 was National Co-ordinator for Language in the National Curriculum.

Foreword

Describing English Language

The Describing English Language series provides much-needed descriptions of modern English. Analysis of extended naturally-occurring texts, spoken and written, and, in particular, computer processing of texts have revealed quite unsuspected patterns of language. Traditional descriptive frameworks are normally not able to account for or accommodate such phenomena, and new approaches are required. This series aims to meet the challenge of describing linguistic features as they are encountered in real contexts of use in extended stretches of discourse. Accordingly, and taking the revelations of recent research into account, each book in the series will make appropriate reference to corpora of naturally-occurring data.

The series will cover most areas of the continuum between theoretical and applied linguistics, converging around the mid-point suggested by the term 'descriptive'. In this way, we believe the series can be of maximum potential usefulness.

One principal aim of the series is to exploit the relevance to teaching of an increased emphasis on the description of naturally-occurring stretches of language. To this end, the books are illustrated with frequent references to examples of language use. Contributors to the series will consider both the substantial changes taking place in our understanding of the English language and the inevitable effect of such changes upon syllabus specifications, design of materials, and choice of method.

John Sinclair, *University of Birmingham*
Ronald Carter, *University of Nottingham*

English Conversation

In this book Amy Tsui subjects patterns of conversational interaction to detailed scrutiny. Using authentic, naturally-occurring data as a source for examples, she offers refinements and extensions to well-developed descriptive frameworks for the analysis of conversational data, and establishes in the process important new insights into the sequencing of patterns of interaction. Dr Tsui is distrustful of traditions in the analysis of conversation which prioritize the negotiable, interpreted, and participant-centred nature of events; instead she is deeply committed to a view of conversation as rule-governed and specifiable. Her study presents a range of carefully-formulated arguments and a wider range still of replicable analyses in support of this view of conversation. It is to her credit that the analyses she provides are sufficiently explicit to encourage further refinement and development in an area of vital importance to the description of longer stretches of text, the teaching of the spoken language, and to linguistic understanding in general.

Ronald Carter

Transcription notations

Data with a label beginning with [B] are telephone conversations and those with a label beginning with [C] are face-to-face conversations. [BCET] stands for Birmingham Collection of English Texts, and the data from this corpus used here consists of face-to-face conversations. [Fieldnotes] consist of conversations which are taken down verbatim after occurrence and texts which are taken from real-life communication such as letters, advertisements, notices, etc. [I] stands for invented data. (Other abbreviations within the square brackets are references to location of the data, and may be ignored by the reader.)

Where the data is taken from published studies, the original notations are retained. Where the data is my own, the following notations are used:

[	Overlapping utterances.
=	A single speaker's utterance which is a continuous flow of speech but has been separated graphically in order to accommodate intervening interruption; or A second utterance being latched immediately to the first utterance with no overlap.
–	Short untimed pause within an utterance.
((*pause*))	Long untimed pause within an utterance.
((*2 sec*))	Timed pause. Pauses are timed only when they illustrate a certain point made.
(( ))	Description of non-verbal elements in the conversation, e.g. ((*laugh*)), ((*knock*)).
(NV)	Non-verbal action.
( )	Doubtful transcription or indecipherable part of the conversation.
capitals	Prominence, e.g. I have THIRty at one point.
...	Intervening utterances which have been taken out.
// //	Tone unit boundary.
p	Proclaiming tone.

r+/r	Referring tone.
Ø	Oblique orientation (i.e. a level or neutral tone).
<u>YES</u>	Capitals underlined: tonic syllable.
$\frac{\underline{YES}}{// \quad //}$	High key.
//<u>YES</u>//	Mid key.
$\frac{// \quad //}{\underline{YES}}$	Low key.
bc	Back-channel cues.
< >	Interpolated utterance.
{ }	Attempted utterance: an utterance which was started but abandoned because of interruption or overlap.

PART ONE
Overview

1
Overview

1.1 Introduction

The bulk of the work on analysing conversation has been carried out by sociologists and anthropologists who are interested in the social and cultural aspects of conversation. Their studies of conversational data have focused largely on how conversation is socially organized and managed by participants, and how participants are observed to do this. The term Conversation Analysis has been coined to describe this area of study.

The concern of this book is distinct from the concerns of Conversation Analysis, although it shares the same object of study — conversation. This study focuses on the linguistic aspects of conversation. This necessarily involves the study of the use of language in communication and the relations between linguistic features and contexts of situation. To some linguists, this kind of study belongs more properly to the realm of pragmatics (see Levinson 1983 for various definitions of pragmatics). However, it is difficult to see how any useful study of language can be conducted independent of context and use. This is why I consider this study a 'linguistic description'.

Lee (1987), in expounding the differences between linguistic approaches to conversation and Conversation Analysis, maintains that linguists often work with a priori theories and conversational data is used to confirm a theory or a model. In this volume, although linguistic concepts and models are borrowed in setting up a descriptive framework for conversation, the aim is not so much to confirm a theory or model but rather to facilitate the formalization of observations of regularities exhibited. The setting up of this framework is a two-way process in which linguistic concepts and models, which provide the theoretical motivation for the framework, are tested out by data, and data, in turn, provides the insights and bases for revision of the framework.

3

1.2 Questions addressed

The following piece of data is the beginning of a conversation between two colleagues, J and S. J goes to S's office to ask if she can borrow a stamp from her:

(1) [C:2:A:2]

J and S are colleagues. J knocks on S's office door.

    1   J: ((knock))
    2   S: Come in.
    3   J: ((knock))
    4   S: Come in.
    5   J: ((enters))
→   6   J: I didn't come in because it was so noisy
→   7   I couldn't hear if anyone said come in.
→   8   I just wanted to ask you if you happen to
→   9   have one more stamp, do you by any chance.
    10 S: I might, yeah. ((looks for stamps in drawer))
                                    [
    11 J: 'cos I'm totally unorganized and
    12   have
→   13 S: I have a one-thirty and I have thirties.
→   14   ((pause)) Okay, you can have a choice.
→   15   You can either have – three thirties – or =
                                          [
    16 J: uhuh
→   17 S: = you can have a one-thirty.
    18 J: Three thirties is fine.

In making a linguistic description of conversational data like (1), the questions that this book addresses are as follows.

Firstly, what exactly do we mean when we identify utterances as performing a certain kind of act? What criteria do we use in identifying them? For example, in line 8, when J says 'I just wanted to *ask* you if you happen to have one more stamp, do you by any chance', is she 'asking a question'? Is she 'making a request'? Or is she doing both at the same time? Similarly, in lines 14–17, when S says 'Okay, you can have a choice. You can either have – three thirties – or you can have a one-thirty', is she 'giving J a piece of information'? Is she 'offering' J a choice of stamps? Or is she doing both at the same time?

Secondly, how do we analyse conversational data in terms of meaningful chunks? That is, how do we decide what the units of conversational interaction are? For example, how do we decide how many units of interaction there are in J's entire stretch of talk in lines 6–9, and S's entire stretch of talk in lines 13–17?

Thirdly, what are the patterns of conversational organization? In lines 6 and 7, J explains why she did not go in the first time she knocked. In other words, if J had heard S's response to her first knock, she would have responded by entering, as she did the second time she knocked. This suggests that there are certain patterns of conversational organization: a knock on the door expects a response which, in turn, expects a further response. How do we describe these patterns?

Fourthly, are there any constraints governing the possible ways in which a conversation can develop? For example, if J had heard S's first response, then the course of the conversation would have been different. J would not have had to knock again and S would not have had to invite J to come in for the second time, and J, in turn, would not have had to explain why she did not go in the first time she knocked, and so on. In other words, how a conversation develops depends on the interlocutors. What one speaker says at any point in the conversation process affects what other speakers can or will say. What starts off as a friendly conversation can inadvertently turn into an acrimonious argument. Does this mean that a conversation can go in any direction, or are there, in fact, constraints operating?

To summarize, there are four areas of linguistic description of conversation that this volume deals with:

1 criteria for characterizing functions of conversational utterances;
2 descriptive units of conversational interaction;
3 the structure of conversation; and
4 conversational processes.

1.3 Data

The investigation into the above four areas is based on a corpus of 'natural conversation'. The term 'natural conversation' refers to conversation which occurs spontaneously, without any planning or prompting beforehand: this is as opposed to conversational data which is intentionally solicited by the linguist, often with interlocutors being assigned roles, or conversational data which is produced by the linguist's intuition or as a result of the linguist's introspection.

The reasons for using data from 'natural conversation' are obvious. Firstly, role-play conversational data may appear to bear a strong resemblance to natural conversation, when, in fact, it does not. What we think we will say in a certain role under particular circumstances is often different from what we will actually say when we find ourselves in those circumstances. Secondly, as Stubbs (1983) points out, introspective data is often thought through for a long time with a particular theoretical problem in mind. Hence, it is not representative of the normal use of language (see also Heritage 1989: 21–47).

The corpus of conversational data used in this book was collected over three years. It comprises telephone and face-to-face conversations between mainly middle-class British and American academics working in universities, and British university undergraduates from working-class families. While a fair portion of the data represents the upper end of the polite-consensus scale, examples are also drawn from near the lower end of the scale.

1.4 Units of conversational description

1.4.1 Turn, pair, sequence

I would like to begin by addressing first the second question raised in section 1.2: what are the descriptive units of conversational interaction? This is because before we can make any descriptive statements about a piece of conversation, we need to decide how we are going to break it up into meaningful units. Important criteria in proposing descriptive categories in a linguistic description are that the labels that are used must be well-defined, explicitly relatable to data, and replicable (see Firth 1935; Sinclair and Coulthard 1975: 17).

The descriptive units that Conversation Analysts have been using in describing conversational organization are: *turn*, *pair*, and *sequence*. A *turn* is seen as everything one speaker says before another speaker begins to speak (see Sacks *et al.* 1974). A *pair* is made up of two turns made by two different speakers. It has been referred to as an *adjacency pair* (see Schegloff and Sacks 1973). For example, in (1), lines 6–9 form a turn taken by J, and line 10 is another turn taken by S. These two turns constitute an adjacency pair of 'request–compliance' or 'question–reply'. A *sequence* is made up of more than one turn. For example, a pair embedded inside another pair is labelled an *insertion sequence* (Schegloff 1972; see (2) below).

Turn and pair are well-defined in the sense that they are identifiable. However, they are not without difficulties. When we apply the descriptive unit turn to conversational data, we come across problems. In (1), lines 6–9 comprise one turn, but it is evident that J is not just doing one thing—making a request or asking a question. She is doing two things—explaining why she did not enter the first time she knocked and making a request for a stamp. Similarly, in lines 13–15 and line 17, which also comprise one turn, S is doing two things: she is answering J's question concerning whether she has any stamps and she is offering J a choice of stamps. In both cases, there are two units within one turn. As Goffman (1981: 23) points out:

> the talk during an entire turn can't be used [for a unit of analysis] ... for ... one of the main patterns for chaining rounds is the one in which whoever answers a question goes on from there to provide the next question in the series, thereby consolidating during one turn at talk two relevantly different doings.

While a considerable portion of most conversations are analysable in terms of pairs, there are certain contributing elements which are not part of a pair. For example, in (1), lines 3 to 5 constitute a bound interactional unit which is made up of three contributing elements. If we say that lines 3 and 4 constitute a pair, we will not be able to analyse line 5 which is clearly bound to line 4 and yet is not part of a pair. (For the concept of 'pair', see section 1.5.1 on 'adjacency pair', and a critique of this concept in Chapter 2, section 2.2.)

Sequence is the least well-defined descriptive unit. Sometimes a sequence is actually a pair, at other times it is made up of three or four turns. Schegloff's example of an insertion sequence is a pair:

(2) [Schegloff 1972: 107]

	Q1	**A:**	I don't know just where the – uh – this address//is
insertion	→Q2	**B:**	Well, where do – which part of the town do you live
sequence	→A2	**A:**	I live at four ten east Lowden
	A1	**B:**	Well you don't live very far from me.

However, Jefferson's (1972) proposal of a *side sequence* which she considers to be different from Schegloff's insertion sequence is made up of more than an adjacency pair; for example:

(3) [Jefferson 1972: 318]

	statement	**A:**	If Percy goes with – Nixon I'd sure like that
	misapprehension	**B:**	Who?
side	clarification	**A:**	Percy, that young fella that uh – his daughter was murdered
sequence		(1.0)	
	terminator	**A:**	Oh yea:h. Yeah.

Jefferson initially suggested that the side sequence in (3) which she labelled *misapprehension sequence* consisted of three turns, a 'statement', a 'misapprehension', and a 'clarification'. She later included the 'terminator' as a potential component of the sequence (1972: 317), resulting in a four-turn sequence. The fact that sequence is not well-defined and that it overlaps with pair undermines to a considerable extent its validity as a descriptive unit of conversational organization.

1.4.2 Act, move, exchange

Sinclair and Coulthard (1975) have proposed a descriptive framework for analysing spoken discourse, using classroom data as a starting point. They borrowed the concept of a rank scale from Halliday's (1961) descriptive units at the grammatical level, and suggest the following descriptive units: *act, move, exchange, transaction,* and *lesson.* These units are ordered in a hierarchical manner such that acts combine to form moves, moves combine to form exchanges, and so on.

In the description of conversation that I shall make subsequently, I have borrowed the descriptive units act, move, and exchange. Therefore, in the following, I shall first give an account of these three units in Sinclair and Coulthard's descriptive framework.

The best starting point is to look at a piece of classroom discourse data:

(4) [Sinclair and Coulthard 1975: 67]
   T: What does the next one mean? You don't often see that one around here. Miri.
   P: Danger falling rocks.
   T: Danger, falling rocks.

This is a typical classroom exchange. According to Sinclair and Coulthard, it is made up of three moves: an *initiating move* from the teacher, a *responding move* from the pupil, and a *follow-up move* from the teacher. A move is the smallest free unit of discourse and is made up of one or more than one act (ibid.: 23). The teacher's initiating move in (4) is made up of three acts: a question, 'What does the next one mean?'; a statement, 'You don't often see that one around here'; and a nomination, 'Miri.'. The responding and follow-up moves, however, are each made up of one act.

It should be noted that the concept of act as proposed by Sinclair and Coulthard is different from the concept of act proposed in Speech Act Theory (Austin 1962). In Speech Act Theory, an *act* refers to the action that is performed in making an utterance. Utterances are taken in isolation and the kind of speech act being performed is determined by considerations like the meaning conveyed by the words and the structures of utterances, the psychological conditions of the speaker, and so forth. No consideration is given to the discourse context in which the utterance occurs.

In Sinclair and Coulthard (1975), *act* is a unit in discourse, and it is characterized according to its function in the discourse. According to this view, '...the *discourse value* of an item depends on what linguistic items have preceded it, what are expected to follow, and what do follow' (ibid.: 34). In (4), the discourse function of the first act, commonly referred to as a question, is to elicit an answer from the pupils. It is therefore characterized as an *elicitation*. The second and the third ones are auxiliary acts in the sense that they help to solicit an answer to the elicitation. The second one, commonly referred to as a statement, is characterized as a *clue*. The third one, which gives permission to pupils to answer the elicitation, is characterized as a *nominate*. In other words, the acts are characterized in terms of how they are related to each other in the discourse rather than the kind of function they are independently used to perform.[1] (The importance of discourse context in determining what act is performed will be discussed in section 1.6.1.) In order to avoid confusion with speech acts, they will be referred to as *discourse acts* hereafter.

As far as the conversational data in (4) is concerned, it appears that a move is no different from a turn, and that it is equally valid to say that a typical classroom exchange is made up of three turns. However, the difference becomes immediately apparent when we consider the following piece of data:

(5) [Sinclair and Coulthard 1975: 21]
Teacher: Can you tell me why do you eat all that food? Yes.
Pupil: To keep you strong.
Teacher: To keep you strong. Yes. To keep you strong.
→ Why do you want to be strong?

There are three turns (or in Sinclair and Coulthard's terms *utterances*[2]) in (5), but there is more than one exchange. When the teacher says 'Why do you want to be strong?', he is clearly starting another exchange. In other words, within the same turn made by one speaker, there can be two moves. In fact, it is in handling data such as (5) that Sinclair and Coulthard decided to abandon 'utterance' as a descriptive unit and proposed the unit *move*. The teacher's second turn therefore consists of two moves: a follow-up move which provides feedback to the pupil's answer, and an initiating move which solicits an answer from the pupil.

Similarly, in (1), the accomplishment of two things within the same turn by J in lines 6–9, and by S in lines 13–15 and line 17, can be captured by describing them as consisting of two moves.

10

1.5 Conversational organization

1.5.1 Adjacency pair

We pointed out in section 1.2 that the conversation in (1) proceeds in an organized manner. An utterance made by one speaker is responded to by another utterance from another speaker. And when the expected response is not forthcoming, interlocutors often give an account of why it is not forthcoming. This kind of conversational organization is clearly captured by Schegloff and Sacks's concept of *adjacency pair*. They point out that an organizational pattern recurrent in conversation is that of two adjacent utterances, which are produced by different speakers, and are related to each other in such a way that they form a *pair type*. They call them an *adjacency pair*. 'Question–answer', 'greeting–greeting', and 'offer–acceptance/refusal' are some examples of adjacency pairs. Their basic rule of operation is:

> Given the recognizable production of a first pair part, on its first possible completion its speaker should stop and a next speaker should start and produce a second pair part from the pair type of which the first is recognizably a member. (Schegloff and Sacks 1973: 296)

Hence, according to Schegloff and Sacks, utterances are related to form pair types so that a particular *first pair part* sets up the expectation of a particular *second pair part*. For example, a 'question' expects a 'reply' and they form a pair type; an 'offer' expects an 'accept' or a 'decline', and each of the latter forms a pair type with the former. So strong is this expectation that if the second pair part does not occur, its absence will be noticeable and noticed by participants. Sacks (1972) provides the following example:

(6) [Sacks 1972: 341]

	1	WOMAN:	Hi.
	2	BOY:	Hi.
	3	WOMAN:	Hi, Annie.
→	4	MOTHER:	Annie, don't you hear someone say hello to you?
	5	WOMAN:	Oh, that's okay, she smiled hello.
→	6	MOTHER:	You know you're supposed to greet someone, don't you?
	7	ANNIE:	[*hangs head*] Hello.

11

The 'greeting' from the woman in line 3 sets up the expectation of a 'return greeting' from Annie. When the latter does not occur, its absence is 'noticed' by her mother (see lines 4 and 6). The necessity of a 'return-greeting' from Annie is further confirmed by the woman's saying 'Oh, that's okay, she smiled hello.' (see line 5), and by Annie's concession to return the 'greeting' in line 7 (see also Schegloff 1968: 1083).

While the adjacency pair accounts, to a considerable extent, for the orderly fashion in which conversation proceeds, it is not without problems. In (1), lines 1 and 2, J's knocking on the door and S's granting permission for J to enter constitutes an adjacency pair in the sense that one sets up the expectation of another. But it is obvious that following S's invitation to enter, a further response is expected. This is why, in lines 6 and 7, J has to explain why she did not enter the first time she knocked. This is further confirmed by the fact that lines 3–5, which constitute a bound interactional unit, comprise three parts and not two.

1.5.2 Three-part exchange

In section 1.4.1, we mentioned that, according to Sinclair and Coulthard, a typical classroom exchange is made up of three moves: an initiating move, a responding move, and a follow-up move. In formalizing their observation of the pattern exhibited in an exchange, they have borrowed the concept of *structure* from Halliday (1961) which accounts for similar patterns between one stretch of language and another. They propose that a typical exchange has three *elements of structure*: an *initiation*, a *response*, and a *follow-up*. An exchange which consists of two parts, or two elements of structure, is perceived as the 'marked form' in which the third part is withheld for strategic reasons. An example would be when a student gives the wrong answer and the teacher withholds the evaluation and goes on to provide clues in order to help the student reach the right answer.

The concept of exchange structure, similar to the concept of adjacency pair, captures the relationship between utterances in which one component sets up the expectation for another. It differs from an adjacency pair in that it proposes that a unit of interaction consists of three parts rather than two. This proposal has been criticized as classroom-specific and of little generalizability. Discourse analysts who have examined exchange structure in non-classroom discourse suggest that exchanges in social discourse typically consist of two parts (see, for example, Burton 1980; Stubbs 1981). This criticism has an immediate appeal because providing an evaluative third part is characteristic only of classroom exchanges. We do not go around evaluating other people's responses—not if we want to keep friends. Whether this criticism is valid, however, depends on whether three-part exchanges are only peculiar to classroom discourse and whether providing an evaluation is the *only* function of the third part of an exchange, the follow-up move. In Chapter 2, we shall examine in detail the question of whether conversation is basically organized in terms of three-part exchanges or two-part adjacency pairs.

1.5.3 Move structure

In section 1.4.2, we saw that a move can be made up of more than one act. According to Sinclair and Coulthard (1975), when a move consists of more than one act, then one of the acts is the main act (which they call *head act*) which carries the discourse function of the entire move. It is obligatory. The rest are auxiliary or subsidiary acts (which they call *pre-head act* if they precede the head act, or *post-head act* if they follow the head act). They are optional.[3]

Hence, the first move in (3), 'What does the next one mean? You don't often see that one around here. Miri.', has a structure of a head act, which is an elicitation, followed by two post-head acts, a clue, and a nominate. 'What does the next one mean?' is obligatory in the sense that the discourse function of the entire move is to get the pupil to provide an answer to this question. 'You don't often see that one around here.' and 'Miri' are optional in the sense that even if they are not produced, the function of the move would still be the same. By contrast, if the teacher had said 'You don't often see that one around here. Miri.', then the discourse function of the entire move would no longer be an elicitation but an informative.

Let us apply Sinclair and Coulthard's concept of move structure to the following conversational utterance which is directed by A to a visitor (B) at his home:

(7) [I] **A:** Why are you standing? Do sit down.

There are two acts here. Taken independently, one is a question realized by 'Why are you standing?', and the other is an invitation to sit down realized by 'Do sit down.'. But our knowledge of conversation tells us that the discourse function of this move is an invitation to sit down and the visitor's response to the invitation is obligatory. Consider the following response to A's utterance:

(8) [I]
    A: Why are you standing? Do sit down.
    B: Thanks. (*sits down*)

In (8), B's response will be interpreted as accepting the invitation to sit down. A cannot and will not challenge B for not responding to his question. If, however, instead of sitting down, B says, 'Well, I've been sitting all day.', B's response will not be interpreted as only an answer to the question, but rather a declination of the invitation. A will not challenge B for having only responded to the question but not the invitation.

This is strong evidence that in these two acts, 'Do sit down' is a head act which is obligatory, and the question 'Why are you standing?' is an optional pre-head act.[4]

Let us now try to apply move structure to the conversational data in (1). Consider the move in lines 14–17: 'Okay, you can have a choice. You can either have – three thirties – or you can have a one-thirty.'. The discourse function of this move is to offer J a choice of two kinds of stamps. 'Okay' marks the beginning of another move. It is therefore a pre-head act. Sinclair and Coulthard call this class of act a *marker*. 'You can have a choice' on its own can be an act of offering. But when it is followed by 'You can either have – three thirties – or you can have a one-thirty.' which elaborates on the offer, then it becomes a pre-head act (which Sinclair and Coulthard call a *starter*) whose function is to direct J's attention to the choice that she is going to be offered. In other words, the obligatory head act is an offer, to which J is expected to respond, and the marker and starter are optional pre-head acts.

In the description of discourse acts to be presented in subsequent chapters, I shall be focusing on the head acts of moves.

1.6 Characterization of conversational utterances

1.6.1 Structural location

In examining the conversation data in (1), we raised the question of what criteria we use in characterizing the function of an utterance and how we define the labels 'making a request', 'asking a question', 'making an offer', and so on.

One of the criteria that Sinclair and Coulthard (1975) use in identifying the discourse acts to account for all the utterances in their data is where they occur in the exchange structure. They write:

> It is place in the structure of the discourse which finally determines which act a particular grammatical item is realizing. (ibid.: 29)

Hence, in characterizing an utterance as performing a certain act, the questions that they ask are 'whether it is intended to evoke a response, whether it is a response itself, whether it is intended to mark a boundary in the discourse, and so on' (ibid.: 14). An elicitation is intended to solicit a response and it occurs at the head of the initiating move. This distinguishes it from a reply which is a response and occurs at the head of a responding move.

That structural location is an important criterion in the identification of discourse acts can be best seen in linguistic items whose communicative value depends entirely on where they are placed in the discourse. A classic example is an 'answer' to a 'question'. Take B's utterance in (9) and X's utterance in (10), for example:

(9) [I]
       A: What's the time?
→ **B:** It's nearly three.

(10) [I]
→ **X:** It's nearly three.
       Y: Oh my God!

They have identical linguistic forms. Yet their structural locations are different. While B's utterance occurs in the responding move, X's utterance occurs in the initiating move. They are therefore two different acts although they both tell the time. We may differentiate them by labelling the former a *reply* to an elicitation and the latter an *informative*.

The importance of structural location in determining the functions of conversational utterances has also been observed by Conversation Analysts. Schegloff and Sacks (1973) point out that the status of an utterance as an answer can only be derived from the fact that it occurs after a question. They write:

> there do not seem to be criteria other than placement (i.e., sequential) ones that will sufficiently discriminate the status of an utterance as a statement, assertion, declarative, proposition, etc., from its status as an answer. Finding an utterance to be an answer, to be accomplishing answering, cannot be achieved by reference to phonological, syntactic, semantic, or logical features of the utterance itself, but only by consulting its sequential placement, e.g., its placement after a question.
> (Schegloff and Sacks 1973: 299)

The importance of this criterion can also be seen from utterances which have been referred to as 'pre-closing' initiations by Schegloff and Sacks (ibid.). In looking at the unit 'a single conversation', Schegloff and Sacks observe that a conversation does not simply end; interlocutors do not just stop talking. They have to bring the conversation to a close. Therefore, preceding the 'closing section' of a conversation which typically consists of pairs like 'Goodbye – goodbye', 'See you – see you', and so on, there are utterances which signal the speaker's intention to bring the conversation to a close. They call such utterances 'pre-closing' initiations. It is this structural organization which assigns meaning to the arrowed utterances in the following piece of data:

(11) [Schegloff and Sacks 1973: 313]
B has called to invite C, but has been told C is going out to dinner.

pre-closing section
→ B: Yeah. Well get on your clothes and get out and collect some of that free food and we'll make it some other time Judy then.
→ C: Okay then Jack.

closing section
B: Bye bye.
C: Bye bye.

16

Schegloff and Sacks point out that the function of B's utterance (arrowed) is not to command C despite its imperative form, but rather to signal his intention to close the conversation; and C's 'Okay' is not an agreement to a command to get dressed, but rather an agreement to an invitation to close the conversation. They write:

> no analysis—grammatical, semantic, pragmatic, etc.—of these utterances taken singly and out of sequence, will yield their import in use, will show what co-participants might make of them and do about them. That B's utterance here accomplishes a form of closing initiation and C's accepts the closing form and not what seems to be proposed in it, turns on the placement of these utterances in the conversation. Investigations which fail to attend to such considerations are bound to be misled. (ibid.: 313)

From the above observations made by Sinclair and Coulthard and by Conversation Analysts, we can see that structural location is a very important criterion in utterance characterization (see also Schegloff 1988: 61).

1.6.2 Prospective classification

To make a finer classification of discourse acts which have the same structural location, Sinclair and Coulthard propose the concept of 'continuous classification' and assert that 'the meaning of an utterance is its predictive assessment of what follows' (Sinclair and Coulthard 1975: 12). In other words, utterances occurring in the same move are characterized according to the kind of response they expect. For example, in the initiating move, an utterance which expects a linguistic response of supplying a piece of information is characterized as an elicitation, one that expects a non-linguistic response is characterized as a directive, and one that expects a linguistic response of acknowledgement is characterized as an informative.[5]

1.6.3 Retrospective classification

Conversation is a co-operative achievement between at least two participants. One produces an initiating utterance with the intention of soliciting a particular response from the other. However, whether it will indeed succeed in getting the expected response depends on the other participant who can deliberately or unwittingly produce an unexpected response. When this happens, the *discourse value* of the initiating utterance may not be the same as intended by its speaker. Let us take the following example:

(12) [Labov and Fanshel (1977: 75)]
     A: Would you mind taking the dust rag and dust around?
     B: No. (*does not move*)

A's utterance is intended to be a request which prospects a non-verbal action from B of dusting the room. However, it is reclassified (in this case deliberately) as an elicitation by B which prospects only a verbal response.

This kind of reclassification is retrospective in focus and is often used as a conversational strategy or as a means of generating 'conversational implicature' (see Grice 1975). For example:

(13) [B:D:B:1:1]
     M has a bad cold and H could not recognize her voice.

     H: You sound terrible, you sound like a man.
→   M: Thank you.

H's comment on M's voice is clearly not complimentary at all. However, M, by saying 'Thank you.' which is commonly used to respond to a compliment, is reclassifying H's comment as a compliment, hence generating sarcasm.

Retrospective classification is therefore another important dimension in utterance characterization.

In the description of discourse acts in conversation presented in subsequent chapters, I shall be using the criteria of structural location and prospective classification. I shall also bring in the dimension of retrospective reclassification in determining the discourse value of an utterance.

1.7 Conversational processes

In section 1.5, we looked at the structural organization of conversation in terms of what is expected to occur. However, the fact that an initiating move sets up the expectation of a responding move does not mean that the former will always be followed by the latter. As

I pointed out in the previous section, conversation is a co-operative achievement of at least two participants. There is no way in which one speaker can put an absolute constraint on what the next speaker will say (see Coulthard and Brazil 1981). This does not mean, however, that one utterance can be followed by any other utterance in conversation. As Firth (1935: 31) points out:

> The moment a conversation is started, whatever is said is a determining condition for what, in any reasonable expectation, may follow. What you say raises the threshold against most of the language of your companion, and leaves only a limited opening for a certain likely range of responses.

At any one point in the discourse, there are only a limited number of choices available to the next speaker *if the discourse is to remain coherent*. The concept of *system* proposed by Halliday (1961) in accounting for grammatical choices is helpful in describing the choices that are available to speakers as the conversation unfolds.

According to Halliday, a system is a set of choices that are available in a given environment (see Halliday 1963: 5, 1984: 9). To better understand the concept of system, let us draw an analogy with systems in grammar. In grammar, present tense, past tense, and future tense form a system of tenses. This means that when we talk about an event, we can choose to mean the event already happened (by using past tense), to mean that it is happening now (by using present tense), or to mean that it will happen in the future (by using future tense) (see Berry 1977: 143). We can represent the system of tense in English as shown in Figure 1.1.

Figure 1.1: System of tense in English

Similarly, in spoken discourse, there are various systems operating. For example, in making an initiating move, a teacher has the choices of eliciting an answer from the pupils, directing pupils to do something, or informing them of something. These three choices form a system. Once the teacher has produced an initiating move, a different set of choices is opened up. After the teacher has made an elicitation, the pupils can give a reply, or they can produce another elicitation asking the teacher to explain the question a bit more, or they can even comment on the question, for example, 'This is a very difficult question.'. However, they cannot produce an acknowledgement like 'Oh I see.' without being incoherent.

Stubbs (1983) proposes that after the production of an initiation, the next speaker makes a systemic choice of whether to support or reject it. According to Stubbs, to support would be to produce an utterance which fulfils the structural prediction set up by the preceding utterance and to reject would be to break the discourse expectation. If the choice is to support the preceding discourse, then another system of choices is set up: the choice of questioning or not questioning the presuppositions of the preceding utterance. Stubbs calls the former 'canonical support' and the latter 'query' (see Stubbs 1983: 100). He represents the systems as shown in Figure 1.2.

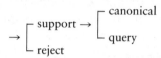

Figure 1.2: Systems following an initiating utterance (Stubbs 1983)

The following is an illustration of how the systems work in conversation. Suppose a tourist in Birmingham City Centre asks a passer-by 'Can you tell me where New Street Station is?', the following are examples of the choices that are available to the passer-by:

(14) [I]
    Tourist: Can you tell me where New Street Station is?
    Passer-by: (a) It's just round the corner.
               (b) Do you know where the Shopping Centre is?
               (c) Sorry, I'm a stranger here.

The passer-by has the choice of supporting the utterance or rejecting it altogether. If he chooses the former, then he has the choice of producing a response, which supplies the information (see (14a)), or he may produce another elicitation before supplying the information (see (14b)). If the choice is to reject the utterance, he may reject the assumption that he is able to supply the requested information (see (14c)). Figure 1.3 provides an exemplification of Stubbs's systems. Hence, the different systems operating at different moves represent the choices that are available to the speaker at different points in

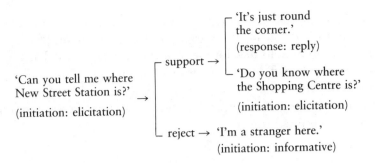

Figure 1.3: Exemplification of Stubbs's systems (1983)

the discourse. Each choice made opens up another set of choices. The actual development of conversation represents a selection of choices that are made by speakers as the discourse unfolds (see also Halliday 1984: 10).

1.8 Towards a linguistic description of conversation

In this first part of the book, I have provided a brief overview of how the four areas of linguistic description identified in section 1.1 will be dealt with. In subsequent parts, I shall discuss in detail each of these areas.

Part Two provides an analytical framework for our description: Chapter 2 looks at the structure of conversation, and addresses the question of whether conversation is basically organized in terms of two-part adjacency pairs or three-part exchanges. Chapter 3 proposes a taxonomy of discourse acts drawn up according to the criteria of structural location and prospective classification. The dimension of retrospective classification will also be brought in to determine the actual discourse value of utterances.

Parts Three and Four give detailed descriptions of the primary classes and subclasses of acts in the taxonomy. Part Three (Chapters 4 to 7) discusses in detail four subclasses of acts in the initiating move: *elicitation*, *requestive*, *directive*, and *informative*. Part Four (Chapters 8 and 9) looks at much-neglected aspects in conversational studies: responses, and third parts of exchanges which we will refer to as *follow-ups*, following Sinclair and Coulthard's model.

Part Five (Chapter 10) focuses on conversational processes. It spells out the systems of choices available at various points in conversation, and demonstrates how each choice made by an interlocutor affects the subsequent development of the conversation. The chapter applies the proposed descriptive framework to the analysis of a piece of telephone conversation, and ends with a discussion of the aspects of conversational patterning and utterance characterization that have yet to be accounted for.

PART TWO
Analytical framework

2
The structure of conversation

2.1 Introduction

In Chapter 1, we saw that the basic unit of organization of classroom discourse is a three-part exchange. We mentioned that this organizational unit has been considered by some as peculiar to the classroom and that it cannot be generalized to non-classroom discourse. It has been suggested that non-classroom discourse is organized in terms of two-part adjacency pairs (Burton 1981) or two-part exchanges with an optional third part (Coulthard and Brazil 1981: 98). This chapter argues that a three-part exchange is more powerful as a description of the basic unit of conversational organization than an adjacency pair.

2.2 Adjacency pair as an organizational unit

Let us start by applying the notion of an adjacency pair to the following piece of conversational data:

(1) [BCET:A:51]
    C: Can I just use your lighter? I've
       ran [run] out of matches.   (1st pair part)
    B: Oh aye ahhh (+NV)   (2nd pair part)
→ C: Ta.   (?   )

The three parts in the exchange are coherent and form a bounded conversational unit. If we analysed them in terms of adjacency pairs, we would have difficulties in characterizing C's second utterance. It is not a second pair part because it follows a second pair part, nor is it a first pair part because it does not invite a second pair part.

Yet it is a very important contribution to the interaction. It is a display of gratitude for the service rendered. It shows that C is fully aware of the virtual offence he has committed by asking B to lend him the lighter and the favour that B has done him. It also informs B that his generosity is appreciated. Goffman calls this kind of utterance an 'appreciation' (see Goffman 1971: 141–2; 1976: 265).

Consider now the following piece of data:

(2) [B:G:A:3:2]
   M has told J that he would not be able to teach a course for him.

   I   J: Even even on a once-a-week basis.
   R   M: Even once a week, 'cos I'm just so exhausted, I have
            late classes and then and then and then I have =
                                                    [
   <F>   J: Yes.
          M: = research I have to do which makes it which
             complicates things ((*laughs*)).
   → F   J: Yeah I understand.

J's request that M teach a course for him is being turned down. M tries to repair the face damage by providing reasons for not being able to comply. J then produces what Goffman refers to as a 'minimization' in the follow-up move to indicate that he understands the situation M is in and that no offence is taken. This third move is very important. As Goffman points out, when the addressee provides reasons for being unable to comply (which Goffman (1971: 109) refers to as an 'account'), he needs a comment of some kind in return. This is because 'only in this way can he be sure that his corrective message has been received and that it has been deemed sufficient to reestablish him as a proper person' (ibid.: 119). Compare (2) with the following:

(3) [Owen 1983: 103]
   I   M: . . . but I mean we just didn't know what this meant
          at all we were just totally confused//(and . . .)
   R   G: hhhh sorry about that I didn't think (I was) spoiling
          your weekend//(. . .)
   → I M: well we did have rather a miserable time I can tell you.

In contrast to (2) above, G's apology for spoiling M's weekend is not followed by a third move in which M minimizes the debt incurred or accepts the apology as sufficient. Instead, M continues to tell G about his unpleasant experience. The absence of a redressing third move implies a rejection of G's apology.

We can see from the above discusson that 'ritual interchanges' (Goffman 1967: 19–22) such as those given above are typically three-part. Goffman notes:

> A response will on occasion leave matters in a ritually unsatisfactory state, and a turn by the initial speaker will be required, encouraged, or at least allowed, resulting in a three-part interchange; or chains of adjacency pairs will occur (albeit typically with one, two, or three such couplets), the chain itself having a unitary, bounded character. (Goffman 1981: 23)

In fact, not only are ritual interchanges made up of three parts, so are non-ritual interchanges. Mishler (1975), in a study of the structure of natural conversation in first-grade classrooms, makes the following observation: a basic unit of conversation is a three-part unit which is a sequence of three successive utterances initiated by an utterance, including a question, from the first speaker, followed by a response from the second speaker, and terminated by a further utterance from the first speaker. He points out that the question–answer sequence, which is widely accepted as an appropriate and coherent unit of communication, may be applicable to testing and interview situations, but is totally inapplicable in 'more "open" natural conversation' (Mishler 1975: 33). He argues that just as a question 'demands' a response, a response also 'demands' a further response from the questioner. This further response, according to him, is 'a "sign" on the part of the questioner that his question has received a response, adequate or inadequate, appropriate or inappropriate' (ibid.: 32). The following piece of data illustrates Mishler's argument:

(4) [B:B:A:2:1]
    Y: is is John there?
    X: Oh y– I think he's in class.
→ **Y:** Oh I see.

The third move from Y indicates that the response has been received and that it is an appropriate one.

Goffman (1981) also points out that sometimes what appears to be a two-part interchange, or an adjacency pair, is, in fact, a three-move interchange. For example:

(5) [Goffman 1981: 47]
  A: [*Enters wearing a new hat*]
  B: No, I don't like it.
  A: Now I know it's right.

Here, B's utterance is not a first pair part, but rather a second pair part (a response) to A's wearing a new hat. Hence, taking into account the non-linguistic first part, we have a three-move interchange. Goffman notes:

> Bringing together these various arguments about the admixture of spoken and nonlinguistic moves, we can begin to see how misleading the notion of adjacency pair and ritual interchange may be as basic units of interaction. (Goffman 1981: 48)

2.3 Three-part exchange as an organizational unit

Burton (1981: 63) considers three-part exchanges highly classroom-specific because, according to her, the follow-up move hardly occurs outside the classroom. She argues that a three-part exchange like the following is deviant in non-classroom discourse:

(6) [I]
  A: What's the time please?
  B: Three o'clock.
  *__A:__ Well done.

She maintains that if a follow-up move does occur in casual conversation, it will be a sarcastic device.

There is some truth in Burton's observation. Exchanges like those in (6) are atypical in conversation. We do not go around asking questions to which we already know the answer. And if we did, the follow-up move would be produced to achieve certain effects. The following are some examples:

(7) [Coulthard and Brazil 1981: 90]
  I **Mother:** Have you brushed your teeth yet?
  R **Child:** Yes.
→ F **Mother:** No you haven't.

(8) [ibid.]

   I **A:** What time did you come home last night?

   R **B:** About midnight.

→ F **A:** No you didn't.

In both exchanges, the follow-up moves are produced to show that the responders are lying. In the case of (8), which is adult–adult interaction, the follow-up move is face-threatening, as noted by Coulthard and Brazil (ibid.).

But how do we explain the follow-up move in (1) and (2)? They are not intentionally produced to generate conversational implicature. In (3), it is the withholding of a 'minimization' in the third move that generates the implicature of rejecting the apology.

And how do we explain the follow-up move in exchanges such as (4) and (9) below which are frequently found in conversational data?

(9) [B:C:A:3:1]

   I **B:** Where where is he staying?

   R **A:** He's staying at the ah the Chung Chi Guest House.

→ F **B:** Oh I see.

Unlike the teacher, B does not have an answer to his own question. Yet, like the teacher, he produces a third move. This third move, however, is not to evaluate the correctness of the reply but to indicate that A's response has been received.

Berry (1981: 123) tries to account for both kinds of exchanges by suggesting that in certain types of non-classroom exchange, the follow-up move is obligatory, whereas in others it is optional. She proposes that the distinguishing criterion is which of the two interlocutors is the *primary knower*. For example:

(10) [Berry 1981: 122]

   I **Quizmaster:** In England, which cathedral has the tallest spire?

   R **Contestant:** Salisbury.

→ F **Quizmaster:** Yes.

(11) [Berry 1981: 122]

   I **Son:**   Which English cathedral has the tallest spire?

   R **Father:** Salisbury.

→ F **Son:**   Oh.

According to Berry, the follow-up move in (10) is obligatory, whereas that in (11) is optional, because, in the former, the quizmaster is the primary knower and therefore a follow-up move to evaluate or confer the correctness of the response provided is necessary. In the latter, however, because the son is the secondary knower, there is no need, or rather, he is not in a position to evaluate or confer the correctness of the response. The correctness of the information provided in the response is already conferred by the father who is the primary knower. Hence, the follow-up move is optional.

Heritage's (1984) study of the conversational particle 'oh' makes similar observations about the state of knowledge of the interlocutors. However, he does not share Berry's conclusion that the third move is optional. He suggests that in conversational sequences like (4), (9), and (11), 'oh' is used to indicate that the information delivered in the preceding move has been received and that a change of the state of knowledge of the questioner has taken place; he labels it an 'oh'-receipt token. He points out that the questioner, upon receiving the requested information, is, in fact, committed to produce an 'oh'-receipt to indicate that he, a previously uninformed party, is now informed. This is evidenced by the fact that in his study, a substantial number of 'oh'-receipts occur early; they are often either latched onto, or slightly overlap with, the answers provided, and they are rarely delayed longer than a micro-pause (Heritage 1984: 309, 339). In other words, a follow-up move in this kind of exchange is by no means optional.

2.4 Functions of the follow-up move

As we can see, there is no consensus with regard to whether conversation is *basically* organized in terms of two-part adjacency pairs or three-part exchanges. The answer to this question hinges on how we perceive the function of the follow-up move.

From the above debate, it is apparent that the function of the follow-up move is perceived by some as solely evaluative (e.g. Berry 1981; Burton 1981; Coulthard and Brazil 1981). If providing an evaluation of the correctness of information supplied in the response were indeed the *only* function of this third move, then I would agree with Burton's observation that it seldom occurs outside the classroom. I would also agree with Berry (1981, 1987), and Coulthard and Brazil (1981) that the third move is optional in speech events other than quizzes or puzzle-solving sessions. However, Heritage's study of 'oh'-receipt tokens supports the observation that providing an evaluation is not the *only* function of the follow-up move.

This has also been noted by Mehan (1979: 194) who maintains that the third component in a three-part sequence which occurs in classroom discourse is different from that which occurs in everyday conversations. For example:

(12) [Mehan 1979: 194]
    A: What time is it, Denise?
    B: Two thirty.
→ **A:** Very good, Denise.

(13) [ibid.]
    A: What time is it, Denise?
    B: Two thirty.
→ **A:** Thank you, Denise.

He points out that while the third component in (12) evaluates the content of the response, that in (13) seems to be more an acknowledgement of the previous reply than an evaluation of it.

Berry (1987: 47), on examining three-move exchanges in doctor–patient interviews, revises her initial position, and asserts that third moves of these exchanges are usually different in character from those of classroom exchanges: they do not have an evaluative function. For example:

(14) [Coulthard and Ashby 1976: 80]
    Doctor: How long have you had those for?
    Patient: Well I had'm a week last Wednesday.
→ **Doctor:** A week last Wednesday.

(15) [Coulthard and Montgomery 1981: 21]
    Doctor: How long have you had these quick pains on the right side of your head?
    Patient: Well again when this trouble started.
→ **Doctor:** Again for about two years.

Berry (1987: 84) comments, 'And intuitively, one feels that they are not so much commenting on the quality of the patient's reply as acts of noting and/or reinterpreting the reply for the doctor's own benefit.'

Clearly, the follow-up move has functions other than making an evaluation of the response. An investigation, in the following section, into what these functions are will help us decide whether it is an important element in conversational organization.

2.5 Pragmatic motivation of the follow-up move

Let us begin with a consideration of the pragmatic motivation for the follow-up move. Conversation is an interactive process, during which the meaning and illocutionary force of utterances are negotiated between the speaker and the addressee, not an interchange of utterances with speaker-determined illocutionary forces (see Franck 1981: 226). Hence, the initiating utterance that the speaker produces is subjected to the interpretation of the addressee who displays his or her interpretation in the response. However, the interaction does not stop there. The addressee may need to know whether the speaker has understood his or her response, whether the response is acceptable, and whether the addressee has correctly interpreted the speaker's utterance. This may require a further contribution from the speaker (see Tsui 1987a: 337; 1987c: 375; see also Mishler 1975: 32, 38). Therefore, just as Schegloff and Sacks (1973: 297–8) argue that a second pair part is necessary to show that the addressee (who produced the second pair part) understood correctly the first pair part and to let the speaker (who produced the first pair part) know whether the first pair part was accepted or not, I argue that the third move is likely for the same reason: to let the addressee know that the speaker has understood the addressee's response, that he or she has provided an acceptable response, and that the interaction has been felicitous. I shall support my argument with some examples:

(16) [Labov 1972: 123]
   Linus: Do you want to play with me Violet?
   Violet: You're younger than me. (*shuts the door*)
   Linus: [*puzzled*] She didn't answer my question.

Here, Violet's response is a way of saying 'no' to Linus's question. She assumes that Linus will be able to interpret her response as a version of 'no', on the basis of the shared knowledge among children that big girls don't play with little boys. It is only when Linus produces a comment on her response that we know her assumption is wrong: he fails to see the relevance of her response. If Violet had waited for Linus's reaction (instead of shutting the door), she would have known that, in fact, the interaction had been infelicitous because Linus did not have the shared knowledge and therefore her response had not been understood.[1]

The following piece of data is another example:

(17) [Davidson 1984: 102]
    A: What time you wanna leav:ve.
       (0.3)
    B: ((*smack*)) Uh:: sick clo:ck?
       (0.5)
    A: Six (uh) clo:ck? hh =
→ **B:** = Is that good.

Here, B proposes a time to leave in response to A's question. However, the interaction is not completed at B's making a proposal, because he needs to know if his proposal is acceptable to A. In other words, after producing a second pair part to A's first pair part, B is looking to a third move to see if his proposal is acceptable. This is supported by the fact that when the proposal is not immediately endorsed by A, but followed by A's repetition with rising intonation, B interprets the latter as expressing some doubt. B therefore immediately checks to see whether his proposal is acceptable.

Finally, consider the piece of data below:

(18) [BCET: A:A:25–6]
  1 **B:** Mind you it's not bad really, banking business, I
        suppose, it's a clean job.
  2 **C:** Yeah, it's that kind of image. I don't really go for
        that, you know.
→   ((*2 sec*))
→ 3 **C:** Do you know what I mean though, I mean it suits
        you.
  4 **B:** Yeah.
→ 5 **C:** I mean, I'm not being insulting or anything, but I
  6   can't see myself being a bank manager.

7 **B:** ((*laughs*)) Oh I can see myself being a bank manager.
8 **C:** You could, yes, that's what I mean, – (   )

After C's response, there is a pause of about two seconds. The fact that a third move to acknowledge the response is not forthcoming from B is 'noticed' by C as an indication that the interaction may have been infelicitous: B may have interpreted his response as an insulting remark (see line 5). Therefore, in the following exchanges, C tries very hard to clarify his own intentions.

From the above examples, we can see that the follow-up move is a very important element of an exchange, not only in classroom discourse, but in conversation as well. It is the element on which further interaction is based. We may say that it has a general function of acknowledging the outcome of the interaction that has taken place in the initiating and the responding moves. As Heritage and Atkinson (1984: 10) observe:

> Any third action, therefore, that implements some normal onward development of a sequence confirms the adequacy of the displayed understandings in the sequence so far. By means of this framework, speakers are released from what would otherwise be the endless task of explicitly confirming and reconfirming their understanding of one another's actions.

In other words, a three-part exchange is the basic unit of organization in conversation. The three moves are related to each other in such a way that each move sets up the expectation of the subsequent move. This does not mean, however, that in all conversational exchanges, the three moves *actually* occur, but rather that whatever occurs will be interpreted in the light of this expectation. As Berry (1981: 38) points out:

> a rule such as *A predicts B* is not to be taken as a claim that A always *will* be followed by B; it is a claim that A will always be *expected* to be followed by B and that whatever does follow A will be interpreted in the light of this expectation.

Hence, when the third move does not occur, we may say, following Sacks (1972: 341), that it is absent. However, as Sacks points out, in order to show that the absence of something is not trivial, that its absence is not just one among a host of other things that might equally be said to be absent, we need to show its *relevance of occurrence*:

> Nontrivial talk of an absence requires that some means be available for showing both the relevance of occurrence of the activity that is proposedly absent and the location where it should be looked for to see that it did not occur. (ibid.: 342)

2.6 The relevance of occurrence of the follow-up move

2.6.1 Classroom exchanges

A classroom exchange provides us with a very good starting point. In a classroom exchange, as Sinclair and Coulthard (1975: 51) point out, when the follow-up move is not found after an initiating move and a responding move have occurred, one is confident that it has been withheld by the teacher for some strategic purpose. For example:

(19) [Sinclair and Coulthard 1975: 65]
    1 I   T: Can you think why I changed 'mat' to 'rug'?
    2 R P: Because er
    3 I   T: Peter.
    4 R P: Mat's got two vowels in it.
→ 5 I   T: Which are they? What are they?
    6 R P: 'a' and 'f', 'a' and 't'.
→ 7 I   T: Is 't' a vowel?
    8 R P: No.
→ 9 F T: No.

In (19), the follow-up move is not found until line 9. Yet we can clearly see that it could have occurred after lines 4 and 6 where the teacher could have provided an evaluation of the pupil's response. But, because the evaluation would have been a negative one had it occurred, its absence could be seen as deliberate withholding by the teacher in order to avoid giving an explicit negative evaluation. This is supported by the fact that the follow-up move occurs when the pupil produces a correct answer. Teachers who do not want to discourage pupils from answering questions often use this strategy. The absence of the follow-up move implies that the answer is incorrect, hence implying a negative evaluation. A comparison of the following two pieces of classroom data supports this point. ((20) occurs immediately before (21))[2]:

(20) [Tsui 1985: 20]
    I **Teacher:** Are you hungry now? Have you had your
                    breakfast? Is it a good breakfast?
    R **Pupil:** Yes.
→ F **Teacher:** Right.
    I   Sit down.

(21) [ibid.]
  1 I **Teacher:** (name) Are you hungry now? Did you have
                    breakfast this morning?
  2 R **Pupil:** Yes.
  3 F **Teacher:** Yes.
  4 I   Good breakfast?
  5 R **Pupil:** No.
→ 6 I **Teacher:** Sit down.

In (20), a follow-up move which gives a positive evaluation occurs after the pupil has provided a response. In (21), the teacher asks more or less the same question. However, a follow-up move which accepts the pupil's answer is found after the first response but not the second.

In both (20) and (21), the teacher's questions are intended as language practice questions and she expects the pupils to give 'yes' as an answer. This is why in (20), the pupil's reply is evaluated as 'right'. However, in (21) the teacher's questions are taken as genuine questions by the pupil. The pupil's reply in line 5 (which is a perfectly appropriate answer) does not match the response that the teacher intends to solicit. It is considered unacceptable by the teacher, who withholds the follow-up move to imply a negative evaluation (see also Hewings 1987: 227).

2.6.2 Conversational exchanges

Just as we can account for the *relevance of occurrence* of the follow-up move in classroom exchanges, so can we in non-classroom exchanges. In the following, I shall make a detailed examination of the circumstances under which the follow-up move does not occur and those under which it does. By examining when, where, and why it is absent, and when, where, and why it is present, we will hopefully be able to gain further insights into its functions. But before we do that, it must be pointed out that in face-to-face interaction, the follow-up move is often realized by non-verbal means such as a nod, a smile, an eyebrow raising, and so on. For example:

(22) [C:2:A:2]
  J wants to pay S for the stamps that S has given her.
  S: I think you better just keep it because I don't have change anyway.
  J: Well, next time I'm in the money as far as stamps are concerned.
→ S: ((*laughs*))

S's laugh is a contributing move in the exchange. It is a non-verbal acknowledgement of J's accepting her suggestion to just take the stamps for free.

Non-verbal gestures such as the above are often not recorded in transcriptions, giving the illusion that the follow-up move is absent. Stenström (1984), in her study of transcriptions of telephone conversations and face-to-face conversations, observes that the follow-up move occurs much more frequently in the former than in the latter. This observation is likely to be the result of not taking into account those follow-up moves which are realized non-verbally in face-to-face interaction. In telephone conversations, the follow-up move must be verbalized, since it cannot be conveyed otherwise. This gives the false impression that it occurs more frequently than in face-to-face conversations.

What are the circumstances under which the follow-up move may not occur and what are those under which it may?

First, in conversations between interlocutors who know each other very well, the follow-up move is more frequently absent. Stenström (1984: 243), in her study of eleven transcribed texts, discovers that the conversations between a married couple have far fewer follow-up moves than any of the other texts. This can be explained by the fact that interlocutors who know each other very well share a large common ground so that there are not likely to be hitches in their interpretation of each other's utterances. Hence, an explicit follow-up move to acknowledge the outcome of the interaction may not be necessary. Moreover, for interlocutors such as husbands and wives, the ritual constraint (Goffman 1981: 19) which necessitates the production of a follow-up move to express an appreciation of service rendered can be relaxed. The following exchange is by no means uncommon:

(23) [I]
    Wife: Will you pass that paper dear.
    Husband: Yup. (+NV).
    Wife: Ø

Second, since to acknowledge the outcome of an exchange is an important function of the follow-up move, it stands to reason that when the interaction has not been felicitous, the speaker is likely to withhold it. The infelicitous interaction may be due to some misunderstanding or mishearing on the part of the addressee. It may be due to some mispronunciation or misuse of words on the part of the speaker. It may also be due to a gap in shared knowledge. The following is an example in which the follow-up move is not forthcoming because of a gap in shared knowledge:

(24) [BCET:A:34]
    I   C: Do you get satisfaction though?
    R B: Yes, I reckon you get more satisfaction as you go up the the scale as well.
→ I   C: What do you mean, the money scale?
    R B: No, the job the job.

B assumes that it is shared knowledge between himself and C that 'the scale' means 'the job scale'. As we can see, his assumption is wrong. Hence C, instead of producing a follow-up move to indicate that he has understood B's response, produces an initiating move to ask for clarification of the meaning of 'the scale'.

The following piece of data is a case of misuse of words by the speaker. It contains what Schegloff (1979) refers to as a 'third position repair':

(25) [BCET:A:4–5]
    A was telling C about a friend who used to live very far from
    her workplace and was getting travelling allowance. When

she moved to a bedsitter very near her workplace, she did
not inform the authority about the move and kept getting the
allowance.

  I **A:** Y'know she kept it up for a couple of months and
            then decided to sort of cut her losses.
  R **C:** It's not that bad.
→ I **A:** Cut her gains, I mean.
  R **C:** Cut her gains.
  F **A:** Yeah.

In (25), A mistakenly said 'Cut her losses', when he meant 'Cut her gains'. Upon hearing C's response, A realized that he had made a mistake and repaired his utterance in the third move. If there had been no mistake, the third move might have been A acknowledging that C had correctly understood what he had said, as in (4) and (9). As we can see, after the 'third position repair' in which A corrected himself, and C had responded to it adequately, A produced another move to acknowledge that the interaction had been felicitous. (See Heritage 1984: 311) where he points out that the third turn in a Question–Answer–'oh'-receipt sequence may be avoided by questioners to propose that they have not been informed.)

It should be noted, however, that sometimes even when there is misunderstanding, mishearing, or a gap in shared knowledge, the speaker may choose to go along with the misunderstanding, and so forth, and produce an acknowledging third move, rather than a 'repair'. For example:

(26) [Heritage and Atkinson 1984: 14]
    E: <u>She</u> gets awful depressed over these things <u>y</u>ihknow <u>she</u>'s
        rea:l (0.2) p'litical <u>mi</u>:nded'n,
        (0.3)
    L: Ye:ah
    E: <u>wo</u> rk –
          [   ]
    L: She a <u>Democra</u>:t?
→ **E:** .t.hhh <u>I</u> vote <u>ee</u>ther <u>wa</u>:y.h
        (.)
→ **L:** Yeah,

Heritage and Atkinson (1984: 14–15) point out that the piece of data in (26) above is a clear case of the speaker (L) not making any attempt to correct the addressee's (E) mishearing, or mistreating, of her prior utterance. When this happens, the speaker is behaving as though the addressee has provided an adequate response and the interaction has been felicitous (see also Tsui 1987a: 338).

Third, a follow-up move possibly will not occur when the speaker is not happy with the response provided, as in (27), or the outcome of the interaction, as in (28):

(27) [BCET:A:1]
    I C: Do you get the bus?
    R B: Yeah.
→ I C: The bus?
    R B: And the – tube.

In contrast to (24) and (25), there is no misinterpretation of meaning or intention here. Rather, C finds the response hard to believe. He therefore re-initiates the question to seek confirmation.

(28) [BCET:A:43]
ex.1 I C: Are you sure you don't want a cigarette?
      R B: No, I couldn't take your last but one.
ex.2 I C: Well, the last one actually – that would be my last
           one.
      R B: No thanks.
ex.3 I C: Go on, have it Rob.
      R B: No, no I'm not having it, I'd feel too bad.
→ F C: Okay.

In this piece of data, the follow-up move is not found until the third exchange, when C finally accepts B's refusal of his offer, after which B and C move on to another topic. It does not occur in the first two exchanges because C is not happy with the negative outcome, or at least he behaves as though he is not happy about the fact that his offer is refused. This is supported by the fact that in the third exchange, C re-offers. It is only when he concedes to accept the negative outcome that he produces the follow-up move. Some further examples are given in (29) and (30):

(29) [Davidson 1984: 127]
    A: You wan' me <u>b</u>ring you anything?
    (0.4)

   B: <u>N</u>o: no: <u>n</u>othing.
→ **A:** <u>AW</u>:kay.

(30) [B:A:A:4:3]
   I **M:** So so do you want me to pick you up, are you in
          your office now?
   R **X:** No, I'm I'm going to the h– I'm at the Great Hall, I
          have to go to the head's office.
→ F **M:** Alright, maybe afterwards.

In (29), A is happy to accept B's rejection of his offer and he produces
a follow-up move to accept the negative outcome. Similarly, in (30),
M produces a follow-up move to accept the negative outcome and
a 'minimization' to save the loss of face resulting from his offer being
declined. (For more examples, see Davidson 1984). She refers to
third moves which accept rejections as 'rejection finalisers'.)

From the above discussion and the examples given, we can see
that the follow-up move has a general function of acknowledging
the outcome of the interaction. To evaluate the correctness of the
response is only one of the realizations of this general function. Other
realizations are: to accept the outcome of the preceding interaction
(examples (28) to (30)); to show an appreciation of the response
(examples (1) and (13)); to minimize the face damage that has been
done (example (2)); and to show a change of state of knowledge
(examples (4), (9), (11), (14), and (15)).

With this characterization of the function of the follow-up move,
it is now not difficult to see that three-part exchanges are by no
means classroom-specific.

2.7 Concluding remarks

In this chapter, we have seen that the follow-up move, which is the
third component part of an exchange, is an important element in
conversational interaction with the function of endorsing the felicitous outcome of the interaction. Its occurrence is pragmatically
motivated.

It may be too strong a statement to say that when the follow-up
move does not occur, its non-occurrence is noticeable and noticed
in the way the absence of a second pair part is, but it is certainly
true that when it does not occur, it is often perceived by participants

to be deliberately withheld for social or strategic reasons. This suggests to us that a potentially three-part exchange which may contain non-verbal component parts, is a more powerful description of a basic unit of conversational organization than an adjacency pair.

It should be noted, however, that while a potentially three-part exchange is the basic organizational unit, it is possible for exchanges to consist of more than three parts. This happens when, following a follow-up move, the next speaker produces a further response to it. Goffman provides the following example:

(31) [Goffman 1981: 16]
    A: Do you have the time?
    B: Sure. It's five o'clock.
    A: Thanks.
→ **B:** (*gesture*) t's okay.

Here, A's 'appreciation' is responded to by a 'minimization', in which the speaker indicates that enough gratitude has been displayed, resulting in a four-part exchange (see Goffman 1981: 16).

A four-part exchange may also result when, following a follow-up move, the next speaker produces a further move in which he indicates that he wishes to relinquish the floor. For example:

(32) [Coulthard 1981: 19]
  I   **D:** but it's only the last three months that it's been
         making you feel ill.
  R **P:** ill with it yes
  F **D:** yes yes
→ F **P:** yes doctor

The last move in (32) follows a follow-up move and yet it is clearly not a new initiating move because it does not expect a further response from the doctor. What the patient is doing here, instead of taking the floor and introducing a new topic or continuing with the current topic, is indicating that he has no more to say and wishes to relinquish the floor. (See turn-taking rules in conversation in Sacks, Schegloff, and Jefferson 1974.) We could say that the patient's last move serves as a turn-passing signal. Coulthard (1981: 19) characterizes such utterances as second follow-up moves. He observes that, theoretically, it is possible to have an infinite repetition of the follow-up move, but in real life, exchanges which have more than three follow-up moves seldom occur.

Taking into consideration data such as (31) and (32) above, we could say that the basic organizational unit of conversation is a potentially three-part exchange with an optional fourth or fifth part. Applying Halliday's concept of structure, we can say that conversation is organized in terms of exchanges which have three elements of structure, an *initiation*, a *response*, and a *follow-up* which is optionally recursive.

3

A taxonomy of discourse acts

3.1 Introduction

In Chapter 1, we established two criteria for characterizing the functions of conversational utterances: structural location and prospective classification. In Chapter 2, we argued that conversation is basically organized in terms of three-part exchanges, with the third element being optionally recursive. In this chapter, we shall look at the primary classes and subclasses[1] of acts which can be identified on the basis of these two criteria.

Before presenting the descriptive categories, we shall need to consider the influential claim that it is not possible to characterize utterances in terms of unit acts and to delimit a finite set of speech action categories (see Leech 1983; Levinson 1983).

3.2 Multiple functions of utterances

Levinson (1983) suggests that it is not possible to characterize an utterance as performing a certain speech act because it often has more than one function. He gives the following example:

(1) [Levinson 1983: 290]
→ A: Would you like another drink?
   B: Yes, I would, thank you, but make it a small one.

According to him, A's utterance is both a question and an offer. He argues that this is supported by the surface form of the response in which 'Yes, I would' responds to the question and 'thank you' responds to the offer (Levinson 1981: 476). He writes:

44

> Single sentences can be used to perform two or more speech
> acts in different clauses, and each clause ... may perform more
> than one speech act at the same time.
> (Levinson 1983: 291)

Moreover, he argues, the source of multiple functions often lies in
the sequential environment of the conversation in which the utterance occurs; that is, in the discourse context. Since the latter is not
restricted in kind, it is not possible to delimit a finite set of speech
act categories which can be mapped onto utterances. Along similar
lines, Leech asserts that utterances are highy ambivalent and their
illocutionary forces are often indeterminate. Therefore, characterizing them in terms of action-categories represents an unrealistic and
unsubtle view of what communication by means of language is all
about. He further asserts that it is pointless to attempt a rigid taxonomy of illocutionary acts (see Leech 1983: 23, 225).

Before we examine Levinson's example, it must be pointed out
that when we say that utterances have multiple functions, it is essential that we make clear what the term 'function' means. If it is used
as a general term encompassing discourse function, psychological
function, social function, and so on, then it is true that utterances
often have multiple functions. We may offer to do something for
somebody, not only to get it accepted, but also to try to impress
him or her, to show solidarity, to get the favour done returned in
future, and so forth.[2] It is also true that it is impossible to characterize all of the above functions by imposing a single categorial
label on the utterance. However, this is clearly not what Levinson
meant by 'multiple functions'. In the above quotation, he is explicitly
referring to the function of an utterance in the performance of a
speech act.

It should be noted that when we characterize the issuance of an
utterance as the performance of a particular speech act, we are characterizing the performance of an illocutionary act. The latter should
be strictly distinguished from the perlocutionary effect that the
speaker intends to achieve (see Austin 1962).[3] For example, the host,
in saying 'Would you like another drink?', may have the intention
of embarrassing the guest who has already finished several bottles
of wine, or he may have the intention of getting the guest to take
the hint and leave, and so on. While offering a drink is an illocution-

ary act, trying to embarrass the guest and trying to get the guest to leave are perlocutionary effects. In other words, a host who by saying 'Would you like another drink?' succeeds in getting the guest to say 'No, thank you. I must be going', has *not* performed two illocutionary acts of offering and asking a covert information question as to when the guest is leaving, but rather has performed an illocutionary act of offering and has succeeded in achieving the perlocutionary effect of getting the guest to leave.

Let us now consider the example in (1). Levinson's analysis of A's utterance as performing two speech acts, a question and an offer, at the same time is problematic.

First of all, the labels 'question' and 'offer' have not been defined. We can only assume a common-sense understanding of a question being an utterance which seeks information and an offer being an utterance in which the speaker commits himself to doing something for the addressee. Let us now imagine that the exchange occurred at a party and B replied, 'Yes I would', which is a perfectly acceptable response between interlocutors who know each other well. Can we then say that B's response indicates that A has asked a question and not made an offer? Apparently not. Given the context of situation, A has still made an offer because after B's response, *A has the obligation to give B a drink*. If A's utterance were a question, there would be no obligation involved.

Secondly, there is no reason to assume that 'Yes, I would' is necessarily a response to a question and not an offer, as there is no necessary relation between grammatical form and communicative function.

In labelling an utterance as performing a particular speech act(s), or discourse act(s), it is essential that we define the labels and the criteria for identification.

If we characterize a question as a speech act, or discourse act, which prospects a verbal response and *only* a verbal response and an offer as one which, if responded to positively, prospects a non-verbal action on the part of the offerer, then 'Would you like another drink?' in (1) cannot possibly be labelled as both a question and an offer in that particular context of situation because it would be contradictory to say that it prospects a verbal response and *only* a verbal response and yet *at the same time* it also prospects a non-verbal action, if responded to positively.

Consider the following piece of data:

(2) [C:2:A:1]

   S bumps into M in the corridor of their offices.

   S: Hi, would you like a piece of apple cake?

   M: //r have you <u>GOT</u> some //

   S: I've got some next door. I'll just get it.

In (2), according to Levinson's argument, 'Would you like a piece of apple cake?' should have been responded to by 'Yes, I would, but have you got some?', where 'Yes, I would' responds to the question and 'but have you got some?' addresses one of the pre-conditions of an offer, which is that the speaker must have some apple cake before she can offer it to the addressee.[4] However, in this piece of data, the addressee, M, responds by only ascertaining that the pre-condition obtains, hence indicating that she is interpreting S's utterance as an offer.

Consider also the following pieces of data:

(3) [B:D:B:2]

   H: Why don't you just can you come up here for a minute? Or or you want me to come down there?

   X: No, ah I was just I was just um I'm calling from the Staff Club and I'm I'm going ah home in a minute. I just
   → wanted to see how we can get in touch. Do you want to call me at home whenever you're finished with Rowena?
   → **H:** Alright.

   X: I'll be there for the next mm mm twenty minutes or half an hour maybe.

   H: Alright.

(4) [C:2:A:5]

   P: Hi, I'll leave my door open so you can check for *TESOL Quarterlies.*

   S: Oh thank you.

   P: I'm off to a meeting right now.
   → **S:** Okay. Do you want me to lock it afterwards?
   → **P:** Ah alright. Yeah, I'll have my key.

   S: Okay, thanks.

In (3), we can see from H's response that the polar-interrogative 'Do you want to call me at home whenever you're finished with

Rowena?' is interpreted by H as a request to call X, rather than both as a question and a request. By saying 'Alright', H has committed himself to carrying out the action. Polar-interrogatives which realize questions asking for information will not be responded to by 'Alright'. Consider the oddity of the response in the following:

(5) [I]
    A: Do you live in Hong Kong?
    *B: Alright.

Similarly, in (4), S's utterance 'Do you want me to lock it afterwards?' is responded to by 'Alright', which commits S to lock the door for P. In other words, P is responding to S's utterance as an offer to lock the door rather than as both a question and an offer.

3.2.1 Ambiguity and multiple functions

Saying that an utterance cannot realize two speech acts, or discourse acts, *at the same time* is not to deny that an utterance can be ambiguous in a given context. But ambiguity is quite different from multiple functions. The former means that in a given context, an utterance can realize act A *or* act B, and it is not clear which one the speaker intends it to be. The latter, however, means that the utterance realizes both act A *and* act B, and the speaker intends it to be both.

Take, for example, the following piece of data from Schegloff (1978). The excerpt is taken from a conversation in a radio phone-in show, A being the radio personality and B a student who calls in. B has been describing to A the difference in opinion between himself and his teacher over the morality of American foreign policy since the time of George Washington.

(6) [Schegloff 1978: 81]
    1 B: An' s- an' ( ) we were discussing, it tur-
    2   it comes down, he s- he says, I-I-you've talked
    3   with thi- si- i- about this many times. I said,
    4   it come down t' this:=
    5 B: = Our main difference: I feel that a
    6   government, i- the main thing, is- th-the
    7   purpose a' the government, is, what is best for
    8   the country.
    9 A: Mmhmm

<pre>
  10 B: *He* says, governments, an' you know he keeps – he
  11   talks about governments, they sh- the thing that
  12   they sh'd do is what's right or wrong.
→ 13 A: for *whom.*
  14 B: Well he says – // he-
  15 A: By what *stan*dard
  16 B: That's what – that's exactly what I mean. He s-
  17   but he says . . .
</pre>

The utterance in line 13 is ambiguous, because it can be a question asking for clarification *or* an agreement. At first, B interprets it as a question asking for clarification and starts to clarify (see line 14). When A interrupts and puts in another rhetorical question (see line 15), B realizes that line 13 was intended to be an agreement, as can be seen from line 16. If the utterance in line 13 had multiple functions, then it would have been both a question asking for clarification *and* an agreement, and A would not have to interrupt B's clarification to make his intentions clear.

Although there are utterances which are 'empirically' ambiguous (to use Schegloff's term), that is, utterances which are found in naturally-occurring data to be ambiguous and not theoretically conjured, it is important to bear in mind that they do not constitute the majority. As Schegloff (1978) points out, most theoretically conjured ambiguities never actually arise. This is because 'actual participants in actual conversations do not encounter utterances as isolated sentences, and . . . they do not encounter them in a range of scenarios, but in actual detailed single scenarios embedded in fine grained contexts' (ibid.: 100). The function of an utterance is often quite straightforwardly interpretable and analysable. Otherwise, human communication would not be possible.

3.2.2 Multiple functions and retrospective classification

In section 1.6.3, we pointed out that it is possible for an addressee, either deliberately or unwittingly, to interpret the speaker's utterance as performing a speech act which is different from what the speaker intends it to be. When this happens, an utterance is being reclassified retrospectively by the addressee. It is important to note that saying that an utterance can be reclassified retrospectively is very different from saying that an utterance is multi-functional.

Retrospective classification is possible when an utterance is 'empirically ambiguous', as in (6) above. The utterance 'for whom' was intended to be an agreement, but was unwittingly reclassified by B as a clarification-seeking question. If it had been performing both an agreement and a clarification-seeking question, the issue of retrospective classification would not even arise.

Retrospective classification is also possible when an utterance has the potential of realizing different speech acts in different contexts of situation. Let us take Labov and Fanshel's example given in section 1.6.3:

(7) [Labov and Fanshel 1977: 75]
    A: Would you mind taking the dust rag and dust around?
    B: No. (*does not move*)

Here, the intended illocutionary force of A's utterance is perfectly clear to both parties. It is a request for B to clean the room. There is no ambiguity at all in the function of the utterance. However, B exploits the fact that it is in interrogative form which can realize an information-seeking question in a different context, and deliberately interprets it out of context as a question. This exchange is funny precisely because both A and B know, and they know that the other party knows, that the interpretation is a deliberate misinterpretation or retrospective classification. If the utterance were multi-functional, the exchange would not be funny at all.

Finally, retrospective classification is possible even when an utterance is *not* 'empirically' ambiguous, and even when it does not have the potential of realizing the discourse value that the addressee assigns to it. For example:

(8) [B:D:B:1:1]
    M has a bad cold and H couldn't recognize her voice.

    H: You sound terrible, you sound like a man.
→ **M:** Thank you.

Here, there is no question that H is making a negative comment on M's voice. The utterance is not ambiguous, nor does it have the potential of realizing a compliment in a different context. However, by deliberately reclassifying an uncomplimentary comment as a compliment, M is generating sarcasm.

3.2.3 Nature of categorial labels

In arguing for multiple functions of utterances, Levinson provides a further example:

(9) [Levinson 1981: 476]
→ A: What are you doing tonight?
   B: Nothing. Why?
   A: I was thinking of going to a movie, wanna come?

According to him, A's utterance is not just a question but also a pre-offer,[5] otherwise B's response would be clearly false: one cannot literally do nothing. He argues that it is only when we see A's utterance as a pre-offer that we would be able to interpret B's response as meaning 'nothing that would make the offer of an evening's entertainment irrelevant' (Levinson 1981: 476).

While one can say that the utterance is both a question and a pre-offer in this particular instance, one cannot say that the utterance is therefore performing more than one speech act. Question and pre-offer are different kinds of label. The former is a speech act label, whereas the latter is a sequential or structural label. Pre-offer denotes the sequential location of the utterance in relation to the rest of the discourse. It is seen as a pre-offer in the light of the way the discourse is structured to avoid the upcoming offer being rejected (see section 1.6.1). The use of categorial labels of different nature is again the consequence of not clearly defining them (see Coulthard (1985) for a detailed discussion of structural and semantic labels).

From the above discussion, we can see the claim that utterances have multiple functions is based on using labels which are ill-defined. This, in turn, leads to the use of different labels for the same speech function, hence giving the illusion that it is impossible to delimit a set of speech action categories. As Searle (1979: 29) points out:

> There are not, as Wittgenstein (on one possible interpretation) and many others have claimed, an infinite or indefinite number of language games or uses of language. Rather, the illusion of limitless uses of language is engendered by an enormous unclarity about what constitutes the criteria for delimiting one language game or use of language from another.

3.3 Primary classes of acts

In the rest of this chapter, I shall present a taxonomy of discourse acts identified on the criteria of structural location and prospected response. Primary classes of acts are identified on the basis of where they occur in the exchange structure. Within each of the primary classes, subclasses are identified on the basis of the response prospected. Further subclasses are identified only if the responses prospected are different enough to warrant the setting up of separate subclasses.

Applying the criterion of structural location, we can identify three primary classes of acts which are head acts of the three moves of an exchange. The class occurring at the head of the *initiating move* can be identified as *initiating acts* (also referred to as *initiations*); that occurring at the head of the *responding move* can be identified as *responding acts* (also referred to as *responses*); and that occurring at the head of the *follow-up move* can be identified as *follow-up acts* (also referred to as *follow-ups*).

3.4 Subclasses of initiating acts

Within each of these three primary classes, we can identify subclasses by looking at the responses they prospect.

The first distinction we can make within the class of initiating acts is between acts which expect an obligatory non-verbal response accompanied by an optional verbal response, and those which expect an obligatory verbal response or its non-verbal surrogate.[6] A non-verbal response refers to an action to be performed, whereas a non-verbal surrogate refers to a non-verbal way of expressing a verbal response. The following examples illustrate the difference:

(10) [I]
    A: Could you please close the door.
    B: Sure.   ← optional verbal response
       ((*closes door*))   ← obligatory non-verbal response
    A: Thanks.

(11) [I]
    X: Are you going home now?

Y: ((*nods head*))   ← non-verbal surrogate of obligatory
                          verbal response, meaning 'Yes'.

X: Oh good.

Let us first examine initiating acts which prospect an obligatory non-verbal response. Consider the following pieces of data:

(12) [B:C:A:1]
    X: Good morning, Braemar Hill School.
    H: Hello, ah I'd like some – ah I make a request, . . .
→   I was wondering if you could send me the application
        form.
    X: Yes um

(13) [B:A:A:4]
→   M: So we– we're thinking about all going down to Chung
→   Ying at about twelve. I booked a table. Well, =
                                                    [
    X: Mhm
→   M: = simply because she'd like to meet the teachers
→   and find out what we're doing, like first year
→   English – the electives and stuff. So if you're
→   free.
    X: Okay.

(14) [C:2:A:1]
→   S: Hi, would you like a piece of apple cake?
    M: Have you got some?
    S: I've got some next door. I'll just get it.

(15) [C:2:A:4:1]
→   R: Could I get some handouts?
    S: Yeah, help yourself.

(16) [Sinclair and Coulthard 1975: 91]
→   **Teacher:** You go and show me one David piece of metal.
    Pupil: (NV)
    Teacher: Yes that's a piece of metal well done a team point
                  you can have one.

(17) [Ervin-Tripp 1976: 29]
    Head of office to subordinate.
→   I want you to check the requirements for the stairs.

All of the arrowed utterances in (12)–(17) prospect a non-verbal response (+NV). It should be noted that in (13), the non-verbal response, which is X's turning up at Chung Ying restaurant for lunch, occurs some time after the exchange. We may refer to the action as a 'non-verbal sequel' (+NV sequel), for the sake of clarity and precision.[7] Those in (12)–(15) are different from those in (16) and (17). In the former, in each instance, the speaker is giving the addressee the option of responding positively or negatively, whereas in the latter, the speaker is not. A response of 'No, I won't' challenges the pragmatic presuppositions of the utterance. (A detailed discussion of the presuppositions of this kind of utterance will be given in Chapter 6; see also Lyons 1977: 767.) In other words, the latter prospects only compliance from the addressee, whereas the former prospects either compliance or non-compliance—although the former is more strongly prospected than the latter. To put it in Pomerantz's terms, a compliance is a 'preferred' response, whereas a non-compliance is a 'dispreferred' response (see Pomerantz 1978, 1984). Let us label those which prospect either compliance or non-compliance *requestives* and those which prospect only compliance *directives*.

Consider now utterances which prospect an obligatory verbal response:

(18) [B:A:2:1]
→ H: What time will you be finished?
   X: Lecture finishes at about quarter past twelve.

(19) [B:B:A:3]
→ B: Do you do you have wheels?
   A: Yes, I drive, it's Donald's car.

(20) [C:4:1]
→ S: John Fraser is a personal friend of ours – Michael went
      to school with him in Canada.
   G: Oh really.

(21) [B:A:A:3:5]
→ K: I think he's a y'know serious scholar, he's got his own
      little thing.
   H: Yeah, he's he IS very scholarly.

In all of the above data, the arrowed utterances prospect verbal responses only. However, the kinds of verbal response they prospect are different. In (18) and (19), the verbal responses prospected are, in very general and grossly simplified terms, the supplying of the missing information indicated in the initiating moves (this will be discussed in detail in Chapter 4). In (20) and (21), the verbal responses prospected are, again in very general terms, acknowledgement that the initiating moves have been heard and understood (this will be discussed in detail in Chapter 8). Let us identify utterances like (18) and (19) as *elicitations* and those like (20) and (21) as *informatives*. Hence, we may say that there are four subclasses of initiating acts: *directives*, *requestives*, *informatives*, and *elicitations*.

That utterances realizing the head act of an initiating move can be classified into these four subclasses is supported by the way they are reported. All utterances can be reported by the general speech act verb 'say', which describes or reports the locution of the utterance.[8] Initiating utterances can be reported by two general speech act verbs, 'ask' and 'tell', which report or describe their general discourse function. Lyons (1977: 766) observes that questions and requests are reported as acts of asking, whereas commands and categorial assertions are reported as acts of telling. This suggests that asking and telling are two distinguishable subtypes of saying. I suggest that a further distinction can be made within these two subtypes of saying. Consider the following sentences (the first of which in each pair of examples is taken from [BCET]):

(22a) 'Would you please remove your glasses?' he asked.
(22b) He *asked* me *to* remove my glasses.

(23a) 'Would you like to come round for a drink tonight?' she asked.
(23b) She *asked* me *to* come round for a drink tonight.

(24a) 'How many languages do you speak?' she asked.
(24b) She *asked* me how many languages I speak.

(25a) 'What do you think of the town so far?' she asked.
(25b) She *asked* me what I thought of the town so far.

The utterances in (22a) and (23a) which realize requestives can be reported as 'asked to'. The utterances in (24a) and (25a) which realize elicitations can be reported as 'asked'.[9]

Consider now the following sentences (the first of which in each pair of examples is again taken from [BCET]):

(26a) 'Get out of my house,' I told them.
(26b) I *told* them *to* get out of my house.

(27a) 'Stay away from this man, he's dangerous,' I told him.
(27b) I *told* him *to* stay away from this man because he was dangerous.

(28a) 'I'm a farmer,' he told me.
(28b) He *told* me *that* he was a farmer.

(29a) 'Very good,' he told me.
(29b) He *told* me *that* it was very good.

The utterances in (26a) and (27a), which realize directives, can be reported as 'told to'. The utterances in (28a) and (29a), which realize informatives, can be reported as 'told that'.

The above linguistic evidence strongly suggests that there are four subclasses of initiating act, represented in Figure 3.1 below.

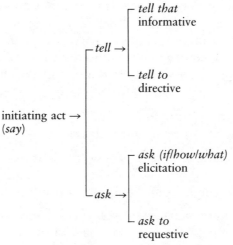

Figure 3.1: *Reporting verbs and subclasses of initiating acts*

Within each of the four subclasses of initiating acts, further subclasses can be identified on the basis of the different responses they prospect. Detailed discussions of each of the subclasses and their further subclasses will be found in Chapters 4 to 7.

3.5 Identification of a response

Before we present the subclasses of *response*, we need to define what constitutes a *response*. Consider the following piece of data:

(30) [C:1:A:2]
     1 **H:** Do you get the *TESOL Quarterly*?
     2 **S:** Yeah.
     3 **H:** Did you get this issue?
→   4 **S:** What – month is it?
     5 **H:** um number two, June eighty-three.
     6 **S:** Yeah, I think I probably did.

The utterance in question here is line 4. It is produced in reply to H's elicitation in line 3. Yet it does not provide the information that is solicited. Furthermore, it elicits a further reply from H. Is it a *response* or is it an *initiation*? Or is it both a response and an initiation?

In the present description, a *response* is characterized as an utterance which fufils the interactional expectation set up by the preceding initiating act. Hence, S's utterance in line 4 is not a response because it does not supply the information solicited. In order to account for the fact that the utterance is indeed produced in reply to H's elicitation in line 3, we shall borrow the concept of a *challenging move* from Burton (1980).

Burton (1980), in looking at utterances such as that in line 4, introduces the notion of 'discourse framework' which pertains to the presuppositions of the initiating move and the interactional expectation set up by that move. She proposes that any move which maintains the discourse framework is a 'supporting move'. It facilitates the progress of the topic presented in the preceding move. Any move which breaks up the discourse framework and holds up the progress of the topic is a 'challenging move'. A challenging move challenges the pragmatic presuppositions of the preceding utterance and may open up another exchange.

The move in line 4 challenges the presupposition that S knows which issue of the *TESOL Quarterly* speaker H is referring to. It is therefore a challenging move[10] (a detailed discussion of presuppositions will be given in Chapter 8). A challenging move is realized by an initiating act. For example, the move in line 4 is realized by an elicitation.

3.6 Subclasses of responding acts

In characterizing responding acts, the notion of 'preference organization' proposed by Conversation Analysts will be adopted. This notion accounts for the fact that not all responding utterances are of equal status; some are 'preferred' and others 'dispreferred'. Schegloff, Jefferson, and Sacks (1977: 362) point out that the notion of 'preference' does not refer to the psychological state of the interlocutors, but to the formal features of the design of turns (cf. Taylor and Cameron 1987[11]). Typically, 'preferred' seconds to first pair parts contain less linguistic material and are given without delay. 'Dispreferred' seconds not only contain more linguistic material, but also contain common features of delay. For example, an invitation sets up the expectation of an acceptance and of a refusal. However, an acceptance is the 'preferred' response, whereas a refusal is the 'dispreferred' response. The following examples will make this clear:

(31) [Schegloff 1972: 107]
    A: Why don't you come up and see me some//times
→ B: I would like to.

(32) [Schegloff 1972: 98]
    A: Uh if you'd care to come and visit a little while this
       morning I'll give you a cup of coffee
→ B: hehh Well that's awfully sweet of you, I don't think I can
       make it this morning . . . hh uhm I'm running an ad in
       the paper and − and uh I have to stay near the phone.

In (31), the acceptance of an invitation is simple and given without delay. By contrast, the refusal of an invitation in (32) contains features of delay (hehh, hh, uhm), the use of the particle 'Well', mitigated refusal ('I don't think I can'), and an explanation of the refusal. The same regularities can be observed in responses to other subclasses of initiating acts (see Chapter 8).

We may say, on the basis of such linguistic evidence, that there are two types of responding acts. One which responds positively and the other negatively. Let us label them as *positive responding acts* and *negative responding acts*, respectively.

There is also a third type of responding act. Consider the following piece of data:

(33) [BCET:A:22]
    C: Could I stay at your place for a bit Rob?
→ D: um I don't know.

D's response does not fulfil the interactional expectation set up. Yet it does not challenge the presuppositions of the requestive either. It is neither a positive nor a negative responding act. D is postponing the decision-making. We may identify this type of responding act as a *temporization*.[12] A temporization is a dispreferred response and it also contains linguistic features of delay such as fillers, particles, and so on (see Chapter 8).

3.7 Follow-up acts

In addition to the linguistic evidence given above, the identification of three subclasses of responding act is also supported by the different kinds of follow-up acts that they prospect. Let us look at the following pieces of data:

(34) [BCET:A:51]
    C: Can I just use your lighter, I've run out of matches.
    B: Oh aye ahhh (+NV)
→ C: Ta.

(35) [B:G:A:3:2]
    M has told J that he would not be able to teach a course for him. J then makes the request again but asking if M cannot do it even once a week.

    J: Even even on a once-a-week basis.
    M: Even once a week, 'cos I'm just so exhausted. I have late classes and then and then and then I have research =
                                    [
    J: Yes.
    M: = I have to do which makes it which complicates things ((*laughs*))
→ J: Yeah I understand.

B's positive responding act in (34) is followed by an appreciation of what B has done for C. Positive responding acts can also be followed by remarks such as 'Great', 'Wonderful', 'Smashing' which are enthusiastic endorsements of the positive outcome of the interaction. We shall identify this kind of follow-up as an *endorsement*. In (35), the negative responding act is followed by a minimization of the face damage done. It is a way of accepting the negative outcome. We shall identify this kind of follow-up as a *concession*.

Let us now consider the follow-up that follows a temporization:

(36) [B:H:B:8:3]
  D: Alright, well em what what em what what time d'you what time would you like to do it.
  H: I'll I'll let you know, let me see, let me see h– if I can get the thing done by the end of the week.
→ D: Okay.

In (36), D and H are working on a book together. D tries to arrange for a time when they will meet and discuss the progress. H postpones the commitment. His temporization is followed by D's accepting the postponement. This kind of follow-up differs from those in (34) and (35) in that H has the obligation to get back to D. We shall identify this kind of follow-up act as an *acknowledgement*.

Apart from the different types of follow-ups prospected, different responses often lead to different developments in the subsequent discourse. This will be discussed in Chapter 9.

Besides the above three subclasses of follow-up act, we can identify a further subclass of follow-up act which is the head act of a second or subsequent follow-up move. It differs from the above three subclasses in that the move in which it occurs is an optional element of structure of an exchange. Therefore, it is not prospected by a responding act. It is a subclass which functions as a 'turn-passing' signal. For example:

(37) [Coulthard 1981: 19]
 I D: but its only the last three months that it's been making you feel ill
 R P: ill with it yes
 F$_1$ D: YES YES
→ F$_2$ P: yes doctor

According to the turn-taking rule of conversation, the patient P has the floor after the doctor D has produced a follow-up move. He can continue to speak on the current topic, introduce a new topic, or terminate the conversation. But P is doing none of the above. By saying 'yes doctor', he is indicating that he has no more to say and wishes to relinquish the floor. Similarly to the head act of the first follow-up move, it prospects an initiating move (although it can be followed by yet another follow-up move, in which the other party indicates that he also wishes to relinquish the floor). I shall identify the subclass which realizes a second follow-up move as a *turn-passing act*.

3.8 A taxonomy of discourse acts

We can now summarize the above discussion by presenting a taxonomy of the subclasses of discourse acts in Figure 3.2.

Elements of structure	I	R	F_1	F_2
Move	Initiating	Responding	Follow-up (1)	Follow-up (2)
Head act: primary class	Initiating (Initiation)	Responding (Response)	Follow-up (1)	Follow-up (2)
Head act: subclass	Elicitation Requestive Directive Informative	Positive Negative Temporization	Endorsement Concession Acknowledgement	Turn-passing

Figure 3.2: A taxonomy of discourse acts

PART THREE

Characterization of discourse acts: initiating acts

4
Elicitations

4.1 Introduction

In this chapter, we shall be looking at the first subclass of initiations, *elicitations*, whose discourse function is to elicit an obligatory verbal response or its non-verbal surrogate.

Utterances which realize this subclass have often been referred to as 'questions' in the linguistic and speech act literature. The term has been used as though it is generally understood what a question is. Unfortunately, an examination of the studies on questions shows that the term has never been clearly defined. It has been used as a semantic category (see Quirk *et al.* 1972, 1985), as an illocutionary act (see, for example, Lyons 1977, 1981; Huddleston 1984), and as a kind of request or directive (see, for example, Katz and Postal 1964; Gordon and Lakoff 1975; Katz 1977; Labov and Fanshel 1977; Burton 1980). Sometimes an utterance is identified as a question because it is interrogative in form, and sometimes because it expects an answer or some verbal performance from the addressee. In other words, the term 'question' is sometimes taken as a syntactic category and sometimes a discourse category: as a result, the term remains vague and ill-defined. I shall examine some of the studies of questions in sections 4.2 to 4.4 below.

4.2 Quirk *et al.*'s study of questions

Let us start with the study of questions by Quirk *et al.* (1972, 1985).[1] Quirk *et al.* define questions as a semantic class which is primarily used to seek information on a specific point (see Quirk *et al.* 1985: 804). They propose that there are three major classes of question according to the answer they expect:

1 Those that expect affirmation or negation, as in 'Have you finished the book?' YES–NO questions.

2 Those that typically expect a reply from an open range of replies, as in 'What is your name?' or 'How old are you?' WH-questions.
3 Those that expect as the reply one of two or more options presented in the question, as in 'Would you like to go for a WÁLK or stay at HÒME?' ALTERNATIVE questions. (ibid.: 806)

Let us examine these three classes one by one.

4.2.1 Yes–no questions, tag questions, and declarative questions

Yes–no questions

According to Quirk *et al.*, yes–no questions are usually formed by placing the operator before the subject and using question intonation—that is, a rise or fall-rise. Another typical characteristic of yes–no questions is the use of non-assertive forms 'any', 'ever', and so on, which denote neutral polarity that leaves open whether the answer is 'yes' or 'no'. However, Quirk *et al.* point out that a yes–no question can be biased towards a positive or a negative answer. For example, assertive forms such as 'someone' may be used, in which case, the question has a positive orientation, e.g. 'Did *someone* call last night?', 'Has the boat left *already*?'. These questions are biased towards a positive answer. They indicate that the speaker has reason to believe that the answer is 'yes'; he/she is asking for confirmation of this assumption (see 1972: 389). This means that the expected answer is 'yes', and thus a 'no' answer would be contrary to that expectation. As for questions like 'Isn't your car working?', Quirk *et al.* suggest that they have negative orientation. This negative orientation, however, is complicated by an element of surprise or disbelief. The implication is that the speaker had originally hoped for a positive response, but new evidence suggests that the response will be negative. There is therefore a combination of old expectation (positive) and new expectation (negative) (1985: 808). The expected answer is 'no', and 'yes' would be contrary to expectation. Quirk *et al.* further remark that because the old expectation tends to be identified with the speaker's hopes and wishes, negatively orientated questions often express disappointment or annoyance. The examples they give are 'Can't you drive straight?' and 'Aren't you ashamed of yourself?'

From Quirk *et al.*'s analysis of yes–no questions so far, we can detect three problems. Firstly, if the classification of questions is made on the basis of the answer they expect, then there should be three classes of questions: one class expecting a 'yes' answer, a second expecting a 'no' answer, and a third with no expectations. However, it should be noted that there are three classes of questions only in terms of the predicted *form* of the answer. In terms of the *communicative choice* realized by the answer, there are only two classes of questions because a 'yes' answer to a positively biased question realizes the same communicative choice of confirming the speaker's assumption or expectation as a 'no' answer to a negatively biased question. This can be supported by the fact that sometimes negatively biased questions can get a 'yes' or a 'no' answer, both realizing a confirmation. For example, the question 'You mean he didn't recognize you?', which is negatively biased, can be responded to by 'Yes' meaning 'you are right, he didn't recognize me, or 'No' also meaning 'you are right, he didn't recognize me'. Both answers confirm the speaker's assumption. Hence, both negatively and positively biased questions belong to the same functional class: questions whose discourse function is to elicit confirmation.

Secondly, if we are looking at the function or the communicative choice realized by the expected answer and not its form, then a 'yes' answer to the question 'Have you been to Paris?' and a 'yes' answer to the question 'Has the boat left *already*?' have different functions. The first 'yes' is an elliptical form of 'Yes, I have been to Paris', which supplies the information, whereas the second 'yes' is an elliptical form of 'Yes, your assumption is correct', which confirms the speaker's assumption. In other words, the difference between these two questions is not so much that one has neutral polarity and the other has biased polarity, but rather that one seeks information and the other seeks confirmation. The former is therefore similar to wh-questions which seek information, such as 'What country have you been to?', except that the information it seeks is more specific (cf. Churchill 1978). It is only because English has a yes–no answering system that we are misled into believing that the function of questions like 'Have you been to Paris?' is to elicit a 'yes' answer (hence a confirmation) or a 'no' answer (hence a disconfirmation) and therefore they have a different function from wh-questions (see the discussion on Alternative Questions in section 4.2.3).[2]

That the so-called neutral polarity yes–no questions are, in fact, information-seeking questions can be further supported by the fact that they do not necessarily expect either a 'yes' or 'no' answer. The utterance 'Are you still here?' spoken with high termination by the speaker to his colleague working in the office at seven o'clock in the evening does not expect either a 'yes' or 'no' answer. It functions as an information question tantamount to 'Why are you still here?'. A mere 'yes' or 'no' response from the addressee would be odd or interpreted as unwillingness to interact with the speaker. The following piece of data supports this observation:

(1) [BCET:A:10]
  → **B:** Did you have a good time in Soho?
     C: It was alright, you know, bit of rip-off place. We found –
         we walked – ((*laughs*)) we were trying to pluck up
         courage to go in a strip club, right, because I hadn't been
         to a strip club before, Mike hadn't either and we thought
         . . .

B's yes–no question is tantamount to 'What did you do in Soho?'. As can be seen, C gives an account of what he and his friends did in Soho.

Thirdly, those questions which express disappointment and annoyance seem to expect neither a 'yes' nor a 'no' answer. Either a 'yes' or a 'no' answer to 'Can't you drive straight?' would be considered cheeky or brusque. Silent acquiescence or an apology is likely to be the expected response. Hence, it is doubtful whether such utterances should be considered as belonging to the category of questions at all, as defined by Quirk *et al.*

Tag questions
Similar problems can be found in their handling of tag questions. Tag questions are considered a further type of yes–no question which conveys negative or positive orientation. Quirk *et al.* propose four types of tag questions:

> Type 1: He likes his JÒB, DÓESn't he? (Rising tone)
> Type 2: He doesn't like his JÒB, DÓES he? (Rising tone)
> Type 3: He likes his JÒB, DÒESn't he? (Falling tone)
> Type 4: He doesn't like his JÒB, DÒES he? (Falling tone)

Each of these four types asserts the speaker's assumption and invites a response. Each, they say, has different assumptions and expectations:

68

Type 1: Positive assumption+neutral expectation
Type 2: Negative assumption+neutral expectation
Type 3: Positive assumption+positive expectation
Type 4: Negative assumption+negative expectation
(Quirk *et al.* 1985: 811)

Quirk *et al.*'s analysis of tag questions is problematic. According to their analysis of the expected answers, there are three and not four different expected answers to tag questions. Both Types 1 and 2 expect either 'yes' or 'no'. But, again, it should be noted that this is a classification in terms of form; in terms of communicative choice, there are only two types, because the 'yes' answer in Type 3 and the 'no' answer in Type 4 both realize the same communicative choice of agreeing with the speaker's assumption.

Further, one can question whether a tag question can have neutral expectation. The very constructon of a tag question suggests that the speaker has certain assumptions and is biased towards a certain answer. As Hudson (1975: 24) points out, tags are always conducive; they cannot be neutral. For a tag question with a rising tone, the discourse context or the context of situation has led the speaker to cast doubt on his assumption and he invites the addressee to confirm it (see also Brazil 1984: 43).

In other words, a tag with a rising tone (i.e. Types 1 and 2) is biased towards an expected answer rather than neutral. It invites the addressee to confirm the speaker's assumption. This can be supported by the fact that a confirmation will be spoken in mid key, indicating that the answer fulfils the expectation, whereas a denial is likely to be spoken in high key, indicating that the answer is contrary to the expectation (see also Brazil *et al.* 1980). For example:

(2) [C:4:14]
                    THINK you did that
     S: //p I   THIS year //r+ DIDn't you //
     G: //p oh YEAH //

G's response is spoken in mid key. If the answer had been 'no', it would have been spoken in high key. For example:

(3) [BCET:A:20]
     B: //p it's not TOO late to apPLY now //r+ IS it //

YEAH
C: //p   //p I <u>THINK</u> so //r+ they're <u>ALL</u> full up //

C's response, 'yeah', which disconfirms the speaker's assumption, is spoken in high key, indicating that it is contrary to B's expectation. As for a tag spoken with falling tone, the speaker has no doubt about his assumption and the addressee is invited to agree with him. For example:

(4) [C:4:3]
    G: //p Fox is his <u>FIRST</u> name //p <u>IS</u>n't it //
    S: //p <u>RIGHT</u> //

(5) [C:4:26]
    G: //p sounds like a soCIety of <u>MOLE</u>s //p <u>DOES</u>n't it //
    S: ((*laughs*))

In (5), S responds to G's tag question by laughing, which is commonly used as a minimal indication of agreement. This kind of response would be unacceptable for a tag with a rising tone, because it would require a more explicit response of a confirmation or disconfirmation.

Thus, although both types of tag question expect a 'yes' (or 'no') answer from the addressee, the functions that they realize are different. While a 'yes' (or 'no') answer to a rising tag realizes a confirmation, a 'yes' (or 'no') answer to a falling tag realizes an agreement. The difference can be best seen by comparing (2) with (6) below:

(6) [I]
    On a sunny day.

    A: //p it's a <u>LOVE</u>ly day //p <u>IS</u>n't it //
    B: //p <u>YES</u> //

While S's question in (2) seeks confirmation from G, A's question in (6) cannot possibly seek confirmation from B that it is a lovely day, because the truth of the asserted proposition is self-evident. It functions to get B to agree with him that it evidently is a lovely day (see Brazil 1984: 36). Thus we can see that, in terms of the function or communicative choice realized by the expected answers, there are only two types of tag question, not four: one which expects *agreement* and one which expects *confirmation* from the addressee.

Declarative questions

The third type of question which falls under yes–no questions, according to Quirk *et al.*, is declarative questions which are items that are identical lexico-grammatically to declaratives but function as questions because they are spoken with rising intonation. For example, 'You've got the exPLÓsives?'. Declarative questions are said to invite the hearer's verification; that is, either a 'yes' or a 'no' answer (see Quirk *et al.* 1985: 814).

This analysis of declarative questions is questionable. Firstly, the very fact that the question should be presented in declarative form suggests that the speaker has certain assumptions and the utterance is biased towards an expected response. Brazil (1985) suggests that in the utterance //r+ you preFER THAT one//, the speaker is heard as 'proffering a tentative assessment of common ground' and the response expected is a 'confirmation of a proclaimed endorsement, yes' (ibid.: 155–6). A response which denies the tentative assessment of the speaker can, of course, occur, but it will be contrary to the expectation and is likely to be spoken in contrastive high key. Secondly, Quirk *et al.* have overlooked the fact that declarative questions can also be realized by a declarative sentence spoken with a falling intonation. For example, the arrowed utterance in (7):

(7) [B:C:A:1:2]
    H: I I don't know, see, he has a son at, was in the school last year ah does he have to re-apply?
    X: Ah yes, I think so.
→ **H:** So we'll have to fill out one of those forms again.
    X: Yes.

H is not telling X that he has to fill out a form, but asking for confirmation. As Brazil (1985) points out, in saying 'you prefer that one' with a proclaiming (i.e. falling) tone and mid-termination, the speaker is not likely to be telling the hearer about his preference, but rather asking him to respond to the tentative assertion. Similarly, the utterance 'John prefers that one' spoken with a falling tone in a situation where the addressee is privy to John's preference functions as a question. Labov and Fanshel (1977) have made similar observations. They state that if the speaker makes a statement about a B-event, which is an event known only to the addressee, with a falling intonation (which they call declarative intonation), then it is heard as a request for confirmation. This is supported by their findings in a series of interviews: negative responses to the declarative question 'and you never called the police' were in the form of a simple 'No', whereas positive responses required some indication of surprise as well, such as 'Oh yes, I called them' (Labov and Fanshel 1977: 101). The requirement of an indication of surprise for positive responses shows that they are contrary to the expectation of the declarative question.

Thirdly, declarative questions can also function as information questions in certain contexts and the answer expected is a supply of information. Consider the following example given by Brazil (1985):

(8) [Brazil 1985: 159]
Doctor: //p where do you GET this pain //
Patient: //p in my HEAD //
→ **Doctor:** //p you GET it in your HEAD //

As is evident from the discourse context, in the arrowed utterance, the doctor is not so much asking the patient to confirm but rather, as Brazil points out, is 'asking for greater precision—a recycling of the question so to speak by behaving as though the patient had not yet selected a response, and leading perhaps to ' "Yes. Behind my eyes." ' (ibid.) (see also example (33), in section 4.6.1).

4.2.2 Wh-questions

The second class of questions is wh-questions which are information-seeking and seem to be the least problematic category. They are realized by wh-words, usually spoken with falling intonation, and the answer expected is the missing piece of information denoted by the wh-word. They are considered to constitute a category distinctly different from questions seeking neutral polarity and questions seeking confirmation. However, things are not quite so simple; consider the following wh-questions:

 (9) [I] What did you say?

(10) [I] What do you mean?

We can say that they expect the answer to be the supplying of information. But they are different from questions like 'What did you do yesterday?', in that they invite the addressee to repeat and/or to clarify whatever was said previously. In other words, these questions take the discourse backwards: they are about the discourse itself. Coulthard distinguishes them from information-seeking questions realized by wh-interrogatives by calling those which seek clarification of the preceding utterance 'Return' and those which seek repetition 'Loop' (see Coulthard 1981: 21ff.).

Consider also the following questions:

(11) [I] What time shall we meet?

(12) [I] Where shall I meet you?

These questions invite the addressee not only to supply the missing information signalled by 'what time' and 'where', but also to commit to a specific time and place of meeting. Take the following piece of data, for example:

(13) [B:B:A:3:3]
→ **A:** What time?
   B: Let's say about seven.
   A: Seven o'clock huh, okay.

Once the 'information' supplied by B is endorsed by A, both A and B have committed themselves to doing something at the specified time. That wh-questions like the above are not simply information-seeking can be seen firstly by comparing (14) with (15) and (16):

(14) [I]
   A: What's the time?
   B: Seven.
   A: Thanks.

(15) [I]
   A: What time shall we meet?
   B: Five o'clock.
→ ? **A:** Thanks.

(16) [I]
   A: Where shall we meet?
   B: At the Peninsula Hotel.
→ ? **A:** Thanks.

(14) is a perfectly acceptable exchange, whereas (15) and (16) are not. In (14), speaker A asks for a piece of information, and when B supplies the information, a thanking from A is in order. By contrast, in (15) and (16), A's thanking B is odd, because B is not merely supplying a piece of missing information.

Secondly, comparing (13) and (14), we can see that the 'information' supplied in B's utterance in (13) is negotiable, whereas that in (14) is not. In the former, A may not accept the time specified by B, in which case further exchanges will be produced until a time acceptable to both is settled upon, as we can see in the following piece of data:

(17) [B:B:B:6:2]

    X: When are we going to get together?

    H: Anytime. How about tonight?

    X: Well, I, I, ((*pause*)) I can't get together until um maybe Sunday.

    H: Alright, Sunday.

H's suggestion of 'tonight' as a time for meeting is not accepted. A further exchange results, in which H and X agree to meet up on Sunday.

The above discussion suggests that wh-questions can realize various functions, and that it is therefore doubtful whether wh-questions constitute a single class.

4.2.3 Alternative questions

The third class of questions proposed by Quirk *et al.* is alternative questions. According to them, there are two types of alternative question: the first type resembles a yes–no question and the second a wh-question. For example:

(18) [I] Would you like CHÓcolate, vaNÍLla, or STRÀWberry?

(19) [I] Which ice cream would you LÌKE, CHÓcolate, vaNÍLla, or STRÀWberry?

The first type is said to differ from a yes–no question *only* in intonation (my emphasis). Instead of the final rising tone, it contains a separate nucleus for each alternative; that is, there is a rise on each item except for the last one where a fall occurs, indicating that the list is complete (see Quirk *et al.* 1985: 823). The second type is a compound question: a wh-question followed by an elliptical alternative question. Its full form is something like the following:

(20) [I] Which ice cream would you LÌKE? Would you like CHÓcolate, vaNÍLla, or STRÀWberry?

There are two points that I wish to raise here: firstly, it is true that alternative questions have at least two different syntactic forms, but do they realize two different categories of questions in terms of the expected answer? Secondly, is it justified to establish alternative questions as a third category? In other words, do they constitute a class of question distinctly different from yes–no and wh-questions?

To address the first point, let us look at the answer expected to (18) and (19). For both, the expected answer is one of the three stated choices. In other words, classified in terms of prospected answer, they belong to the same type of question, although they have different syntactic structures. They both invite the addressee to inform the speaker of his choice. To address the second point, let us compare alternative questions and wh-questions. Look at the following exchanges initiated by an alternative question and a wh-question:

(21) [I]
   A: How are we going to get there?
   B: By BÙS.

(22) [I]
   A: Will we get there by BÚS or TRÀIN?
   B: By BÙS.

In both exchanges, A's utterance invites B to supply a piece of information. The only difference is that in (22), the information that B supplies is one of the alternatives offered by A. In other words, both are *information-seeking* questions.

Let us now compare alternative questions with yes–no questions. Quirk *et al.* differentiate them as follows:

(23) [I] (Alternative)
   A: Shall we go by BÚS or TRÀIN?
   B: By BÙS.

(24) [I] (Yes–no)
    A: Shall we go by bus or TRÁIN?
    B: No, let's take the CÀR.

(24) is considered to be a different category of question from (23) because (24) can be responded to by 'yes' or 'no', whereas (23) cannot. The answer to (23) must be lexicalized. However, what Quirk *et al.* have overlooked is that the 'yes' or 'no' answer to (24) is only a preface to the stating of a choice which must also be lexicalized. This is supported by the fact that a response consisting of only a 'yes' or 'no' without the stated choice is self-evidently incomplete. Consider the following:

(25) [I]
    A: Shall we go by bus or TRÁIN?
  ? **B:** No.

Hence, like (23), the expected answer to (24) is the stating of a choice. The only difference between the two is that in the former, the choice is selected from a restricted set, whereas in the latter, it is selected from a potentially unrestricted set. In this sense, alternative questions and yes–no questions are similar (see also Jespersen 1933). In fact, in some languages, for example Portuguese and Mandarin Chinese, which do not have a 'yes/no' answering system, the answer to a yes–no question is always lexicalized as in alternative questions.[3]

We may conclude by saying that in terms of expected answer, alternative questions do not constitute a separate category, but rather belong to the category of information-seeking questions.

4.2.4 Exclamatory questions

Finally, I wish to discuss briefly what Quirk *et al.* call 'exclamatory questions' which are considered a minor type of question. Exclamatory questions are considered to function like exclamations, although they have the form of a question. They can take the form of a negative polar question with a final falling instead of rising tone, such as 'Hasn't she GRÒWN!', and 'Wasn't it a marvellous CÒNcert!', or they can take the form of a positive polar question, also with a falling intonation, such as 'Am I HÙNgry!', 'Did he look anNÒYed!'. Quirk *et al.* point out that the first form invites the addressee's agreement. This suggests that the answer expected would be the same as for questions which seek agreement with the speaker's assumption or belief, for example, 'She has grown, HÀSn't she?'. Hence, the former belongs to the same category as the latter. As for the second form of exclamatory question, the expected answer is more often an acknowledgement than an agreement. This is true for exclamatory questions such as 'Am I HÙNgry!', where the experience is entirely personal and therefore can only be acknowledged; but it is also true for questions like 'Did he look anNÒYed!', which are often responded to by an acknowledgement such as 'Oh DÍD he'. Here we can see that exclamatory questions which elicit agreement in fact belong to the same category as tag questions which elicit agreement, and those which elicit an acknowledgement belong to an entirely different category.

4.2.5 Form versus communicative choice

From the above discussion, it can be seen that the characterization and classification of questions proposed by Quirk *et al.* is unsatisfactory. Although they claim that their classification is made according to the response expected, the above discussion reveals that very often precedence is given to syntactic form rather than expected response. The three major classes of questions that they propose are, in fact, based on surface form. Even when they do look at the expected response, it is often the form of the response that is being attended to, rather than the function or the communicative choice realized by the response.

4.3 Question as illocutionary act

Let us now look at the characterization of questions as illocutionary acts. Lyons (1977) characterizes a question as an utterance with a particular illocutionary force. He asserts that the difference between a question and a statement is that the former contains a feature of doubt, and that one of its felicity conditions is that the speaker should not know the answer to his question. He asserts that although questions are normally associated with the expectation of an answer from the addressee, this association is conventional and is independent of the illocutionary force of the question. He argues that this analysis of questions enables us to subsume various kinds of rhetorical questions instead of having to treat them as abnormal or parasitic upon information-seeking questions (ibid.: 755). The inconsistency of this characterization of question can be seen from two objections that I shall raise below.

Firstly, if the expectation of an answer is independent of the illocutionary force of a question, then there is no need to differentiate the following two sentences:

(26) [I] Is the door open?

(27) [I] The door is open, isn't it?

In both sentences, the speaker expresses doubt as to whether the door is open. Yet Lyons distinguishes between the two by pointing out that a sentence like (27) 'puts to the addressee the positive proposition p (which the speaker is inclined to believe to be true and assumes the addressee will accept), but at the same time explicitly admits in the tag the possibility of its rejection' (ibid.: 765), and that the function of the checking tag is 'expressly to solicit the addressee's acceptance or rejection of the proposition that is presented to him' (ibid.). A sentence like (26), however, is 'neutral with respect to any indication of the speaker's beliefs as to the truth value of p, and when they are asked of an addressee, unless they are given a particular prosodic or paralinguistic modulation, they convey no information to the addressee that the speaker expects him to accept or reject p' (ibid.). In other words, while one expects the possibility of rejection in the tag, the other has no expectation of rejection or acceptance. Hence, by differentiating the two, Lyons is, in fact, taking the expected answer into consideration.

Secondly, according to Lyons' characterization of questions, it is difficult to see how rhetorical questions can be handled. Consider the following example:

(28) [B:H:B:5:5]
    H and M are talking about a colleague who has just joined the department.

    H: But I think he might be a threat a threat to the very insecure Chinese folk around here.
→ M: Who cares?
    H: And ah that that sh-

M's utterance 'Who cares?' is commonly referred to as a rhetorical question. But it does not express doubt, nor does it imply that M does not know the answer to the question. It is a remark on H's opinion that the new colleague will be a threat to his Chinese colleagues. This is supported by the fact that after M's remark, H does not supply an answer, but rather continues to express his opinion.

What Lyons, as well as Quirk *et al.*, seem to be doing is trying to offer a description which takes into account both syntactic form and discourse function. Therefore, different and inconsistent criteria are used in the identification and classification of questions. The result is that the category of question becomes a half-way house between a syntactic category and a discourse category. As Anthony points out:

> A definition which attempts to cover utterances as syntactically and functionally disparate as those which we intuitively label questions necessarily reduces itself to near-vacuity. (Anthony 1974: 6, quoted in Stenström 1984)

4.4 Question as request

Let us now turn to the characterization of questions which moves completely away from syntactic form to function—the characterization of questions as requests and directives. Questions have been characterized by some as requests which have the purpose of eliciting information (see, for example, Katz and Postal 1964; Katz 1972, 1977; Gordon and Lakoff 1975; Labov and Fanshel 1977). It has been suggested that the logical form of questions should be REQUEST (a, b, TELL (b, a, S)) and not ASK (a, b, S); 'a' being the speaker, 'b' the addressee, and 'S' the proposition in the question (see Gordon and Lakoff 1975: 87). In other words, it should be 'I request that you tell me', instead of 'I ask you'. Questions have also been characterized by others as a kind of directive on the grounds that a directive is an instruction to perform something and questions are instructions to make a verbal performance. For example, according to Burton (1980), 'Tell me your name' is a directive to make a verbal performance, and according to Willis (1981), a question in which a student is instructed to say something is characterized as 'Direct: verbal'. While this kind of characterization does not confuse form and function, it is not without problems.

Sadock (1974) points out that it is wrong to say that all questions are to be represented as requests, specifically requests for information. He provides the following evidence to support his argument: requests can take sentence-adverbial 'please', but there are many types of questions that can be used as indirect requests with which 'please' cannot occur, for example, *'Don't you think you should please take out the garbage?'; true questions allow the pre-tag 'tell me', but requests do not, for example, *'Tell me, take out the garbage, will you?'; and so on (see Sadock 1974: 90). Lyons (1977) points out that questions are not a kind of request because 'No' in response to yes–no questions such as 'Is the door open?' is an answer to the question, whereas 'No' to 'Open the door, please?' is refusing to do what is requested.

To Sadock's and Lyons' arguments I wish to add that there is a crucial difference between the two, which is that utterances referred to as 'questions' elicit or prospect a very different response from requests. A question elicits an obligatory verbal response (or non-verbal surrogate) and the interaction between the speaker and the addressee is completed entirely at the verbal level. A request, however, elicits an obligatory non-verbal response with perhaps an accompanying verbal response, and the interaction is completed at the non-verbal level. In other words, questions have a different discourse function or consequence from requests and therefore they should not be subsumed under the latter (see also Stubbs 1983: 75).

Since the category 'question' is vague and ill-defined and cannot be subsumed under either requests or directives, I propose to call those utterances which elicit solely a verbal response *elicitations*.

4.5 Elicitations

The term 'elicitation' is first introduced by Sinclair and Coulthard to describe utterances in the classroom which elicit a verbal response. They write:

> An elicitation is an act the function of which is to request a linguistic response—linguistic, although the response may be a non-verbal surrogate such as a nod or raised hand. (Sinclair and Coulthard 1975: 28)

The term *elicitation* is used here as a discourse category to describe any utterance, both inside and outside the classroom, which functions to elicit an *obligatory* verbal response or its non-verbal surrogate.

I shall now attempt to identify further subclasses of elicitations according to the different responses prospected.

4.6 Subclasses of elicitations

4.6.1 Elicit:inform[4]

Let us start with the kind of elicitation which invites the addressee to supply a piece of information. Consider the following data:

(29) [B:A:A:2:1]
→ H: What time will you be finished?
X: Lecture finishes at about quarter past twelve.

(30) [B:E:A:4:3]
→ X: Are you a literature section or a language studies.
　　　　　　　　　　　　　　　　[
H:　　　　　　　　　　No no I'm I'm not I'm
language side, but I would like to see the two sides bridged myself.

(31) [B:B:A:3]
→ B: Do you do you have wheels?
A: Yes, I drive, it's Donald's car.

(32) [Schegloff 1972: 107]
→ A: I don't know just where the – uh – this address // is
B: Well, where do – which part of the town do you live.
A: I live at four ten east Lowden.
B: Well, you don't live very far from me.

(33) [B:C:B:1:9]
E: D'you have an OUP here, or you haven't got it?
F: No, ah I asked them, they haven't got it, so I got it from New York.
→ E: You have to get it from New York huh?
F: Yeah just write, just write them a letter, they'll probably send it by air mail too, for free.

For (29), it will be generally agreed that H's utterance asks 'for a piece of missing information. X's utterance in (30) is similar to H's utterance in (29) in that it also invites the addressee to supply a piece of information, except that the answer prospected here is one of the alternatives supplied. B's utterance in (31) is what Quirk *et al.* refer to as a 'neutral polarity yes–no question', in which the speaker does not have any assumptions as to whether the answer is 'yes' or 'no'. As mentioned before, although the prospected answers to this kind of utterance are usually in the form of 'yes' or 'no', they do not, and cannot possibly, realize a confirmation or disconfirmation, because there is no speaker assumption to confirm or disconfirm. They are, in fact, the missing information that the speaker seeks. A's utterance in (32) is declarative in form. However, we can see that A is not giving B a piece of information, but rather seeking information. It is equivalent to 'Where is this address?'. Finally, E's utterance in (33) is a declarative plus a questioning particle. This kind of surface form commonly realizes a confirmation-seeking elicitation. But, in this particular context, its function is obviously not to seek confirmation, since what it appears to seek confirmation of has already been given in the preceding utterance and there does not appear to be any hitch in communication between E and F. E's utterance is therefore seeking further information about obtaining the book from New York. Hence, we can say that the arrowed utterances in (29) to (33) all realize the same discourse function. Let us call them *elicit:inform*.

4.6.2 Elicit:confirm

The second subclass consists of elicitations which invite the addressee to confirm the speaker's assumption. This subclass can be realized by tag interrogatives (both reversed polarity tags and copy tags), declaratives, and positive and negative polar interrogatives. The following arrowed utterances are all instances of *elicit:confirm*:

(34) [C:4:14]

              THINK you did that

→ S: //p I   THIS year //r+ DIDn't you //

     G: Oh yeah.

(35) [B:B:A:1:2]

→ F: //p JOHN would know //r+ WOULD he //

     H: Yeah, John would know.

(36) [B:E:A:4:3]
  → X: //p these ARE students in the <u>ENG</u>lish department //
     H: That's right, they're all English majors.

(37) [B:D:A:1:2]
  → C: //p the <u>WHITE</u> building //r+ where they have the
        psy<u>CHO</u>logy department and everything //
     D: Psycho, law, you name it, oh they're all in there.

(38) [B:F:A:1:3]
  → E: //p <u>DID</u>n't ah //r YEVtu<u>SHEN</u>ko //r+ write a <u>PO</u>em
        about that //
     F: Yeah, that's right.

(39) [B:B:A:2:1]
  → X: //p is that YOU <u>HEN</u>ry //
     Y: Yes, that's right, yeah.

In all of the above arrowed utterances, the declarative, or the declarative associated with the interrogative, expresses what the speaker assumes to be true and the speaker is inviting the addressee to confirm that his assumption is true.

In (34) and (35), the rising tags invite the addressee to confirm the speaker's assumption. The arrowed utterances in (36) and (37) are declarative in form, with the former spoken with a falling tone (p) and the latter a rising tone (r+). In both cases, the addressee has better knowledge of the subject matter than the speaker. Hence, they realize the function of seeking confirmation from the addressee. If it were vice versa, (36) would realize the function of giving information, and (37) would realize the function of seeking confirmation that the addressee knows which building the speaker is referring to. The following is an example of the latter:

(40) [B:A:A:1]
     H: //p <u>HEY</u> //p I I for<u>GOT</u> something //p I <u>HAVE</u> to go to
        <u>LUNCH</u> today //p with <u>AL</u>ice //((*laughs*))//o to <u>SEE</u> =
                                     [
     X: ((*laughs*))
     H: the//=//p <u>YOU</u> know //o <u>THE</u> //p the ah <u>VID</u>eotape //r+
        of that <u>SHOW</u> //r+ we <u>DID</u> at the ho<u>TEL</u> //
     X: Yup, yup.

Here, H seeks confirmation from X that he knows which video-tape he is referring to.

Hence, the discourse function of an utterance depends not only on the intonation, but also on the situation and who knows what (see Brazil 1985). However, it should be noted that the context of situation does not always help to disambiguate the discourse function. For example:

(41) [Coulthard and Brazil 1981: 84]
    A: So the meeting's on Friday.
    B: Thanks.
    A: No I'm asking you.

In cases like this, the discourse function of the utterance will only be disambiguated as the discourse unfolds.

E's utterance in (38) is a negative polar interrogative. According to Quirk *et al.*, negative questions have a negative orientation: they are biased towards a negative answer. However, E's utterance is not negatively conducive. Quite the contrary, it prospects a positive response confirming the speaker's assumption that Yevtushenko did write a poem. Whether a negative polar interrogative is positively or negatively conducive depends on the context. For example, if A, seeing B still in bed at 11.00 a.m., says 'Don't you have lectures today?', then the expected answer to the utterance is obviously negative. A positive answer would be contrary to the expectation.

Finally, in (39), X assumes that the person on the other end of the line is Henry and he invites the addressee to confirm his assumption. X's utterance is what Quirk *et al.* would describe as a positively biased yes–no question. However, as we can see, there are no assertive forms like 'someone' or 'already' in the utterance. The positive orientation is achieved by making 'you' prominent. Even when an assertive form like 'someone' is used, the utterance is not necessarily positively orientated. For example, the utterance 'Did someone CALL last night?' with the prominence on 'call' is not positively orientated. It is equivalent to 'Did anyone CALL last night?'. Both of them mean 'Was there a caller?'. Unless 'someone' is prominent, the utterance is not positively orientated and 'someone' is not contrastive to 'anyone'.[5] In other words, prosodic features like prominence are important factors in determining what kind of elicitation an utterance realizes.

particularly between strangers. Other examples are the use of elicit:agrees like 'Are you John Matthews?' or 'You must be John Matthews' to start a conversation in an encounter at a party or at the beginning of an interview when names are already known. Since what the addressee is invited to agree with is self-evidently true, the speaker is bound to be successful in eliciting the expected response. This establishes the common ground between the speaker and the addressee, serves to 'promote social mutuality', and paves the way for further interaction (see Brazil 1984: 34).

4.6.4 Elicit:commit

There is yet another subclass of elicitation which differs from the above three subclasses in that, in addition to a verbal response, it also elicits commitment of some kind. Let us identify them as *elicit: commit*. Consider the following example:

(47) [C:1:A:4:1]
→   J: Can I talk to you?
    S: Sure. Come in. Let's close the door. Have a seat.

The purpose of J's elicitation is not just to elicit a 'yes' answer from S, but also to get S to commit herself to a talking session. As Goffman (1981) points out, the intent of the question 'Have you got a minute?' is to open up a channel of communication which stays open beyond the hoped-for reply that satisfies the opening. The following exchange is, therefore, odd:

(48) [I]
    A: Can I talk to you?
    B: Sure.
?   A: ∅

Hence, this kind of elicitation not only invites an obligatory response, but also invites commitment on the part of the addressee to further interaction.

Another kind of elicitation which can be considered an elicit: commit is that realized by the type of wh-interrogative discussed above (see (11) and (12)) which invites the addressee to enter into some kind of contract with the speaker. The following is another example:

(49) [B:C:A:5:1]
    X: Where shall I meet you?
    H: Well ah I'll be finished with my class at five, it's =
                                                [
    X: uhuh
    H: = right in Tsimshatsui, so maybe we'll meet you at the
       Peninsula, between say five fifteen and five thirty?
→ X: Okay, wonderful.

As I have already pointed out above, utterances like X's elicitation above initiate an exchange in which the speaker endorses the 'information' elicited in the third part. Once the endorsement is given, both the speaker and the addressee have committed themselves to a future action.

This subclass bears strong similarity to requests, in the sense that if responded to positively, it will involve commitment to a further action or a further exchange. There is, nevertheless, an important difference: a verbal response is obligatory in elicit:commit, whereas it is not in requests.

4.6.5 Elicit:repeat and elicit:clarify

Finally, there are two subclasses of elicitation which refer to the discourse itself. One prospects a repetition and the other prospects the clarification of a preceding utterance or preceding utterances. We may label the former as *elicit:repeat* and the latter as *elicit: clarify*. The former is realized by wh-interrogatives such as 'Who/When/Where/What did you say?', 'Say that again?', or words such as 'Sorry?', 'Pardon?', or 'Huh?'. It should be noted, however, that the utterance 'What did you say?' realizes an elicit:repeat only when 'what' is prominent and is usually spoken with a rising tone (r+). If 'you' is prominent, then it realizes an elicit:inform. The following is a possible contextualization of the latter:

(50) [I]
    A: He asked me if he could borrow my car.
→ B: And what did YOU say?

Here, B is not asking A for a repetition, but rather to report what he said. It is therefore an elicit:inform and is usually spoken with a falling tone.

Elicit:clarify has a greater variety of realizations. It can be realized by wh-interrogatives such as 'What do you mean?', 'Which room?', or 'Where?'.

To summarize, we may say that we can identify six subclasses of elicitation: *elicit:inform*, *elicit:confirm*, *elicit:agree*, *elicit:commit*, *elicit:repeat*, and *elicit:clarify*.

4.7 Concluding remarks

In this chapter, I have characterized any utterance in the *initiating move* which prospects an obligatory verbal response as an *elicitation* irrespective of its syntactic form. On the basis of this, I have identified six subclasses of elicitation. This characterization avoids the inconsistency of using syntactic criteria for some utterances and discourse criteria for others. It avoids confusing labels such as 'exclamatory questions' and 'declarative questions'—where, in the former, the term 'question' refers to the interrogative form, whereas in the latter, the term 'question' refers to the discourse function. It also avoids the lumping together of utterances which have different discourse consequences, such as the characterization of questions as requests.

5
Requestives

5.1 Introduction

The aim of this chapter is to make a detailed examination of utterances which belong to the category of *requestives*. It argues that utterances which solicit non-verbal actions can be classified into two separate subclasses according to whether or not the addressee is given the option of carrying out the solicited action, namely *requestives* which give the addressee the option and *directives* which do not.

Let us compare the following two pieces of classroom data:

(1) [Reading Lesson:5][1]
→   P: Can we give in our grammar on um Wednesday?
    T: Can you give in your grammar on Wednesday?
        You have a lot of homework for tomorrow?
    Ps: Yes yes
    P: We have our last exercise.
    T: You have to do
    P: Our last exercise.
    T: Oh, that's because you have been lazy and didn't do
        your work properly, that's why you have extra work to
        do right? So I'm sorry you have to do it otherwise I =
                [
    Ps: No.
    T: = won't be able to finish marking your books to give
        you before the holidays.

(2) [Sinclair and Coulthard 1975: 91]
→   T: Can you point to a piece of metal in this room anybody
        a piece of metal in this room.
    P: (NV)
    T: Yes.

→ T: You go and show me one David a piece of metal.
    P: (NV)
    T: Yes that's a piece of metal well done a team point you
       can have one.
→ T: Will you show me a piece of metal.
    P: (NV)
    T: Yes the radiator that's a piece of metal.

The first arrowed utterances in (1) and (2) are both interrogative in form and both concern a non-verbal action. That in (1) involves the non-verbal action of the pupils handing in the grammar exercise on Wednesday, and that in (2) involves the non-verbal action of the pupils pointing to a piece of metal. However, while we will say that in (1) the pupil is making some sort of request, we will say that in (2) the teacher is giving an instruction or issuing a directive. This is because in (1), the pupil's utterance does not assume compliance: whether the teacher will grant them permission to hand in their grammar homework on Wednesday is entirely up to her. As we can see from the data, the teacher chooses not to comply with the pupils' request. By contrast, in (2), the pupils are not really given the choice of not acting according to the teacher's instruction; they are to do it. This can be seen from the fact that the teacher uses the interrogative form interchangeably with the imperative form to get the pupils to perform (see the second and third arrowed utterances). In other words, the responses that they expect are different. While that in (1) expects either compliance or non-compliance, that in (2) expects only compliance. In the present description, they belong to two different subclasses. The pupil's utterance in (1) is characterized as a *requestive*, whereas the teacher's utterances in (2) are characterized as *directives*.

5.2 Requestives versus directives

Requestives subsume utterances which have been referred to, in the speech act literature, as request, invite, ask for permission, and offer. They do not subsume those which have been referred to as order, command, and instruct. The latter are subsumed under a different subclass: directives.

The setting up of requestives and directives as two separate sub-classes departs from most taxonomies in the speech act and linguistics literature. Fraser (1975b) considers request, ask, command, invite, order, instruct, and beg as belonging to the category of 'requesting' which is characterized as 'the speaker's desire for the hearer to bring about the state of affairs expressed in the proposition' (Fraser 1975b: 192). Searle (1979) brings request, invite, and permit together with command and order under directives whose illocutionary point is to get the hearer to do something. Labov and Fanshel (1977) subsume orders like 'Come home!', requests like 'Will you please come home?', and suggestions like 'Isn't it about time you came home?' and hints like 'It's getting late!' under the category of 'request for action'. They assert that the common characteristic of all of these speech acts is that the speaker is using a verbal means to accomplish the end of getting the addressee to come home. (See also Ohmann 1972; Vendler 1972; Katz 1977; Bach and Harnish 1979; Leech 1983.) Therefore, before we characterize the subclasses of requestive, we need to justify the identification of requestives and directives as two separate subclasses.

A requestive such as what is commonly referred to as a 'request' and a directive such as what is commonly referred to as an 'order' do share an important characteristic: they both prospect a non-verbal action from the addressee. However, as I have pointed out above, there is an important difference between them in terms of discourse function.

Searle (1969) suggests that an order differs from a request in that the former has the additional preparatory condition that the speaker must be in a position of authority over the addressee. Others suggest that the difference between an order and a request is one of politeness and deference (see, for example, Green 1975: 120–2). While it is true that orders can only be appropriately performed by a speaker who has authority over the addressee but not vice versa and it is true that requests are generally conceived as polite ways of getting the addressee to do something, these are not the crucial differences. First of all, it is not uncommon for requests to be performed when the speaker has authority over the addressee (see (3) below). Secondly, as Lyons (1977: 748–9) points out, a request can be impolite and an impolite request is not an order.

The crucial difference is that a request gives the addressee the options of complying or not complying, whereas an order does not. In other words, in a request, the speaker acknowledges the addressee's right to withhold compliance (see Lyons 1977: 749; Leech 1983: 219; Butler 1988: 133).[2] An order assumes that the addressee will co-operate, whereas a request does not. This is supported by Lawson's study of the directives of a two-year-old child in which it is discovered that the child uses directives like 'Mommy, I want milk' to her mother, whereas to her father she uses forms like 'Daddy, I want some please? Please Daddy, huh?'. As Ervin-Tripp points out, this is because the mother is the one who supplies food and therefore compliance is assumed, whereas the father does not usually supply food and therefore compliance is not assumed (see Ervin-Tripp 1977: 183–4).

Hence, J's utterance in the following is a request although he definitely has power over H, the secretary:

(3) [Fieldnotes]
J is a professor and H is his secretary.

J: Hazel, could you knock up some coffee?
H: Okay.

Here, serving coffee is not part of the duty of a secretary, and therefore compliance is not assumed. Although we seldom find non-compliance in situations like this, it is, nevertheless, an option open to the addressee. It is only when the utterance prospects compliance *by virtue of* the speaker's right or power/authority over the addressee, or *by virtue of* the defined responsibility that it is an order.

Therefore, it is not accidental that the unmarked form of a request is the interrogative, whereas the unmarked form[3] of an order is the imperative, or a declarative which states the speaker's wants and needs (see also Halliday 1984: 14).[4] A request realized by the interrogative 'Can you close the window?' indicates that the speaker does not assume that the addressee is able to carry out the requested action, hence giving the latter the option of complying or not complying (see also Churchill 1978).[5] An order realized by the imperative 'Close the window', or the declarative 'I want you to close the window', does not indicate the speaker's doubt or query as to the addressee's carrying out the action, hence leaving the latter no option but to comply (see also Leech 1983: 109). This is supported by Ervin-Tripp's study of directives in American English in which she discovers that utterances of the form 'I want you to do X', which she calls needs and wants statements, occur in transactional work settings where who is to do what is very clear and are used between people differing in rank (see (4) and (5) below) and in families where solicitude on the part of the addressee could be assumed (see (6) below; cf. Gordon and Lakoff 1975).[6]

(4) [Ervin-Tripp 1976: 29]
    Doctor to nurse in hospital.
    I'll need a 19 gauge needle, IV tubing and a preptic swab.

(5) [ibid.]
    Head of office to subordinate.
    I want you to check the requirements for stairs.

(6) [ibid.: 30]
    Four-year-old to mother.
    I need a spoon. Mommy, I need a spoon.

The following pieces of data are some further examples:

(7) [Reading Lesson: 1]
    Teacher: Maria, I want to see you. I want to know why the whole exercise book has been marked not by me. I want to see you at the end of the lesson Maria, alright?

(8) [C:1:A:3:1]
    H and S are colleagues who know each other very well. H went into S's office to get teaching materials.
    H: I want to take a few more of these.
    S: ((*nods head*))

In classroom situations, pupils are expected to comply with the teacher's directions (see (2) and (7) above). Hence, needs and wants statements such as the above are frequently used. In (8), S is the co-ordinator of a course and all teaching materials are stored in her office. Teachers are supposed to go to her office whenever they need the handouts. In other words, it is the responsibility of S to provide the handouts. Therefore, a want statement is perfectly acceptable (see also Mitchell-Kernan and Kernan 1977: 194; Leech 1983: 129).[7]

It should be noted, however, that in circumstances like (8), a speaker may decide that there are other dimensions overriding obligation and responsibility, and may choose to use a 'request' rather than a needs and wants statement. For example:

(9) [C:2:A:4:1]
→ **R:** Could I get some handouts?
    S: Yeah, help yourself.

Example (9) occurred in the same setting as (8). R is a junior colleague who does not know S as well as H does. She is also teaching the same course as S and H. Although a want statement is acceptable here, she chooses to use a 'request' which does not assume compliance. It is likely that to R, dimensions of social distance and seniority override the dimension of obligation.

Although both compliance and non-compliance are prospected by a requestive, the former is more strongly prospected than the latter. A compliance is a 'preferred' response, whereas a non-compliance is a 'dispreferred' response (see Pomerantz 1984: 63; see also Churchill 1978; 71; Owen 1983: 42).

Hence, according to the criterion of prospected response, we can say that at a less delicate stage, requestives and directives belong to the same subclass which elicits a non-verbal response, as opposed to the subclass which elicits a verbal response. But at a more delicate stage, they belong to two different subclasses. We can represent the classification as shown in Figure 5.1.

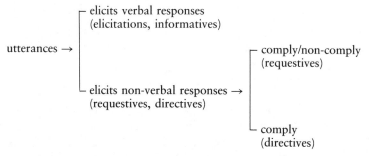

utterances →
- elicits verbal responses (elicitations, informatives)
- elicits non-verbal responses → (requestives, directives)
  - comply/non-comply (requestives)
  - comply (directives)

Figure 5.1: Classification of utterances

In the following, I shall attempt to identify the subclasses of requestives.

5.3 Subclasses of requestives

The classification of requestives into more delicate subclasses is no easy task. Consider the following pieces of data:

(10) [B:G:B:4:3]
    1 D: You're going to China on Friday or Saturday.
    2 R: No, we're going on Saturday and coming back Monday.
    3 D: I'll see if I can f– do you go into Canton?
    4 R: Yes.
→ 5 D: I'll see if I can find an old map of Canton that we had of the city y'know just as reference.
    6 R: Oh Don that's very kind of you.
→ 7 D: I'll sen– I saw it in the book shop but I have to
    8   I'll search again I'll put it in the mail box.
    9 R: Ah thank you very much.

(11) [Fieldnotes]
    A: D'you mind if I smoke?
    B: Go ahead.
    A: Thanks. (+NV)

(12) [B:B:A:3:1–2]
→ H: Well y'know Alice and I were just suggesting that maybe some Friday evening you might be free to come out for supper, right? . . .

(13) [B:C:A:2]
→ J: um I wonder if you might give my apologies I'm – not going to make it tomorrow.
            [
    K: Okay.
    K: Okay Jack sure.

The above arrowed utterances are all instances of requestives. (10) can be labelled an offer, but similar utterances have been labelled a requested permission by some (see, for example, van Dijk 1981). (11) can also be labelled a requested permission, but it is very different from (10). In (10), the speaker's action is for the benefit of the addressee, whereas in (11), the speaker's action is for the benefit of the speaker himself. As for (12), we may say that the speaker is extending an invitation, but we may also say that the speaker is requesting the addressee to come for supper. Brown and Levinson (1987: 125) label the utterance 'I know you can't bear parties, but this one will really be good—do come' as 'request/offer'. Formal invitations are often formulated as 'requests'. For example, 'Mr. and Mrs. Waterson *request* the honour of your presence at their daughter's wedding on 9 March 1985, 10.00 a.m. at St. John's Cathedral.' However, (12) is very different from (13) which is often labelled a request as well. How do we decide what act is being performed in each instance? Let us do so by examining the responses to these requestives.

For (10) and (11), a positive response from the addressee will commit the speaker to some non-verbal action. For (12) and (13), a positive response will commit the addressee him/herself to some non-verbal action. Hence, according to who is to perform the non-verbal action, we can make the first distinction: (10) and (11) prospect potentially a speaker action, whereas (12) and (13) prospect potentially an addressee action.

Let us now see whether we can make further distinctions among them by examining the realizations of the prospected responses to utterances (10) to (13). In both (10) and (11), the non-verbal action is performed by the speaker. In (10), from the fact that R (addressee) expresses an appreciation (line 6) and thanks D (line 9) for getting the map of Canton for her, we can deduce that D's action (speaker action) is for the benefit of R (addressee benefit). By contrast, in (11), B's (addressee) response does not contain an appreciation or thanking. On the contrary, it is A (speaker) who thanks B for allowing him to smoke. We can therefore deduce that A's action (speaker action) is for the benefit of A himself (speaker benefit). In other words, we can make a distinction between who the speaker action benefits: the speaker or the addressee.

In both (12) and (13), the non-verbal action is performed by the addressee.[8] In (12a) below, which is a continuation of the conversation in (12), after extending the invitation, H diverts the conversation to recalling a mutual friend whom he also wants to invite. As soon as the identity of Betty Loo is established, T accepts the invitation by expressing an appreciation. And towards the end of the conversation, T thanks H for the invitation. This indicates that the addressee action is for the benefit of the addressee himself.

(12a) [B:B:A:3:1–2]

    H: Well y'know Alice and I were just suggesting that maybe some Friday evening you might be free to come out for supper, right? Do you remember Betty Loo? She used to work at Wanchai.

    T: Betty Loo.

    H: Yeah, she was she was =

    T: = I would recognize her.

    H: Yeah well she she teaches out here too.

    T: Uhuh.

    H: But she knew Simon very well. She's I think used to (   ) at Wanchai and she teaches in the Business Faculty. So we thought she could come over with her husband =

→ **T:** = That'd be very nice.

    . . . . . .

    H: Yeah okay look forward to seeing you.

→ **T:** Yeah thank you for phoning up for the invite I definitely will be there.

However, in (13), K's action (addressee action) is for the benefit of J (speaker benefit). As we can see in K's response to J's requestive, there is no thanking or appreciation. In fact, it would be out of order if K did this. A plausible continuation would be J thanking K.[9]

From the regularities exhibited in the prospected responses, we can classify requestives into four subclasses. Let us identify (10) as an *offer*, (11) as a *request for permission*, (12) as an *invitation*, and (13) as a *request for action* (see Figure 5.2).

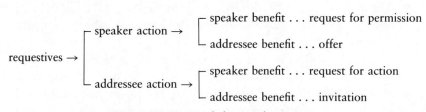

Figure 5.2: Four subclasses of requestives

The subclass request for action subsumes not only acts which have been identified as 'requests' in the speech act literature, but also 'contingent offers'. Consider the following piece of data:

(14) [B:E:A:4:4]

> *H has asked X, a visiting professor, to give a lecture and X said that he would think about it and give him a reply on Thursday.*

→ H: Well, I'll take you to the airport as a as a ah ((*laughs*)) if you if you did it for me, I'll be I'll be very happy to take you to the airport.

X: Well, that's very nice, thank you very much ((*laughs*)) I'll I'll (   ) of you and I =
        [

H: so treat for a treat, treat for a treat.

X: = think Dr. Lee would want to take, would be taking me to =
        [

H: Oh yeah.

X: = the airport, but but if you did it instead, that might be very convenient for him. I'll see you on Thursday.

H: Okay.

H's utterance (arrowed) is considered a 'contingent promise' or a 'contingent offer' in which the speaker commits himself to a future action if the addressee complies. It is considered a kind of 'commissive' which commits the speaker to a future action (see Searle and Venderveken 1985). However, even though part of H's utterance 'I'll be very happy to take you to the airport' may look like a commissive, the purpose of the entire utterance is an attempt to get the addressee X to offer a lecture to his students. Therefore, it is best characterized as a variant of a request for action.

Then how do we account for the fact that H's utterance is responded to by an appreciative remark 'that's very nice' and a thanking, which are only appropriate if the action is for the benefit of the addressee? This can be explained by its 'hybrid' nature: it contains the speaker's commitment to an action as part of the request for action (see Hancher 1979: 6).[10] X has chosen to respond to the commissive part instead of the directive part, out of politeness. It should be noted that this is not to say that this act is multifunctional. Its illocutionary intent is to get the addressee to perform an action, as pointed out above. The speaker's commitment to taking the addressee to the airport is a means to get the latter to comply rather than an illocutionary intent in itself.

In a sense, request for action can also subsume acts which have been referred to as 'suggestions' or 'proposals' which commit both the speaker and the addressee to a future action. For example:

(15) [B:B:B:6:2]

→ X: So why don't we arrange to get together maybe Sunday?
   H: Okay, that'll be splendid, that'll be great.

(16) [B:A:A:1:1]
→ A: So maybe we have we have lunch tomorrow?
   B: Okay yeah it's yes it's fine yes.

In (15), what X is doing is to try to get H to commit himself to a future action; and in this sense X's utterance can be considered a request for action. The same applies to A's utterance in (16). They are also similar to a request for action in the sense that in both cases, the speaker *wants* the action done. This is supported by the fact that if the addressee is unable to comply, he is likely to give a reason for non-compliance, and perhaps an apology as well. The following example illustrates this point:

(17) [B:D:B:2:2]
   S: Or alternatively we could get together at five-fifteen when I'm finished.
→ J: No, I have to babysit, actually, can I – 'cos I think Andrea's going to a Yoga class later.

However, there are three ways in which they differ from a request for action. Firstly, a request for action prospects only addressee action, and it is typically realized by 'Can/Could *you do X*?'. A 'suggestion' or a 'proposal', on the other hand, prospects both speaker action and addressee action, and it is typically realized by 'Can/Could/Shall *we do X*?'. Secondly, while a request for action which is complied with is often followed by the requester's thanking the requestee for complying, a 'suggestion' or a 'proposal' which is complied with is not likely to be followed by 'thanking'. Consider the oddity of the following:

(18) [I]
   J: So why don't we arrange to get together maybe Sunday?
   H: Okay, that'll be splendid, that'll be great.
   *J: Thank you.

100

Thirdly, from the fact that a compliance is often realized by an enthusiastic acceptance *without* thanking and that the proposer does not usually thank the addressee for complying, we can deduce that the action is often not only beneficial to the former but also to the latter.

The above reasons warrant the setting up of another subclass to account for utterances such as the above. Let us call it *proposal*.

The features of these five subclasses of requestives can be summarized as shown in Figure 5.3.

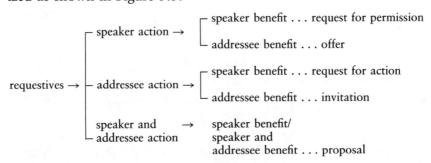

Figure 5.3: *Five subclasses of requestives*

Given the above characterization of the five subclasses of requestives, we are able to determine what acts are being performed in (19) to (22) below:

(19) [van Dijk 1981: 228]
Ticket inspector to passenger.

May I see your ticket please?

(20) [I]
Customer to shopkeeper.

May I use the telephone?

(21) [Leech and Svartvik 1975: 155]
Host to guest.

Please sit down.

(22) [I]
Chairman to panel members who are standing and chatting to each other when meeting is about to begin.

Please be seated.

In its surface form, (19) looks like a request for permission. But a ticket inspector does not have to obtain permission from a passenger to see the ticket; passengers are obliged to show their tickets when required. Hence, the ticket inspector is actually soliciting action from the passenger. The latter's action benefits the speaker in the sense that the ticket inspector wants the action done. Therefore, I would identify it as a request for action. Strictly speaking, the passenger is not really given the option of non-compliance. We may want to argue, therefore, that the ticket inspector is not really performing a request for action, but rather a kind of directive. He is merely putting a directive in the form of a requestive out of politeness. I shall return to this point later (see section 5.4.6).

By contrast, (20) is a request for permission, because, unlike the ticket inspector, the customer has to obtain permission, and there is no obligation on the part of the shopkeeper. However, as in (19), the action is beneficial to the speaker.

Although (21) looks like a request for action, and is often quoted as an instance of it, in this particular context the positive response that it intends to solicit is the guest's sitting down, and this action benefits the guest. It is therefore an *invitation* to sit down.

By contrast, (22) is a request for action because the requested action is beneficial to the chairman whose duty is to conduct the procedures of a meeting. It should be noted that the utterance would be a directive if the panel members are to comply upon hearing the utterance, in which case we would say that, similar to utterance (19), the chairman is putting the directive in the form of a requestive out of politeness.

The apparent ambivalence of (19) and (22) is due to the fact that very often one subclass of requestive is presented in a form which typically realizes another subclass.

In the following, I shall examine this phenomenon and investigate the motivation behind it.

5.4 Requestives and politeness strategies

In (19) above, we have seen that the ticket inspector performed a request for action by using a form which typically realizes a request for permission. This is a linguistic phenomenon prevalent in requestives. The following are some more examples:

(23) [BCET]
It is my pleasure and privilege now to invite her Royal
Highness to announce his name and to present the award.

(24) [Fieldnotes]
Mr. and Mrs. Waterson request the honour of your presence
at their daughter's wedding on 19 March 1985, 10.00 a.m.
at St. John's Cathedral.

(25) [BCET:A:B:49]
→ C: Can I have a match please?
    B: (NV)

(26) [C:1:A:4:1]
Colleague to colleague.

    R: Can I talk to you?
    S: Sure. Come in.
    R: (NV)
→ S: Let's close the door.
    R: (*closes the door*)

In (23), the speaker is, in fact, performing a request for action, but
it is presented in the typical form of an invitation by using the word
'invite'; in (24), the contrary happens: an invitation to a wedding is
presented in the typical form of a request for action, by using the
word 'request'.[11] In (25), a request for action is presented in the
typical form of a request for permission by using 'Can I do X?'
instead of 'Can you do X?'. In (26), a request for action is presented
in the typical form of a *proposal* by using 'Let's'. Why? And why is
this phenomenon so prevalent among requestives?

The reasons are socially motivated. Requestives are intrinsically
face-threatening acts (see Brown and Levinson 1987). They either
predicate a future action of the addressee and in so doing put some
pressure on him to do or to refrain from doing an action, hence
infringing on his freedom of action; or they predicate a future action
of the speaker and in so doing put some pressure on the addressee
to accept or reject it, hence incurring a debt or a responsibility for
the action done. There are various strategies to minimize the threat,
such as using hedges, apologizing for transgression, using softening
mechanisms that give the addressee a face-saving way out, and so

on (see Brown and Levinson 1987 for a detailed discussion). One important way of minimizing the threat is to present one subclass of requestive as another subclass.

How is this done? Recall the network of features of the five subclasses of requestive. We can represent their features in a matrix as shown in Figure 5.4.

	speaker action	addressee action	speaker and addressee action
speaker benefit	request for permission	request for action	—
addressee benefit	offer	invitation	—
speaker and addressee benefit	—	—	proposal

Figure 5.4: A matrix of features of requestives

This matrix enables us to see more clearly what common features one act shares with another. A request for permission shares the feature of soliciting speaker action with an offer, yet it also shares with a request for action the feature of speaker benefit. An invitation shares the feature of addressee action with a request for action, but it also shares with an offer the feature of addressee benefit, and so on. This enables linguistic manipulation to take place when circumstances require, mostly out of politeness. Let us now see how this is done.

5.4.1 Request for action in the form of request for permission

Consider the following pieces of data:

(27) [BCET:B:A:49]
Friend to friend.

→ C: Can I have a match please?
 B: (NV)

(28) [B:H:B:1:1]
Friend to friend.

 J: Hello Henry two things um Johnson speaking here. =

                                              [

 H: Oh.

→ J: = Could I first have the title of the Higgins and John's
       book please (   ) publisher.
                                [

H: Oh I'll give it to you in a second,
    it's right on my desk. It's called *Computers and
    Language Learning*.

(29) [B:G:B:1:1]
    P asked to speak to Dr. Jackson.

    K: He's he's not in but you tr could try ah extension 404
       see if he's there.
    P: I see.
    K: You see he's two offices, the ah ah Translation Centre
       and the English Department.
    P: Yes I see um =
→   = Can I leave a message for him then in case =
       [[
    K: I'll leave a me–   I'll leave a message
    P: = I miss him at the other
                          [
    K: Alright, I'll leave a message on his
       door then.

The above arrowed utterances are all instances of request for action
in which the speaker asks the addressee to do something for him. In
(27), C asks the addressee B to give him a match; in (28), J asks the
addressee H to give him the title of the book; in (29), P asks the
addressee K to take a message. In all three instances, the requests
for action are presented in surface forms which typically realize
requests for permission. This shifts the focus from 'you do X'
(addressee action) to 'I do X' (speaker action). Hence, it sounds less
imposing, as if it requires less of the addressee and is therefore more
polite. It also emphasizes the common feature between the two acts,
which is speaker benefit. As Leech (1983: 134) points out, 'Could I
borrow this electric drill?' is more polite than 'Could you lend me
this electric drill?' and 'I wouldn't mind a cup of coffee' is more polite
than 'Could you spare me a cup of coffee?' because they suppress the
cost to the addressee and emphasize the benefit to the speaker.

5.4.2 Request for action in the form of invitation

Consider the following examples:

(30) [BCET]

It is my pleasure and privilege now to *invite* her Royal Highness to announce his name and to present the prizes.

(31) [Fieldnotes]

Letter from Conference Organizing Committee to a prospective participant.

We would very much like you to consider presenting a paper at the Seminar and therefore *invite* you to send in an abstract for our consideration, to reach us not later than 30 Nov 85.

Both (30) and (31) are requests for action. In (30), the speaker requests her Royal Highness to present the prizes. In (31), the letter requests the participant to send in an abstract. Yet they are both presented in forms which typically realize invitations. In each case, the word 'invite' is used. In a request for action, the addressee's future action is beneficial to the speaker, whereas in an invitation, it is beneficial to the addressee him/herself. Rejections of a request for action and an invitation are both face-threatening. However, it is much less face-threatening to refuse to do something for one's own benefit than for someone else's benefit. Therefore, it is much less face-threatening to decline an invitation than to refuse to comply with a request for action. And because of this, the speaker is putting less pressure on the addressee to comply in an invitation than in a request for action. Therefore, by presenting the latter in a form that typically realizes the former, the speaker seems to be less imposing and hence more polite.

5.4.3 Request for action in the form of proposal

(32) [Ervin-Tripp 1976: 49]

Doctor to technician.

We have to do a few things over.

(33) [C:1:A:4:1]

Colleague to colleague.

R: Can I talk to you?

S: Sure. Come in.
R: (NV)
→ **S:** Let's close the door.
R: (*closes the door*)

The above examples are requests for action in which the speaker is soliciting an action from the addressee. The action is beneficial to the speaker in the sense that he/she wants the action to be carried out. However, they are presented in the typical forms of a *proposal*. By doing this, the speaker is behaving as though the action is to be performed by and is beneficial to both the speaker and the addressee. This kind of strategy is usually used by a person of higher rank to one of a lower rank, as pointed out by Ervin-Tripp (see 1976: 48).

5.4.4 Invitation in the form of request for action

(34) [Fieldnotes]
Mr. and Mrs. Waterson request the honour of your presence at their daughter's wedding on 19 March 1985, 10.00 a.m. at St. John's Cathedral.

(35) [Davidson 1984: 126]
A invites H to a thanksgiving dinner.

A: W'l Helen? now I'd lo:ve tuh have you join us.

Given the reasons for presenting a request for action in the typical form of an invitation, it is not difficult to understand why the latter is often presented in the typical form of the former. As a request for action is more difficult to refuse than an invitation, the host or hostess show their sincerity in having the addressee accept the invitation. In addition, by presenting it as a request for action, they indicate that they take the addressee's coming to the party as solely beneficial to themselves, rather than beneficial to the addressee as well.

5.4.5 Offer in the form of request for permission

Consider the following utterances:

(36) [I] Can I help you?

(37) [I] Let me get a chair for you.

Both a request for permission and an offer commit the speaker to a future action. While the action in an offer benefits the addressee, that in a request for permission benefits the speaker. By presenting an offer in a form that typically realizes a request for permission, the speaker is behaving as though the future action is beneficial to him/herself. This takes away the need for the addressee to be grateful.

Finally, a remark needs to be made about request for permission. It appears that this subclass is seldom presented in a form which typically realizes another subclass. The reason could be that among the five subclasses, request for permission is the least face-threatening and yet is the most compelling. A request for permission involves the speaker him/herself performing the future action which is to his/her own benefit. Therefore, it is very difficult to refuse a request for permission because the action is for the speaker's own benefit and it is least imposing since the speaker is going to perform the action. Hence, there is no need to present it in the typical form of another subclass as a politeness strategy. On the contrary, all other subclasses are often presented in the typical form of a request for permission, as can be seen from the examples quoted above.

5.4.6 Directives in the form of requestives and vice versa

In the above discussion, we have demonstrated how subclasses of requestive are presented in surface forms which typically realize other subclasses as a politeness strategy. This linguistic manipulation is found not only in requestives, although it is most prevalent among them. It happens across subclasses of initiating act. A directive, for example, can be presented in a form that typically realizes a requestive, as in the following:

(38) [Levinson 1983: 276]
> May I remind you that jackets and ties are required if you wish to use the bar on the 107th floor, sir.

The form in which (38) is presented typically realizes a request for permission, yet it is, in fact, a directive because it does not really give the addressee the option of not complying. Someone who walks into the bar in a T-shirt and a pair of jeans is most likely to be thrown out. Example (19) provided another instance. As mentioned above, the ticket inspector's utterance 'May I see your ticket please?' can be characterized as a directive because the passenger is not *actually* given the option of non-compliance, although the ticket inspector is behaving *as though* the passenger is given the option (see also Lakoff 1977: 90).[12]

The following provides a further example:

(39) [Fieldnotes]
Above the hand-basin in an aircraft toilet.

As a courtesy to other passengers may we request that you clean the bowl after washing.

The sentence is, in fact, an instruction to passengers to clean the hand-basin, which does not really give the option of non-compliance. Yet it is presented as a request for action.

The motivation in the above instances is again politeness. A directive which does not give the addressee any option but to comply is even more face-threatening than a requestive. In settings where the duties of each individual are well-defined and where co-operation from each individual is assumed, directives are more permissible, as pointed out earlier. What is interesting, however, is that even in settings like this, where the relationship and the duties are well-defined, forms which typically realize requestives are often used instead of those which typically realize directives. The teacher's utterances in (2) give one example, and (40) below provides another:

(40) [Leech 1983: 127]
Boss to secretary.

Would you like to type these letters.

Example (40) is a directive because typing letters is the duty of a secretary. It does not really give the option of non-compliance. By presenting it in the typical form of a requestive, however, the speaker is being polite to his/her subordinate. In fact, the more power the speaker has over the addressee, the more assured he/she is of the co-operation of the latter, the more polite he/she can afford to be, and the more often he/she can present directives in the form of requestives.

Conversely, requestives are sometimes presented in imperative forms which typically realize directives. As Leech and Svartvik (1975) and Lakoff (1977) point out, what are commonly referred to as 'commands' or 'orders' are often used in making offers, for example:

(41) [I] Do have some more sherry.

(42) [I] You must have some more cake.

(43) [I] Do sit down.

(44) [I] Don't stand on ceremony.

Directives compel the addressee to perform the solicited action. By presenting requestives in forms typically realizing directives, the speaker is putting pressure on the addressee to comply with the requestive. This indicates his sincerity in having the addressee accept the offer or invitation (see also Leech 1983: 109).

5.5 Indirect speech acts

5.5.1 Indirect requests

Finally, I wish to address the issue of 'indirect speech acts' here, since requestives are acts in which indirection is most prevalent.

The concept of indirect speech act is introduced by Searle, who maintains that in saying 'Can you pass the salt?', the speaker is performing a primary illocutionary act of request by way of performing a secondary illocutionary act of asking a question. An act which is performed by way of another illocutionary act is considered an indirect speech act. The speaker is therefore said to be performing an 'indirect request'. Searle further sets out ten inference steps that the addressee has to go through to derive a request from a question (Searle 1979: 33–6).

This characterization is counter-intuitive. Utterances like 'Can you pass the salt?' and 'Would you mind passing the salt?' are directly recognizable as requests. The addressee does not have to go through the literal interpretation of the utterance and a series of inference steps to arrive at this interpretation. As Ervin-Tripp (1976: 52) points out, 'rapid, routinized interpretations are based on the predictability of a large part of human interaction'.

So far, the most satisfactory characterization of the utterances in question is that offered by Conversation Analysts. For them, questions about whether utterances have literal or indirect forces simply do not arise (see Levinson 1983: 363). An utterance like 'Do you have a stamp?' is characterized as a pre-request which serves to ascertain that the preconditions for getting compliance to a request for a stamp obtain before the latter is actually performed. The motivation for performing a pre-request is to avoid getting a rejection, because a potential request which the addressee is not likely to be able to comply with will not normally be extended. This is a face-saving conversational strategy that is so commonly employed that conventionalization occurs. Hence, upon hearing an utterance like the above, the adresssee immediately anticipates an upcoming request (see also Edmondson 1981: 117). Very often, instead of going through the ritual of responding to the pre-request and waiting for the upcoming request, the addressee responds as though a request has already been made.

There are, however, two aspects in this kind of characterization that need commenting on. Firstly, as I have pointed out previously, the term 'pre-request' is a structural label which denotes the sequential location of an utterance in relation to the rest of the discourse. It is not a discourse act label (see section 3.2.3). In terms of discourse function, the utterance 'Do you have a stamp?' is an elicitation if it prospects a verbal response which informs the speaker as to whether the addressee has a stamp. Hence, the following arrowed utterances, which would be characterized as 'pre-requests' by Conversation Analysts, are characterized as elicitations here:

(45) [C:1:A:2]
  → H: Do you get the *TESOL Quarterly*?
      S: Yeah.
  → H: D'you get this issue?
      S: What – month is it?
      H: um number two, June eighty three.
      S: Yeah, I think I probably did.
      H: Can I just borrow this for a day – for a day =
                                        [
      S: Yeah.
      H: = or two?

As I have pointed out before, it is possible for S to respond to H's utterances by the non-verbal response of giving H the *TESOL Quarterly* if S knows exactly which issue H is referring to. When this happens, the discourse value of H's utterances will be reclassified as requests for action. In other words, H's utterance is an elicitation which can be responded to *as though* a request for action has already been made.

Secondly, we need to distinguish between utterances which *are* requests for action and those which are preliminary to them but *can be interpreted* as requests for action. For example:

(46) [I] Can I borrow a stamp from you?

(47) [I] Do you have a stamp?

While the first one is a request for action, the second one is an elicitation which typically occurs before a request for action (cf. Levinson 1983: 362). The difference can be seen from the responses that are acceptable to them.

(48) [I]
    A: Can I borrow a stamp from you?
    B: (a) Yes. (+NV)
       *(b) Yes. (−NV)

(49) [I]
    X: Do you have a stamp?
    Y: (a) Yes. (+NV)
       (b) Yes. (−NV)

In (48), a positive response without the non-verbal action of compliance is very odd. If A's utterance were preliminary to a request for action, B would be entitled to give only a verbal response and wait for the upcoming request for action. This indicates that A's utterance is not preliminary to a request for action, but rather is itself a request for action (cf. Leech 1983: 97).[13] In (49), positive responses with or without the non-verbal action of compliance are both acceptable. X, upon getting only a positive verbal response, cannot accuse Y of responding inappropriately.

The different discourse functions of these two kinds of utterance are supported by the regular pattern exhibited in Merritt's data (1976). Utterances which are in the form of 'Do you have X?' typically occur before utterances of the form 'Can I have X?':

(50) [Merritt 1976: 340]
    restaurant (S6–2).

  → C: Do you have hot chocolate?

S: Mm-hm.
→ C: Can I have hot chocolate, with whipped cream?
S: Sure. (*leaves to get it*)

(51) [ibid.]
indoor market place.

→ C: Do you have the blackberry jam?
S: Yes.
→ C: Can I have a half pint then?
S: OK. (*turns to prepare*).

Finally, their different discourse functions can also be seen from the difference in meaning in their negative responses. Consider:

(52) [I]
A: Can I borrow a stamp from you?
B: No.

(53) [I]
A: Do you have a stamp?
B: No.

B's response in (52) is a refusal, whereas that in (53) is not: it is a piece of information (see Merritt 1976: 347; see also Lyons 1977: 754). Hence, while the former is face-threatening, the latter is not. This is why a requestive is typically preceded by an elicitation to check the preconditions.

5.5.2 Indirect invitations and indirect offers

So far, I have been focusing on requests for action. Similar analysis can be applied to other subclasses of requestives. Consider the following example:

(54) [Davidson 1984: 113]
1 B: So I jus' wan' duh tell yih if you'd come we—
2   we're inviting the kinnergarden teachers too becuz
3   we think it's a good chance tuh get tuh know the
4   mothers.
5 A: Uh huh. =
→ 6 B: = hh So if yer free:, (.) It's et the youth ho:use.
7   (0.2)
8 A: We:ll? (.) ez far ez I kno:w, (0.8) I will be.

113

The utterance in line 6 would be referred to as an 'indirect invitation' by speech act theorists. Here, it would be characterized as an elicitation which typically occurs before an invitation. Its function is to check that the precondition for extending an invitation obtains, namely that A is free. And as we can see from A's response, the precondition does obtain. This kind of elicitation can be responded to *as though* an invitation has already been made, or we can say that it can be retrospectively classified as an invitation, as in the following example:

(55) [B:A:A:4]
```
    1 M: So we– we're thinking about all going down to Chung
    2     Ying at about twelve. I booked a table. Well, simply =
                                                    [
    3 X:                                          mhm
    4 M: = because he'd like to meet the teachers and find out
    5     what we're doing, like first year English – the electives
→   6     and stuff, so if you're free.
→   7 X: Okay.
```

As we can see, the elicitation in line 6 is directly responded to by X *as though* an invitation has already been extended. In other words, X has retrospectively classified the elicitation as an invitation. His 'Okay' realizes an acceptance of the upcoming invitation.

Consider now the following utterance in line 1, which speech act theorists would refer to as an 'indirect offer':

(56) [B:E:A:6:1]
```
→    1 H: Would you wa– you want me to leave a message?
     2 X: Yeah, it would be very kind if you can do that.
                                          [
     3 H:                               Okay. Can you
     4     give me the number?
            . . . . . .
→   10 H: Okay, I'll I'll tell him to give you a call when he
    11     comes out of class.
             [
    12 X:     Thanks so much.
```

It is an elicitation, which typically occurs before an offer, and its

114

function is to check that the precondition for making an offer obtains, namely that X wants H to leave a message. As we can see, after making sure that the precondition obtains, H goes ahead to obtain details of the message. Again, this kind of elicitation can be retrospectively classified as an offer and responded to accordingly, as in the following:

(57) [B:A:A:4:3]
    M: Alright, do you want me to get the paper?
→ **X:** Yeah, why don't you bring the paper.
    M: Alright.

From the above discussion, we can see that in the present descriptive framework, the question of whether a speech act is literally or indirectly conveyed does not arise. An utterance is characterized as performing a particular discourse act according to the response it prospects. The addressee always has the freedom to reclassify the utterance and produce some other response which is appropriate to the reclassification. The discourse function of an utterance is therefore determined by the negotiation of this reclassification between the speaker and the addressee (see section 1.6.3).

5.6 Concluding remarks

In this chapter, we have examined the second subclass of initiating act, requestives. We have identified five subclasses of requestives on the basis of who is to perform the future action and who the action benefits. We have also shown how these two features are reflected in the responses. This description enables us to see that utterances which appear to be ambivalent, or to have indeterminate illocutionary forces or multiple functions, are, in fact, performing a particular discourse act under the linguistic disguise of another discourse act in order to reduce the face-threatening effect. This social motivation of preserving face governs not only the linguistic realizations of acts, but also their sequential organization. The so-called 'indirect speech act' is a case in point.

6
Directives

6.1 Introduction

In the previous chapter, we characterized directives as acts which prospect a non-verbal action[1] from the addressee without giving him/her the option of non-compliance. We also pointed out that directives are typically realized by imperatives (see section 5.2). 'Orders' and 'commands' were referred to as instances of directives. In this chapter, we shall try to offer a more detailed description of this subclass and identify further discourse acts which can be subsumed under it.

In the following pieces of data, we have two utterances (arrowed), both of which are in imperative form and prospect non-verbal actions. Neither of them give the addressee the option of not complying, or at least the options of complying or not complying are not indicated in the utterance. Hence, they are both directives.

(1) [BCET:D:53]
    D: Dave was telling me this joke about this little tramp you know ((*laughs*)) and ah – this tramp's sort of standing at the traffic lights and ah =
→   = Leave my matches alone, I'm telling you a joke.
    C: Right what's that

(2) [C:2:A:6:2]
    S: Anyway um I heard well I know because I went to
→   Taiwan this summer. Don't try to exchange your money at a bank or at the airport but get your friend to take you to ah – like a jewellery store and they'll exchange it =
                                       [
    X: Ah
    S: = a lot cheaper there.

X: They have better rate.
S: mhm
X: Good tip, thanks.

These two directives, however, are responded to differently. In (1), D's directing C to stop fiddling with his matches and listen to his joke is responded to by a complying 'Right'. In (2), S's directing X to go to a jewellery store to exchange her money is responded to by an appreciative remark, 'Good tip' and a thanking. This suggests that they are two different types of directives. Their different responses are due to the different nature of the actions involved. While in (1) the action of not fiddling with the matches and paying attention to the joke is the 'want' of the speaker—or, we could say, for the benefit of the speaker—the action in (2) of going to a jewellery store to exchange money is for the benefit of the addressee, since she can get a better rate by doing so. We may say that there are two major categories of directives: those which are issued for the benefit of the speaker him/herself, and those which are issued for the benefit of the addressee.

6.2 Two major subclasses of directives

The classification of directives into two distinct categories is supported by studies in syntactic structures and speech act theory.

Linguists often refer to the command use and the non-command use of imperatives (see, for example, Bolinger 1967). Schreiber (1972) proposes a distinction between true imperatives and pseudo-imperatives. True imperatives (which he calls command imperatives) have the force of a command, whereas pseudo-imperatives (which he calls hortative imperatives) do not. For example, the imperative 'Go away' can be a command imperative with the underlying structure 'I command that you go away'; or it can be a hortative imperative with the underlying structure 'I suggest that you go away' (see Schreiber 1972: 340–1). S's utterance in (2) would be an instance of a hortative imperative.

McCawley (1977) also proposes that there are two classes within 'exercitives': imperatives and advisories. His distinction is based on the grounds that 'ask' can be used to report imperative acts but not advisory acts. For example, if someone orders you to shine his shoe, we can paraphrase it as 'He asks you to shine his shoe'. However, if someone advises or recommends that you shine his shoe, we cannot paraphrase it as 'He asks you to shine his shoe' (see McCawley 1977: 16–17).

Sadock (1974) makes a distinction between imperatives like 'Leave at once!' and 'why-impositives' like 'Why don't you take an aspirin?', on the basis of their different linguistic behaviours. Why-impositives do not happily take 'please' or 'kindly', whereas imperatives do (see Sadock 1974: 116). For example:

*(3) [I] Why don't you please/kindly take out the garbage?

*(4) [I] Why not please/kindly take out the garbage?

 (5) [I] Take out the garbage, please.

This difference in linguistic behaviours can be explained by pragmatic motivations. Imperatives typically realize what has been referred to in the speech act literature as 'orders', which are acts by which the speaker attempts to get the addressee to perform an action for the speaker's own benefit. Because of this, they can happily take 'please' and 'kindly' which express the speaker's indebtedness to the addressee. Why-impositives, on the other hand, typically realize 'directives' which are advisory,[2] that is, those in which the course of action advocated by the speaker is for the benefit of the addressee, at least partly, if not entirely. There is no indebtedness involved on the part of the speaker. It is the addressee, if anyone, who should be indebted. This is why they do not happily take 'please' or 'kindly'. And this is also why S's directive in (2) is responded to by an appreciative remark and a thanking. The following piece of data provides a further example:

(6) [B:A:B:4]
    X: Hello ah Michael?
    H: Michael's not here.
    X: Is he at 304?
→ H: Yeah. Why don't you call 304?
→ X: Okay thank you I will.
    H: Right.

Here, H's directing X to call extension 304 is for X's benefit. X is indebted to H and this is why he thanks H.

118

Therefore, in addition to the linguistic behaviours outlined above, I would like to add a further dimension for distinction: difference in discourse behaviours. Directives which are advisory can be responded to by thanking and appreciation, whereas those which are mandatory cannot. I shall call directives which direct the addressee to perform an action for the benefit of the speaker *mandatives*, and those which advocate a course of action to be performed by the addressee for his own benefit *advisives*. I use the verb 'advocate' for the second subclass instead of 'direct' because it captures better the less compelling nature of this subclass: the carrying out of the action is entirely up to the addressee (see also Green 1975: 123).[3]

6.3 Advisives

Let us consider advisives first. Compare (2) with the following piece of data:

(7) [B:G:A:1:3]
    H and X are talking about getting research assistants to
    conduct interviews.

    X: Well, if you can get eight that's fine but he needs multiples of two and ah he should alternate those interview topics, that's all um now he's going to need a little training, isn't he Henry.

    H: No, he said he knows this, he was there before when I was going through with ah Andy.

→ X: Well, you'll have to practise with him once or I mean really you can't just throw him in there and monkey =
                                                             [

    H: No, no I –

    X: = around or he'll screw the subject and ruin the data.
                                  [

    H: No, I won't.

In (7), X suggests that H practise with the research assistant before the actual interview. As with (2), the action advocated is for the benefit of the addressee. However, in (2), the consequence of complying is desirable: X would be able to exchange her money at a better rate, 'and they'll exchange it a lot cheaper there', whereas in (7), the consequence of not complying is undesirable: the research assistant may ruin the data, 'or he'll screw the subject and ruin the data'. In other words, there are two kinds of advisives: one in which the desirable consequence of complying is highlighted, as in (2), and the other in which the undesirable consequence of not complying is highlighted, as in (7).

Katz (1977) makes a similar distinction among 'advisive' verbs. He maintains that 'advisive' verbs like 'warn' and 'caution' differ from 'advise' in that the former specifies that the indicated choice is preferable to other choices because it poses least danger to the addressee, whereas the latter specifies that the indicated choice is preferable because it offers more benefit to the addressee. For example:

(8) [Katz 1977: 202]
I warn you not to stick your nose into other people's business.

(9) [ibid.: 201]
I advise you to take off your hat here.

He calls the former 'negative advisives' and the latter 'positive advisives'. This distinction has also been noted by Searle and Venderveken (1985), who assert that in 'warning', the state of affairs that the speaker warns the addressee about is not in the latter's interest, whereas in 'advising', the action that the speaker advises the addressee to do is presupposed to be in the latter's interest (see also Green 1975: 124).[4]

Following the distinction made by Katz (1977) and Searle and Venderveken (1985), I shall identify an act in which the undesirable consequence of not complying is highlighted as a *warning*, and an act in which the desirable consequence of complying is highlighted as an *advice*.

6.3.1 Warnings

In (7) above, we have an instance of a *warning* which *explicitly* states that the course of action is for the benefit of the addressee and *explicitly* specifies the undesirable consequence of non-compliance.

Sometimes, a warning can take the form of stating the action and providing a reason for it. Consider the following pieces of data:

(10) [B:D:A:1:5]
J has been telling H about the lunch he had with Andy and John.

    J: But ah I had a good conversation with Andy, we went to lunch. John John's ah John's a good guy.

    H: Yeah John's nice.

    J: And ah I told Andy that I'd send them this paper but I never did.

→ **H:** You'd better send it because he was bitching about ah people not y'know people not keeping up their professional promises or getting it off to him y'know he's =

                                    [

    J: mhm

    H: = he is very sensitive.

    J: That bastard, you know why, because I sent him up a whole bunch of stuff. I sent him something that it I know he was looking for he couldn't find um y'know what the heck does he want?

(11) [Fieldnotes]
A and B are flatmates. B is about to pick up the kettle.

→ **A:** Don't pick it up, it's burning hot.

    B: Right.

In (10), H provides the reason for suggesting that J send Andy the paper. He is implying that if J does not send his paper, the latter is likely to complain about him. The undesirable consequence is *implied* rather than explicitly stated. In (11), a reason is given for not picking up the kettle. The undesirable consequence of not complying is again *implied*: B will burn her hand. In other words, in a warning, the undesirable consequence of not complying may be explicitly stated or it may be implied.

In the examples of warnings given so far, the course of action advocated by the speaker is explicitly stated. There are cases in which it is implied rather than explicitly stated. Consider the following pieces of data:

(12) [Fieldnotes]
  B is about to take the kettle from the cooker.

→ **A:** The handle is hot.
  B: Oh. (*stops picking up the kettle*)

(13) [Fieldnotes]
  Words printed on a plastic bag.

  This plastic bag is not a toy.

(14) [Fieldnotes]
  Television advertisement.

  Cigarette smoking is hazardous to health.

In all of the above instances, the warnings are realized by the speaker or writer providing a piece of information. The actions to be taken and the undesirable consequences of not taking heed are implied by the information given. The implied action in (12) is do not pick up the kettle, and the implied consequence is that B will burn her hand; in (13), the implied action is do not let children play with the plastic bag, and the implied consequence is children may be suffocated by the bag; in (14), the implied action is do not smoke, and the implied consequence is that smoking will damage one's health.

Hence, a warning may also be realized by a piece of information given for the benefit of the addressee *without* explicitly stating the course of action and the consequence.

6.3.2 Advice

An *advice* is a directive which advocates a course of action for the benefit of the addressee, and in which the consequence of compliance is desirable. In (2) above, we have an instance of an advice in which the desirable consequence is explicitly stated, which is, if X changes her money at a jewellery store, she will be able to get a better rate. Advice of this form is not uncommon. We often hear advice like 'Take an aspirin and you'll feel better' or 'Stop worrying and your headache will go away'. It is equally common, however, for an advice to state only the action but not the desirable consequence. For example:

(15) [C:1:A:4:6]
S is the course co-ordinator and X is a new colleague who has been telling S that she could not cope with the marking.

→   S: I think there are some things you can do, like, I I often
     write yes in the margin if I agree or I even put just an =
                                            [
     X: Okay.
     S: = exclamation point
     X: Or a question mark or
     S: Interesting or y'know so that on every page there's =
                                                            [
     X: there's
     S: = evidence that I read it ((*laughs*))
                             [
     X: that you've read it, yeah. Okay, alright,
        alright, I'll ah that'll help 'cos it just seems ah y'know
     S: TOO much work.

(16) [B:C:B:1:8]
     E: I'd like to get a copy from Singapore in fact. I've got to
        give a course on second language acquisition and I
        thought this would be a nice textbook but I can't get
        hold of the copy.
                  [
     F: It's it's a good one. =
→   = Why don't you call, write ah write to New York and
        ask for an inspection copy.

In (15), S puts forward a list of things that X can do, and the desirable consequence of acting accordingly is implied: X will find the marking much easier. In (16), F suggests that E write to the publisher and ask for an inspection copy, and the desirable consequence of doing so is also implied: E will be able to get the book that he wants.

6.3.3 Advice versus 'advise, suggest, and recommend'

In the present description, *advice* covers acts which have been referred to in the speech act literature as 'advise', 'suggest', and 'recommend'. This is contrary to most descriptions, in which they are treated as three separate 'acts'. In the following, I shall argue that these three 'acts' are, in fact, different labels for the same act.

Searle and Venderveken (1985: 203) distinguish between 'advise' and 'suggest' on the grounds that the former has the additional condition that 'the state of affairs that P is good' for the addressee. However, in the following piece of data (17), we have an utterance which is labelled a 'suggestion' by the speaker himself (see line 1) and it is responded to by the addressee thanking him (see line 41). Therefore, there is no reason to assume that the condition that 'the state of affairs that P is good' for the addressee does not apply to 'suggest' (see also Green 1975 on 'suggestions').

(17) [B:B:B:3:2–3]
    X is the librarian and H is a staff member. H called to make
    enquiries about gaining access to some recently ordered
    books.

→   1 X: . . . so ah, if, I suggest probably you'd better
    2   drop in the book orders department and see if
    3   they're – they are on the way. If not, if they've
    4   gone on into the cataloguing, then they're going
    5   to be on to the shelves before you see them.
    6 H: Yeah, the only thing is, I don't even know the
    7   names of the books that were ordered. I just
    8   heard they were on linguistics, which is my
    9   field, that's why I just want to know
                                    [
  10 X: I'm very hard put to
        s– direct you.
           [
  11 H: Yeah, so you know . . .
       . . . . . .
  36 X: Oh, if that's the case, you better go to the
  37   person who ordered them and get some
  38   bibliographic information, that's something to =
                                  [
  39 H: Alright
  40 X: = deal with.
→ 41 H: Okay, alright, so I'll check that out. Thank you very
  42   much.

It has also been asserted that the verb 'suggest' implies a tentative illocution (Leech 1983: 208). While the verb 'suggest' does have the semantic feature of tentativeness which the verb 'advise' lacks, it is doubtful whether 'advise' and 'suggest' are two distinctly identifiable acts. Take the following piece of data, for example:

(18) [B:B:B:4:3–4]
      G and H are colleagues. G is a sociolinguist. H called G to
      discuss research in this area.

      G: I think that ah a person like Jack's going to be
          very interested in actual speech samples, but he =
                                                          [
      H: Yeah.
      G: = is not going to be very keen and impressed with
   →   that other sort of research. So my suggestion to
          you is to ah to get into that. I've had a couple
          of thoughts in that respect about papers that
          would be good for you to do . . .

It is difficult to decide whether G is giving a suggestion or a piece of advice. He labelled his own utterance as a 'suggestion'. Yet there is no reason why we cannot say that G is giving H a piece of advice since he is an expert in the area. This is not because G's utterance is ambiguous between a 'suggestion' and an 'advise', but rather that the two illocutionary verbs 'suggest' and 'advise' do not, in fact, correspond to two distinctly different acts despite the fact that there are semantic differences between them.

As for 'recommend', Searle and Venderveken (1985) propose that it has the additional preparatory condition that the state of affairs represented is good in general. However, this condition hardly distinguishes it from an 'advise'. We can 'recommend' a course of action which is both good for the addressee and good in general, just as we can 'advise' a course of action which is both good for the addressee and good in general. Consider the following examples:

(19) [Quirk *et al.* 1985: 831]
      Take an aspirin for your headache.

(20) [ibid.]
      Lock the door before you go to bed.

How do we decide whether a 'recommend' or an 'advise' is performed in each instance? For (19), we can say that 'the doctor advises him to take an aspirin for his headache', or 'the doctor recommends that he take an aspirin for his headache'. Similarly, for (20), we can say that 'the security guard advises him to lock the door before going to bed', or 'the security guard recommends that he lock the door before going to bed'. Quirk *et al.* (1985) uses them as examples for both 'advise' and 'recommend'.

To conclude, although there may be semantic differences between the verbs 'advise', 'suggest', and 'recommend', these differences, however, do not warrant the setting up of three subclasses of advisives (see also Katz 1977: 204).[5]

6.3.4 Verb versus act

In the above discussion, we have seen that it is essential not to confuse the meaning of the illocutionary verbs and the acts to which they correspond. We have seen that different illocutionary verbs may, in fact, correspond to the same act (see Tsui 1987c). In the following, we shall discuss briefly 'warn' and 'advise' as verbs and *warning* and *advice* as discourse acts.

The verbs 'warn' and 'advise' can have an assertive or a directive use. The acts *warning* and *advice*, however, are solely directives (cf. Leech 1983: 208; Searle and Venderveken 1985).[6] Consider the following examples:

(21) [Fieldnotes]
Letter from Lloyds Bank to customer.

I write to advise you that this item has been credited to the above-mentioned account today.

(22) [BCET]
I would advise you to take a short break.

(23) [BCET]
The catalogue warned that this lot was 'creased, trimmed or marked with adhesive tape'.

(24) [BCET]
I warn you to stay away from this man.

In (21), the verb 'advise' is used assertively, whereas in (22), it is used directively, as can be seen from the syntactic structures 'advise ... that' and 'advise ... to'. However, only in (22) would we say that the act of *advice* is performed. In (21), although the verb 'advise' is used, the act performed is an *informative*, because no non-verbal action is prospected (see Chapter 7 for a detailed discussion of informatives). In (23), the verb 'warn' is used assertively, whereas in (24), it is used directively. However, despite the fact that it is used assertively in (23), the act performed is similar to that in (24); it is a *warning*. This is because, in contrast to (21), a course of action is implied. In (23), the aim of informing the addressee that the goods were 'creased, trimmed or marked with adhesive tape' is to get the addressee to take a certain course of action to avoid undesirable consequences. As I have pointed out above, many *warnings* are presented as a piece of information and the course of action is implied (see (13) and (14) above).

The importance of not confusing the verb and the act it is used to perform is best seen in the following example:

(25) [Fieldnotes]
Inside a supermarket in Birmingham city centre.

Warning: customers are *advised* that videoscan closed circuit television is in operation with video-recording.

Here, both the verbs 'warn' and 'advise' are used. The verb 'advise' is used assertively and is synonymous with 'inform'. However, the aim of informing the customers is to deter them from shoplifting. Therefore, the act performed is a *warning*, and not an *advice* or an *informative*.

6.4 Mandatives

Mandatives are directives by which the speaker attempts to get the addressee to perform, or to refrain from performing, an action for the benefit of the speaker himself. The following are instances of mandatives:

(26) [BCET:D:6]
D: How how Cathy a book this size how come you don't binds spend.

C: I haven't read it that's why
             [
D: Binds spend. Bend the spine.
C: I haven't read it.
D: Oh you haven't read it.
→ C: Don't for God's sake bend the spine.
D: I WON'T bend the spine.
C: You mean you do it deliberately.
D: No I just can't read it, I can't read round corners
    ((*laughs*))

(27) [Fieldnotes]
→ A: Vote for the Tories and I'll kill you.

In (26), C is trying to stop D from bending the spine of her book. In (27), A is trying to stop his friend from voting for the Tory government. However, there is an important difference between them. In (26), C merely states the course of action that she wants D to refrain from doing, whereas in (27) A not only states the action that he wants the addressee to refrain from doing but also the undesirable consequence that he himself will bring about if the latter refuses to comply. The difference between them can be best demonstrated by comparing the following examples:

(28) [I]
Mother to child.

Pick up your coat.

(29) [I]
Mother to child.

Pick up your coat or I'll spank you.

Examples (28) and (29) are both attempts to get the child to pick up his coat. However, (28) not only states the action, but also the speaker's bringing about the undesirable consequence if the child refuses to do so.

We can, therefore, identify two subclasses of mandatives. One is issued because of the speaker's want, or one can say is issued for the benefit of the speaker himself. The other has the additional feature of explicitly stating that the speaker himself will bring about the undesirable consequence should the addressee refuse to comply. Let us identify the former as an *instruction* and the latter as a *threat*.

An *instruction* is usually given by a person who has the right to get, or who is sure of getting, the addressee to comply. Therefore, there is no need to state the undesirable consequence of non-compliance as a means of getting the latter to comply. By contrast, the right is not inherent for the speaker who performs a *threat*, and therefore he has to rely on the addressee's fear of the undesirable consequence that he will bring about to get the addressee to comply (see also Katz 1977: 190). Mothers often resort to *threats* when they fail to get compliance from their children.

6.4.1 Instructions

As mentioned above, an *instruction* is usually given by a person who has the right to get the addressee to comply. This right is usually due to the power or authority that he has over the latter, but not necessarily so. For example, in (26), C's right to stop D from bending the spine of the book is due to the fact that the book belongs to her. The right may also be due to the work setting in which who is to do what is clearly defined and hence compliance is normally expected (see section 5.2). An example that Ervin-Tripp (1976) gives is the use of 'directives' (which are characterized as instructions here) by blue-collar workers when moving heavy objects. Another example that she gives is a situation in which husband and wife are engaged in persuading a stepfather to eat herring:

(30) [Ervin-Tripp 1976: 31]
Wife to husband, who has herring.

Bring some out, so that Max c'd have some too.

She points out that because serving the stepfather is a central goal to both, compliance is expected. Therefore, an imperative is used. This is compared to the use of a different form by the wife later:

(31) [ibid.]
Wife to husband, as she tastes herring later.

Geschmacht. Mmm. Oh it's delicious Ben c'd you hand me a napkin please.

Because the wife does not have the right to expect the husband to hand her a napkin, an 'embedded imperative' and 'please' are used (see section 5.2 for examples). The imperative in (30) realizes an instruction even though the speaker does not have power over the addressee.

Similarly, in (32) and (33) below, because the speakers and the addressees are collaborating, compliance is expected. Therefore, instructions are acceptable:

(32) [B:G:B:2:7]
H and R are writing a textbook together and they are talking about the publisher being very slow in responding to their manuscript.

H: Alright I'll I'll ah alright I'll shoot it back to you and ah see um I'll I'll probably see him that guy tomorrow by no it's tomorrow no usually Thursday at breakfast I see him 'cos I I have an early class, so usually at Chung Chi staff club for a cup of coffee and he's always there.

R: I see.

H: So you should see him at at breakfast.

R: Yeah.

H: I'll I'll maybe I'll nudge him along.

→ R: Yeah. Oh don't don't tell him we're TOO eager.

H: Yeah, that's true, I I try to be real.

(33) [B:H:B:10:3]
A and H are jointly inviting a scholar to come to Hong Kong in the following year, but received a note from him saying that he will be in Hong Kong in the current year, which is 1984.

H: I don't know what the story is, y'know.

X: I thought it was '85.

H: Yeah I hope I y'know I wanna dash him off a quick note today but I want to check it out with you first ah
      . . . . . .

→ X: anyway ah find out what's going on with with Bernstein and then

H: I'll give I'll give ah I'll try and give Bernstein a call today but I'll um I don't think I'll say anything to Michael, I'll leave it till later.

[

→ **X:**   Oh don't do a thing yeah gee till you're sure, I =

[

H: Yeah

X: = think Peter's got the date wrong and so forth but you can check that out.

The most common realization of an instruction is 'Do X'. But it can also be realized by wants and needs statements (see section 5.2 for examples), and it can also be presented as a piece of information when the necessary action is obvious. For example:

(34) [Ervin-Tripp 1976: 30]
Customer to waitress.

Coffee, black.

(35) [ibid.]
Chef to assistant.

Salt and pepper.

Given the above characterization of an instruction, we would be able to characterize what act is performed in the following:

(36) [Fieldnotes]
During a snooker match, a snooker player missed the ball and the audience is making a lot of noise.

Referee: Thank you.
Audience: (*stop making noise*)

The referee's 'Thank you' is an attempt to get the audience to stop making noises.[7] Compliance from the audience is expected by virtue of his right as a referee to keep order during the match. His utterance is therefore not an act of 'thanking' but rather an *instruction*.

6.4.2 Threats

Threats have always been classified as 'commissives' rather than 'directives' in the speech act literature. Searle and Venderveken (1985) characterize 'threaten' as an undertaking on the part of the speaker to perform a future action to the detriment of the addressee. The undertaking, however, involves no obligation (see ibid.: 193). They assert that 'threaten' differs from the primitive illocutionary force 'commit' only by the fact that in the act of 'threatening', the state of affairs represented in the proposition is bad for the addressee.

Fraser (1975a) argues against considering 'threat' a kind of 'commissive'—or a type of 'negative promise', as he puts it—on the grounds that there is an important difference between the two: a 'promise' involves an obligation to carry out the action, whereas a 'threat' does not: we cannot challenge a person who has 'threatened' for not carrying out the action.

What Fraser has pointed out is one of the differences between a 'threat' and a 'commissive'. The crucial difference, however, is that the purpose of a *threat* is not to commit the speaker to a future action, but to get the addressee to perform an action (see also Harris 1980: 175). This can be best seen in threats issued by mothers in which the aim is clearly to get their children to do something, rather than to commit themselves to carrying out an action. Indeed, children know that, most of the time, mothers will not carry out the 'committed' action, even when they fail to get compliance.

6.4.3 Threats and warnings

The fact that a 'threat' has the feature of an undesirable consequence if not complied with has led some linguists to consider it indistinguishable from a 'warning'. Sadock (1974) argues that 'threaten' and 'warn' are not separate illocutionary acts. 'Warnings' for which we assume the warner has control over the consequences of not heeding the warning are described as 'threats'. He gives the following example:

(37) [Sadock 1974: 143]
Hit me in the knee with that little hammer and I'll kick you in the chin.

He asserts that if the speaker is talking about his strong reflex action, the sentence is a 'warning'.[8] But if he is talking about something malicious that he intends to do, then it is a 'threat'.[9]

Fraser (1975a: 173) proposes an analysis similar to Sadock's. He suggests that a 'threat' is a special type of 'warning' in which the speaker takes on the responsibility for bringing about the disadvantageous action. He argues that if S says to H 'If you do not get there before 8.00 pm, we will start the party anyway', and if H feels strongly about being present at party-beginnings, then S has 'threatened' as well as 'warned' H.

It is true that in both 'warn' and 'threaten', the consequence of not acting accordingly is undesirable. It is also true that 'threaten' often contains a second part of the form 'I'll/We'll do X', indicating the speaker's personal involvement in the impending action. However, it is not true that 'warning' and 'threatening' are therefore not separable or that one is a subclass of the other. There is a very important difference between them. A *warning* is performed in the interest of the addressee, whereas a *threat* is performed in the interest of the speaker himself. This difference is reflected in the response they prospect. A *warning* prospects compliance or minimally an acknowledgement with an optional 'thank you'. A *threat* prospects compliance, usually in the form of silent acquiescence, but it does not prospect a 'thank you'. What usually follows a threat is a challenge like 'Don't you dare', 'You can't do that', or 'You will not'. If it is responded to by 'thank you', then conversational implicature such as sarcasm is generated.

6.5 Concluding remarks

In this chapter, we have made a detailed description of directives. We have pointed out that in identifying acts, it is important not to assume that there is a one-to-one correspondence between illocutionary verbs and acts. In identifying the subclasses of directives, we have examined their discourse behaviours, the nature of the action involved in terms of who the action benefits, whether the speaker has the right or authority to get compliance, the consequence of complying or not complying, and whether the speaker is responsible for bringing about the consequence. We may summarize the subclasses and their features as shown, on page 134, in Figure 6.1.

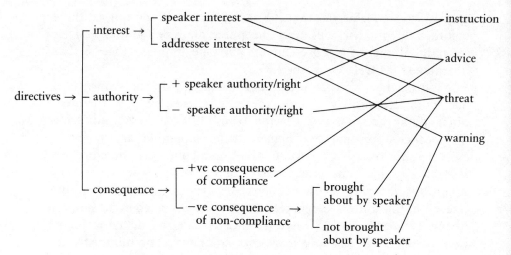

Figure 6.1: Four subclasses of directives

7
Informatives

7.1 Introduction

The term 'informative' is first introduced by Sinclair and Coulthard (1975) as a discourse category which has the function of providing information and prospects an acknowledgement of attention and understanding (see Sinclair and Coulthard 1975: 41). In the present descriptive framework, *informatives* are characterized as a more general category which covers not only utterances which provide information, but also those which report events or states of affairs, recount personal experience, and express beliefs, evaluative judgements, feelings, and thoughts.[1] The following are some examples of informatives:

(1) [C:4:1]
→   S: John Fraser is a personal friend of ours, Michael went to school with him.
    G: Oh really.

(2) [B:A:A:3:5]
→   K: I think he's a y'know serious scholar, he's got his own little thing.
    X: Yeah, he's he IS very scholarly.

(3) [B:C:A:3:2]
→   A: I I still feel very embarrassed about the fact that you weren't introdu– introduced to him.
    B: Mm – well, well, no worry, that's that's the way, =
                                            [
    A: (   )
    B: = yeah.
    A: Alright.

In (1), we have the speaker providing a piece of factual information.

In (2) we have the speaker expressing an evaluative judgement of the referent 'he'. In (3) we have the speaker expressing his feelings towards a past event. They all prospect acknowledgement of some sort by the addressee.

That an acknowledging response is prospected by an *informative*, rather than optional, is supported by Keenan's study (1983) of the conversations between her two twin sons. She discovered that 'comments'—which she characterized as utterances in which the speaker expresses his/her belief about the world, as opposed to trying to get the addressee to carry out some action—were almost always followed by some utterances that addressed themselves to the 'comments'. When a 'comment' received no acknowledgement, it was repeated again and again until it did (see also Goffman 1974: 503; cf. Stubbs 1981).[2] For example:

(4) [Keenan 1983: 8]
→ **Child 1** – [i:] moth/
   Child 2 – goosey goosey ganda/ where shall I wander/
→ **Child 1** – [i:] moth/
   Child 2 – up downstairs lady's chamber/
→ **Child 1** – [i:] moth/
→ **Child 2** – [i:] [le:] moth/

She also discovered that out of the first seventy-six conversational turns containing 'comments', only three received no verbal acknowledgement. She observes:

> A speaker uttering a comment expects the hearer to *acknowledge* that comment. That is, once a comment has been produced by a speaker, the co-present interlocutor is normally obligated to respond to that comment. (Keenan 1983: 6, my underlining)

The following piece of data supports Keenan's observation that an acknowledging response is by no means optional:

(5) [B:G:B:4:2]
  1 **C:** Alright, so that'll be fine then ((*pause*)) I'm ah.
  2 **A:** Okay.
  3 **C:** Alright, so have a nice time in China if I don't see you.

→   *(2.5 sec)*
4 **C:** You're going to China on on Friday or Saturday.
5 **A:** No, we're going on Saturday and coming back on Monday.

In lines 1–2, C and A close the topic regarding arrangements for a dinner gathering on the following Tuesday. In line 3, C wishes A a nice trip to China at the coming weekend. When this well-wishing is not responded to, C immediately checks to see if there are any hitches in communication by asking A to confirm the date of her trip to China.

7.2 Subclasses of informatives

We shall now to try to identify subclasses of informatives on the basis of the data given in (1) to (3).

The three informatives are responded to by different forms of acknowledgement. In (1), G's acknowledgement of the piece of information provided by S is in the form of an 'oh'-receipt token which indicates that the message has been received and understood (Heritage 1984; see also section 7.3). In (2), X's acknowledgement of K's evaluative statement is in the form of another evaluation which strongly agrees with K. In (3), B's acknowledgement is in the form of a minimization of the expressed embarrassment. On the basis of the different responses, we may say that they realize three different subclasses of informatives.

The first subclass comprises those which report events or states of affairs, or recount personal experiences. Let us identify them as *reports*. Example (1) is an instance of a report. They subsume acts which have been identified in the speech act literature as 'state', 'inform', 'report'. The second subclass comprises those which express judgements of some sort, including an evaluative judgement. Let us identify them as *assessments*. Example (2) is an instance of an assessment. They subsume acts which have been identified in the speech act literature as 'praise', 'compliment', 'assess', 'characterize', 'criticize', 'complain', 'blame', 'accuse'. The third subclass comprises those which express the speaker's feelings and attitudes towards certain events or states of affairs. Let us identify them as *expressives*. Example (3) is an instance of an expressive. They subsume acts which have been identified in the speech act literature as 'thank', 'apolo-gize', 'congratulate', 'condole', 'welcome', 'greet', 'wish', and so on.

7.3 Reports

A *report* gives an account of certain events, states of affairs, or per-sonal experience in the past, present, or future.[3] It differs from an assessment in that its primary illocutionary intent is not to assert an evaluative judgement, although it may contain evaluative elements (cf. Drew 1984).[4] The difference between a *report* and an *assessment* can be best illustrated by comparing the following utterances:

(6) [I] **A:** That philosopher downstairs is a bastard.

(7) [I] **B:** That bastard downstairs is a philosopher.

Applying the notion of given and new, in (6), the given is 'That philosopher downstairs' and the new is 'a bastard'; whereas in (7), the given is 'that bastard downstairs' and the new is 'a philosopher'. In terms of illocutionary force, the primary illocutionary intent of A's utterance in (6) is to assert his evaluation of the philosopher downstairs. However, that of B's utterance in (7) is to give a piece of information about the person downstairs whom B considers a bastard.

A report can be responded to by a message-received signal which is typically prefaced by 'oh' (see (1)).[5] As Heritage (1984) points out, 'oh' marks the 'receipt' of information delivered in the previous utterance. It indicates that the addressee has undergone a change of state from uninformed to informed. Heritage refers to it as a 'change-of-state token'. The following are some more examples:

(8) [B:B:A:1:1]
    H was telling F how to get in touch with a postgraduate student from China.

    H: She she's I think she's from Beijing but you can just call just to confirm that there might be ah another person also from from Beijing but I'm pretty sure she's she's from Beijing.
→ **F:** Oh I see.

138

(9) [B:B:B:1:2]
    H: I just had a piece of your pie this morning, it was
       delicious. I'll have it this afternoon. David
             [[
→ X: Oh good.   Yeah ah and
       I also wanted to say that I've sent something up, =
                                       [
→ H: Oh
     X: = something to be xeroxed ah you'll get something ah =
                  [
     H: Good.
     X: = in in the mail next couple of days. It's an article, so I
       think it may be may be what what we were looking for.
     H: Alright, good.

In both (8) and (9), the informatives are responded to by 'Oh I see'
and 'Oh' which are 'change-of-state tokens'.

A message-received signal can also be realized by 'Right', 'Good',
or what Goffman (1974: 540) refers to as 'back-channel' cues, such
as 'mhm', 'uhuh', 'yeah', 'right', showing that the addressee is
listening and wishes the speaker to continue with the reporting.

Responses to reports may be more than a mere message-received
signal or an 'oh'-receipt token. As Heritage points out, 'it is common
for recipients to attend to, and deal with, informings as tellings of
good or bad news. Recipients do so by assessing the news delivered
...' (1984: 302). Drew also observes that the possible implication,
or 'upshot', of a reporting is left to the interpretation of the addressee
(Drew 1984: 137). The latter may acknowledge a report as a factual
account, in which case he produces a message-received signal, or he
may address what the 'upshot' of the report is taken to be. For
example:

(10) [C:1:A:3:9]
    B: My spoken English students are going to take me to
       dinner and we can go–
→ S: That's nice.
    B: Yes.

The 'upshot' of B's report of a future event is taken to be desirable, and S responds by making a positive remark on the reported event. Remarks like the above are often polite and supportive: a reported event which is presupposed to be good or desirable is often responded to by a positive remark, and one which is presupposed to be bad or undesirable is responded to by a negative remark or by sympathy, condolence, and so forth (see Leech 1983: 138–9, 'maxim of sympathy'). The following are some more examples of remarks which are supportive:

(11) [C:1:A:1]
    H: I'll give you ten dollars.
    S: Oh.
    H: My finance my financial situation is improving.
    S: ((*laughs*)) Are you
                  [
    H: My wife gave me a hundred dollars. She says this to me, she controls all the money, alright, I'll give you a hundred dollars, this is the LAST one you're getting this month – till pay day.
→   **S:** Oh no. ((*laughs*))

(12) [C:1:A:4:4]
    P has been telling S that the size of her (P's) class is far too big.
    P: Well, Jane cancelled that one yesterday because it had =
                                       [
    S: Yeah.
    P: = only three people in it and she gave me one of =
                         [
    S: I know.
    P: = her students. ((*laughs*))
→   **S:** Oh. ((*laughs*)) Oh I'm sorry.

In (11), S empathizes with H with regard to the somewhat funny and yet undesirable financial situation that he is in. In (12), S expresses her sympathy with P upon hearing that one more student has been added to her class which was already too big.

A report may also be responded to by remarks like 'that's right', or remarks prefaced with 'yes' if the reported event is also known to the addressee (see also Heritage 1984: 305).[6] For example:

(13) [BCET:A:35]
   C: David Owen was on the box the other night, last night on Question Time.
→ B: Yes, I saw the last minute of it.

Responses like the above indicate that the message is not only received, but also that the reported event is known. This appears to suggest that there are two subclasses of reports: those in which the reported event is not known to the addressee and those in which it is. Labov and Fanshel (1977) classify representations of events which are known to both the speaker and the addressee (i.e. AB-events) as 'refer', and those which are known only to the speaker (i.e. A-events) as 'give information'. However, it is doubtful whether we can distinguish between these two subclasses in the actual process of the conversation, because interlocutors can never be sure of what is known and what is not known to the other party until the response is produced. It is not uncommon for a speaker to repeat something which he has already told the addressee about. For example:

(14) [BCET:D:1]
   C: Lorna bought me that for Christmas.
→ D: Yes, you were saying that.

It is also possible that what was assumed to be an 'AB-event' turned out to be an 'A-event'. For example:

(15) [B:D:A:1:12]
   H: But did you hear what China said? They would be very happy the way Hong Kong handled everything, y'know, like, they'll they'll rush in if there's any law and order problem.
→ J: Oh will they? I didn't know that.

H's report, which could well be an 'AB-event' since it is in the news, turned out to be an 'A-event', as can be seen from J's response. It is equally likely for J to say, 'Yes, it was in the news last night', indicating that it is indeed an 'AB-event'. Sometimes, it is not clear whether the reported event is an 'A-event' or an 'AB-event', even when we look at the addressee's response. For example:

(16) [BCET:A:42]
    B: Arthur Scargill just bought a new fifteen thousand five hundred pound Jaguar.
→ **C:** Bloody hell, communist.

(17) [BCET:A:42]
    B: Randy Andy, his income is five thousand from the navy and twenty thousand from the Royal purse.
→ **C:** Twenty thousand, twenty-five thousand for Randy Andy Windsor – I think it's disgusting.

From the responses in (16) and (17), it is by no means clear whether B is reporting an 'A-event' or an 'AB-event'. As we are dealing with prospective classification and subclasses of acts are set up only if they are identifiable in the discourse, I am therefore reluctant to make further classifications of reports.

7.4 Assessments

Assessments are a subclass of informatives in which the speaker asserts his judgement or evaluation of certain people, objects, events, states of affairs, and so on. The evaluative element can be conveyed by lexical items such as 'good', 'scholarly', 'bastard', and so forth. It can also be conveyed by intonation. Consider the following pieces of data:

(18) [C:1:A:4:1]
    X and S are talking about the size of their classes. The normal size is sixteen to twenty students.
→ **X:** I had THIRty, I told you that didn't I, I had THIRty there at one stage.
    S: I can't believe it, wow.

(19) [C:1:A:1:1]
    H: But I don't know, I reali– I didn't realize why she says

→   we have to save money ah SHE went and bought nine
         hundred dollars of um balcony furniture.
     S: Oh boy.

In (18), by making 'thirty' prominent, X is conveying an evaluative
judgement that her class is far too big. In (19), by making 'she'
prominent, H is contrasting 'she' with 'we', hence conveying the
evaluative judgement that his wife has double standards.

Assessments typically prospect a response in which a second judgement or evaluation is made. In Pomerantz's terms, it typically prospects a 'second assessment'. In the ensuing discussion, I shall refer
to the response as a 'second evaluation' so as not to confuse it with
an *assessment* which is an initiating act.

7.5 Subclasses of assessments

In what follows, I shall identify the subclasses of *assessment* by
examining the object of evaluation and the way they are typically
responded to. I shall start with the kind of assessment which gives
judgement or evaluation of an event, state(s) of affairs, or a third
party—that is, neither the speaker nor the addressee. The evaluation
or judgement can be positive or negative:

(20) [B:D:A:1:8]
     H and J are talking about H's accepting an offer of a job
     from another institution.

     H: But I'm y'know I I think it would be very dicey because
         you don't know, I don't know what the set up is there.
     J: You don't know who and you're gonna go through the
         whole thing again.

(21) [B:D:A:1:6]
     C: And I thought that he was he was very professional
         about it.
     K: Oh he IS very professional, he's good.

In (20), H expresses his reservations about changing his job and J
agrees with him by making a similar judgement. In (21), C makes
an evaluation of a third party 'he'. K agrees with him by giving a
similar evaluation.

This kind of assessment can also be responded to by a second evaluation or judgement which 'upgrades' it. For example:

(22) [B:G:A:2:3]
    H: yeah well I feel very the principles are very important because the fu because of the future future things.
                            [[
  → **X:**   oh extremely   extremely.

(23) [B:C:B:1:9]
    E: They they definitely inflate their findings (   ) =
                                              [
    F: Oh yeah, a =
    E: = (   ) half a dozen (   )
        [[
  → **F:** = lot of it is   I think a lot of it is bullshit.

(24) [B:A:A:3:4]
    K: I think he's a y'know serious scholar, he's got his own little thing.
  → **X:** Yeah, he's he IS very scholarly.

In (22), H's judgement of the principles as being 'very important' is upgraded to 'extremely'. Similarly, in (23), E's negative evaluation of 'they' as 'inflating their findings', is upgraded to 'a lot of it is bullshit', and in (24), K's evaluation of 'he' as 'a serious scholar' is upgraded to 'very scholarly' and upgraded by making 'is' prominent.

This kind of assessment can also be responded to by downgrading the evaluation. For example:

(25) [B:C:B:1:1]
    F: He's a very nice person.
    E: He is, isn't he, yeah.
    F: Yeah just ah
    E: He knows his stuff too, doesn't he, although I don't agree with him (   )
                  [
  → **F:**   I yeah he yeah he's a very good explainer.

E's evaluation of 'he' as someone who 'knows his stuff' is downgraded to 'a good explainer'. In other words, this kind of assessment can be responded to by a second evaluation which is similar to or agrees with it, or which upgrades or downgrades it.[7] While an upgrading evaluation realizes a strong agreement, a downgrading evaluation realizes a weak agreement (see Pomerantz 1978, 1984; Tsui 1991b). Let us identify this kind of assessment as *assessing*.

Assessments can also be evaluations directed at the addressee. The following is an example:

(26) [BCET:A:32]
    C: I mean from what I can see Rob you're in a hell of a good position.
    B: ((*laughs*)) It's okay I suppose.
    (*5 secs*)
    B: Mm It's okay.

In (26), C's assessment is a positive evaluation of B, the addressee. It is responded to by a second evaluation which downgrades 'in a hell of a good position' to 'it's okay'. In contrast to (20) and (21), example (26) shows that it is socially unacceptable to upgrade the assessment, because to do so would violate the social norm of modesty (see Leech 1983: 'maxim of modesty'; Tsui 1991a; see also Pomerantz 1978 for examples).[8] Hence, while it is appropriate for the addressee to agree with or upgrade an assessment which is directed at a third party, it is not acceptable to do so for an assessment which makes a positive evaluation of the addressee him/herself. Let us call this subclass *compliment*.

The following is another example in which a *compliment* is downgraded by the addressee:

(27) [BCET:A:27]
    B: Teacher training is a good thing to be on.
    C: I don't want to be a teacher or anything.
    B: It gives you a year.
    C: Yeah.
    B: A bit slow off the mark here.
    C: It's terribly slow, yes.
→   B: Not like you.
→   C: I'm afraid it's like me of late.

It should be noted that a compliment can be a positive evaluation of a third party in which the credit given to the third party is also a credit to the addressee. For example:

(28) [B:A:A:3:5]

> H: Somebody was saying Mary looks very pretty. Alice didn't recognize her, she's getting very tall, your kids are very tall.
>
> M: Yeah, she's going to be a pretty one, she's pretty.

Mary is M's daughter and Alice is H's wife. By telling M that his daughter is very pretty, H is paying a compliment to him as well (see Manes and Wolfson 1981: 122).[9] Notice that the compliment is downgraded from 'very pretty' to 'pretty'.

The assessment in (29) below is the reverse of those in (26) to (28). It is a negative evaluation of the addressee:

(29) [BCET:D:45]

> *C has been telling D that she has three library books out which are long overdue.*
>
> D: I'll tell you this, Cathy, if I ever buy a bookshop, or own a library, I'm not letting you take any books out.
>
> C: Yeah, I know ((*laughs*)) I'm disastrous.

As we can see, the second evaluation is the complete reverse of those in (26) to (28). C upgrades D's criticism of herself to 'disastrous'. This kind of assessment can also be responded to by a similar evaluation. For example:

(30) [BCET:D:31]

> D: Cathy, do you have to spray that stuff round the place. You're destroying the ozone layer, and my nostrils, oh my god!
>
> C: I know, it's a bit bad isn't it.

(31) [BCET:D:68]

> C: Ow!
>
> D: Watch it.
>
> C: ((*laughs*))
>
> D: Christ! Cathy, you would drive anybody half-way round the goddamn fucking bend.

[

→ **C:**   I once dropped the telephone.
    D: I can imagine you dropping the telephone.

In (30), D's negative evaluation of C's destroying the ozone layer is agreed with by C. In (31), C nearly knocked over a table lamp. D then commented on her clumsiness. By telling D that she even dropped the telephone once, C is implicitly making a similar evaluation of herself: that she is a very clumsy person. An apology is also a possible response. It implicitly agrees with the prior negative evaluation. For example:

(32) [B:H:B:4:1]
    S: Hello.
    H: Oh is is Sally there?
    S: This IS Sally.
    H: Oh Sally, this is Henry calling.
    S: Hi Henry.
    H: Come all the way down the hall.
→   **S:** You sound so secretive.
→   **H:** I'm sorry y'know I think you're with somebody and so
        my voice changed.

The fact that the assessments in (29) to (32) prospect a contrary set of responses suggests that they belong to a different subclass. Let us label them *criticism*. A *criticism* is a face-threatening act which is usually avoided unless the interlocutors know each other very well. For this reason, a criticism is often *presented as* a report. As Drew points out, by giving an account of an event without explicitly stating the implication of the account, 'speakers withhold officially taking positions about the possible implications of their reportings' (Drew 1984: 137). Take the following piece of data, for example:

(33) [BCET:D:63]
→ 1 **C:** You've drunk all that. I only bought that a week or so
         ago.
  2 **D:** I go through one of those every day at least, I do.
→ 3 **C:** That cost me (   ) I haven't got any money to
  4   get any more until I get my dole cheque. You know
  5   the dole cheques have been delayed.
  6 **D:** I'll buy one Cathy and I'll drop – oh watch it, oh why
→ 7 **C:** No, I'm not complaining, I'm saying that my dole

147

8   cheque's – because of the post – because of the strike.
         Apparently the cheque's

In line (1), C 'reports' that D has drunk the entire bottle of wine.
D, however, does not take the upshot of the 'report' as a *criticism*
until C continues to point out that the wine is expensive and that
she has no money to get another bottle. It is interesting to note that
as soon as D attends to the 'upshot' in line 6, C disengages herself
from the upshot by saying 'No, I'm not complaining'. The following
is a further example of a report taken as a criticism, which is
responded to by an apology.

(34) [BCET:D:15]
         C: What was I saying?
         D: I don't know.
    → C: You interrupted me.
         D: I'm sorry, I wasn't listening.

Compliment and criticism are both assessments which are directed
at the addressee. Let us now consider assessments which are directed
at the speaker him/herself:

(35) [Fieldnotes]
         A and S have been discussing the interpretation of certain
         utterances in conversation.
         S: That's very interesting. I don't think I have the guts to
            make it the subject of my thesis. It's very difficult.
         A: No, you'll be able to once you get into it, the ah the
            nuances and all that.

S's assessment in (35) is a negative evaluation of the speaker herself.
It is responded to by a second evaluation which disagrees with her.
In contrast to a criticism, a disagreement with the preceding assessment does not challenge the presuppositions of the latter. Quite the
contrary, it is typically prospected. It is, or it implies, a positive
evaluation of the speaker, and hence saves the face of the latter (see
also Pomerantz 1978, 1984; Leech 1983). The following is another
example from Pomerantz (1984):

(36) [Pomerantz 1984: 85]
         L: . . . I'm so dumb I don't even know it. hhh! – heh!
    → W: y–no, y–you're not du:mb, . . .

148

Apart from disagreement, this kind of assessment can be responded to in the following way:

(37) [B:B:A:3]
  → H: My God, ten years, I can't believe it. It doesn't seem that you were away that long. Maybe it just shows that I'm really getting old.
      X: Eh listen, Henry, that's what's happening to all of us.
      H: Yeah.

By saying that the negative attribute applies to himself as well, X is, in fact, trying to play down the negative aspect of the evaluation (cf. Pomerantz 1984).[10] In other words, negative evaluations directed at the speaker him/herself prospect disagreements or downgradings. We shall identify them as another subclass and label them *self-denigrations*.

H's assessment in (38) below is very different from the assessments in (35) to (37). It is a positive evaluation of the speaker himself:

(38) [B:E:A:1:1]
      H: eh listen I I typed up your paper, it's beautiful, it's =
                                                [
      X: Oh
      H: = beautiful, it's going to be Nobel Nobel ah material.
      X: Great stuff.

H's evaluation of his own typing as 'beautiful' and 'Nobel material', albeit facetious, is responded to by a similar second evaluation, 'great stuff'. Let us call this kind of assessment *self-commendation*.[11] In contrast to a self-denigration, a contrary second evaluation would be socially unacceptable, because it implies a negative evaluation of the speaker and is therefore face-threatening. It usually occurs between interlocutors who know each other very well. Consider the following piece of data:

(39) [BCET:A:32]
      C: I mean from what I can see Rob you're in a hell of a good position.
      B: ((*laughs*)) It's okay, I suppose.
        (*5 secs*)
      B: Mm, it's okay.

C: Yeah well I think ninety quid take home is more than
okay, just for the record.
          [
B: ((*laughs*))
→ B: I work hard.
→ C: DO you ACTually work hard?
B: Well
C: ((*laughs*)) Think about it before you answer.

Here, B's positive evaluation of himself is challenged by C. This is acceptable only because C knows B very well.

We have pointed out above that a *criticism* is often *presented as* a report. Similarly, because making a positive evaluation of oneself violates the social norm of modesty, a *self-commendation* is often *presented as* a report, and the 'upshot', which is the positive evaluation of the speaker himself, is often left to the interpretation of the addressee. Take the following piece of data, for example:

(40) [B:E:A:1:2]
→ B: And and ah they asked me to review it too.
J: Oh they did?
B: Yeah. So I might because it's it's it's kind of in my field.
          [
J: Good.

In (40), B 'reports' that he has been asked by the publisher to review a book. There is no explicit positive evaluation of himself. However, because being asked to review a book implies a positive evaluation, J responds by making a second positive evaluation, 'Good'. The following is another example:

(41) [B:A:A:3:2]
→ K: So he he he asked me to call, he wanted me to call
    Professor Lee, which I at present declined to do.
                                        [
X: Good for
    you.

Here, 'he' is the head of the department in which K works. K 'reports' that he turned down an unreasonable request from the department head. Since to refuse to succumb to authority is seen as

150

something commendable, K's 'report' is responded to by a positive evaluation of him.

Another way that self-commendations can be performed without violating what Pomerantz (1978: 88) refers to as the 'self-praise avoidance' maxim[12] is to incorporate a disclaimer when one praises oneself. The following is an example:

(42) [C:1:A:4:15]

    P: I mean I I mean I I y'know it's it's a problem I mean they asked me oh something about do you give blood. I said well I'm not allowed to give blood. Why not? Well I had malaria and I can never give blood. How did you get malaria? Well I was in the jungles in Zambia. Y'know,

→   and and it's not that I'm boasting or anything but I =

                                                    [

    S: You're not.

    P: = have done certain things in my life and they asked about it.

Similar to (40) and (41), P's disclaimer that she is not boasting is responded to by an agreement from S, which implies a positive evaluation.

The features of the five subclasses identified above are summarized in Figure 7.1.

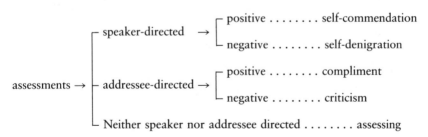

Figure 7.1: Features of five subclasses of assessment

7.6 Expressives

Expressives are ritualistic acts in which speakers express civility and goodwill towards each other. They are what Goffman (1971: 63) refers to as 'interpersonal rituals'. Expressives are easily identifiable because they are often realized by formulaic expressions and the forms of the responses prospected are highly predictable.

Goffman (ibid.) suggests that there are two kinds of ritual interchanges: 'supportive interchanges' and 'remedial interchanges'. Supportive interchanges are those in which signs of goodwill are appreciated. Some serve to affirm and support the social relationship between speakers. Examples include congratulations at marriage, condolences at deaths, and greetings in encounters. Remedial interchanges are those which are performed when an individual violates the social norm of respecting others' privacy. They consist of the offender providing an account and apologizing for the violation and the offended acknowledging the account and apology as sufficient.

Goffman's classification is made from a sociological perspective. From a discourse analysis perspective, however, we can say that there are basically three types of expressives. Firstly, there are those in which the speaker shows concern for and empathizes with the addressee. They typically prospect responses expressing appreciation, often in the form of 'Thank you' or 'That's very kind/nice of you'. They include acts which are commonly referred to as 'congratulate', 'well-wishing', 'welcome', and 'condole'. The following are some examples:

(43) [B:B:B:6:1]
 → H: Welcome back to Hong Kong.
  X: Thank you.

(44) [Fieldnotes]
 → A: I heard that your promotion has come through, congratulations.
  G: Thank you, I'll believe it when I see the piece of paper.

(45) [B:D:B:1:1]
 → H: I hope you'll feel better.
  A: Thanks a lot.

(46) [B:D:B:4:4]
→ **H:** Okay then, well take it easy then.
    X: Thank you very much.

(47) [B:C:B:1:9]
    J: So maybe I'll see you at the next HAAL meeting, alright?
→ **B:** Yeah. Okay then, look after yourself.
    J: Alright.

(48) [Fieldnotes]
→ **A:** I'm sorry to hear that your father is very ill.
    B: Yeah, thanks for your concern.

Secondly, there are those in which the speaker expresses his feelings towards a debt which he has incurred. They typically prospect minimizations or acceptances. They include acts which have been commonly referred to as 'thanking' and 'apologizing'. For example:

(49) [B:C:A:2:1]
    H: Hello.
    G: Hi Henry, Jack here.
    H: Hi.
→ **G:** Sorry to trouble you.
    H: Sure Jack.
    G: um I wonder if you might give my apologies, I'm not
       going to make it tomorrow. =
                [
    H: Okay
    G: = Okay Jack sure.
→ **G:** Sorry about that.
        [[
    H: Right   Right.

(50) [C:1:A:4:9]
→ **P:** Oh that'll be great. ((*laughs*)) Thank you.
    S: You're welcome.

Thirdly, there are those which express goodwill and are typically responded to by a return of goodwill. They include acts which have been commonly referred to as 'greeting', 'leave-taking', 'farewell', and so on.[13] For example:

(51) [B:E:A:1:1]
→ **H:** Eh:: how're you doing, Johnny baby.
   J: Good. How're you doing, Henry baby.

(52) [B:D:A:1:14]
→ **A:** Okay then, we'll keep in touch then.
   B: Okay then.

(53) [B:B:A:3:5]
   B: So, we look forward to seeing you at in ah
                                                      [
   A: Yeah, look forward
      to Friday the fourth, Henry.

We can represent the features of the three types of expressives as shown in Figure 7.2.

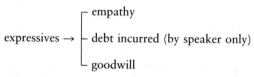

Figure 7.2: Features of three types of expressives

7.7 Concluding remarks

In this chapter, we have characterized the last subclass of initiating act: informatives. We have characterized it as a discourse category which not only provides information, but also reports events and states of affairs, conveys evaluative judgements, and expresses feelings and attitudes. It prospects an obligatory verbal response of acknowledgement. The acknowledgement can be in the form of a message-received signal or a supportive comment, if it is in response to a *report*. It can be a second evaluation which agrees or disagrees with the prior evaluation, if it is in response to an *assessment*. It can also be in the form of reciprocating the goodwill, expressing appreciation, minimization, or empathy, if it is in response to an *expressive*.

The prospected responses to assessments are largely governed by modesty, politeness, and the preservation of face. The agreement with or upgrading of an *assessing* and a *self-commendation* is motivated by politeness and preservation of face: one should avoid threatening others' face and one should be supportive of others. Likewise, the disagreement with a *self-denigration* is also motivated by politeness. To agree with self-denigration is to make a negative evaluation of the self-denigrator which is face-threatening. This is why *criticisms* are often presented as *reports*. On the other hand, the downgrading of a *compliment* is motivated by modesty: to make positive evaluation of oneself violates the maxim of modesty and is socially unacceptable. This is why, similar to *criticisms*, *self-commendations* are often presented as *reports*. Or, if performed, they often contain disclaimers.

Expressives and their typical responses are governed by the social norms of affirming and supporting social relationships and respecting the preservation of self by individuals.

PART FOUR

Characterization of discourse acts: neglected aspects

8
Responses

I THE IDENTIFICATION OF A RESPONSE

8.1 Introduction

(1) [Labov 1972: 299]
   A: What is your name?
   B: Well, let's say you might have thought you had
      something from before, but you haven't got it any more.
   A: I'm going to call you Dean.
   (from Laffal 1965: 85)

The above is an excerpt from a conversation between a doctor and a schizophrenic patient taken from Labov (1972). It has often been quoted as an example of incoherent discourse. What is it that makes it incoherent? Our intuition tells us that it is incoherent because the utterances are totally unrelated: B's 'reply' does not answer A's question and A's second utterance is not a further response to B's 'reply'. But what criteria do we use to decide whether B's utterance constitutes an answer? Compare (1) with the following:

(2) [Labov 1972: 123]
   Linus: Do you want to play with me Violet?
   Violet: You're younger than me. (*shuts the door*)
   Linus: [*puzzled*] She hasn't answered my question.

Despite the fact that there does not seem to be any relation between the surface forms of Linus's 'question' and Violet's 'answer', we feel that it is a coherent piece of discourse (see Grice 1975: 'maxim of relevance'). We also feel that Violet has, in fact, 'answered' Linus's 'question', although Linus said that she has not. But what is it that renders Violet's utterance in (2) relevant and B's utterance in (1)

159

irrelevant? On what grounds do we say that the former constitutes an answer, whereas the latter does not?

In the first part of this chapter (sections 8.1 to 8.4), we shall address these questions. We shall try to establish the criteria for determining whether an utterance constitutes a *response*. In the second part (sections 8.5 to 8.9), we shall examine the responses to the four major subclasses of initiating act.

8.2 Responses in speech act literature

Responses have been given very little attention in the speech act literature. Most of the acts characterized and listed in the various taxonomies are initiating acts (see Austin 1962; Ohmann 1972; Vendler 1972; Fraser 1975b; Bach and Harnish 1979; Searle 1979; Searle and Venderveken 1985). This is because the characterization of illocutionary acts is often done by making a semantic analysis of performative verbs rather than by examining the function of utterances in discourse; and as many responding acts do not have a corresponding performative verb, this kind of analysis inevitably neglects responses. Let us take the following piece of data, for example:

(3) [BCET:A:17]
    C: Could I stay at your place for a bit Rob?
→ B: um I don't know.

B's response to C's request for permission to stay at his place cannot be described by any of the performative verbs. Its illocutionary force can only be captured by expressions like B 'refuses to commit himself either way' (see Tsui 1987c: 365).

The few responses that have been attended to in the speech act literature such as 'agree', 'accept', 'deny', 'permit', and so on, are not clearly differentiated from initiating acts. For example, according to Austin (1962), 'agree' and 'state' are both 'expositives' in which the speaker expounds his/her views; and according to Searle (1979), 'permit' and 'order' are both 'directives' in which the speaker attempts to get the addressee to do something. But 'agree' and 'permit' are clearly different from 'state' and 'order', in that while the former two are usually acts in the responding move, the latter two are acts in the initiating move. This lack of differentiation is a result of characterizing illocutionary acts as isolated units instead of as components in the interaction between the speaker and the addressee. Little attention has been paid to the way an utterance is related to the preceding and following utterances. It is not surprising, therefore, that in Austin's and Searle's taxonomies, as well as in subsequent taxonomies, the structural location of an illocutionary act has never been a criterion for establishing the taxonomy.[1]

A characterization of utterances which is based on observations of real-life discourse is not likely to neglect the importance of responses (see Schegloff and Sacks 1973: 313). As Fries (1952: 172), after examining some fifty hours of surreptitiously recorded conversation, observes:

> as one attempts to survey and describe the structural patterns of English sentences, he cannot escape the necessity of separating sharply the utterances that are used to stimulate various types of responses from those utterances that are themselves the oral responses regularly elicited by certain structural arrangements.

8.3 Responding move and challenging move

In characterizing responding acts, an important question that needs to be addressed is: what are the criteria for identifying a responding move? It is obvious that not any move following an initiating move is a responding move. An initiation can be followed by a move which is totally unrelated, as (1) above or in the case of an interruption. The question is how do we decide whether a related move is a responding move? Consider the following:

(4) [Tsui 1991c: 118]
    A: What's the time?
    B: (a) Eleven.
        (b) Time for coffee.
        (c) I haven't got a watch, sorry.
        (d) How should I know.
        (e) Ask Jack.
        (f) You know bloody well what time it is.
        (g) Why do you ask?
        (h) What did you say?
        (i) What do you mean?

B's possible utterances are all related to A's initiating move whose head act is an elicit:inform. But are they all *responding moves*? To answer this question, we need to look at the illocutionary intent and the pragmatic presuppositions of A's elicitation. The term 'pragmatic presuppositions' is used in the way it is expounded in Stalnaker (1977: 136) They refer to the background belief of the speaker; that is, propositions that the speaker takes for granted to be true in making the utterance. The illocutionary intent of A's elicitation is to get B to provide a piece of information. It presupposes that:

a. the speaker does not have the information and wants to (sincerely);
b. the speaker has the need and the right to ask for the information;
c. the speaker has reason to believe that the addressee has the information;
d. the speaker has reason to believe that the addressee is willing to supply the information (see Searle 1969; Lakoff 1973; Labov and Fanshel 1977; Coulthard 1985: 184).

In addition to the above presuppositions, there are also those which pertain to all illocutionary acts:

e. the addressee can hear what the speaker says;
f. the addressee can understand the meaning conveyed (see Searle 1969: 57; cf. Keenan and Schieffelin 1983: 79).[2]

In (4), both (a) and (b) fulfil the illocutionary intent of A's elicitation. They provide the information that A seeks, although in (b) the information is given indirectly: A has to deduce the information from it on the basis of his knowledge of the world; that is, that coffee time is usually around 11.00 a.m. They both support the pragmatic presuppositions of A's elicitation. They are both responding moves.

The rest of the utterances do not provide the information that A seeks; they do not fulfil the illocutionary intent of A's elicitation. Rather, they challenge its pragmatic presuppositions.[3] Utterances (c) and (d) challenge the presupposition that the addressee has the information (see Katz 1972: 214).[4] Utterance (c) does it in a polite way by providing a reason for his inability to supply the information, whereas (d) does it in an aggressive way. Utterance (e) could be challenging the presupposition that the addressee has the informa-

tion or the presupposition that the addressee is willing to supply
the information. Utterance (f) challenges the presupposition that the
speaker does not have the information. In (g), the presupposition that
the addressee has the need to ask for the information is challenged.
Utterances (h) and (i) challenge the presuppositions that the speaker
can hear and understand what has been said.

Following Burton (1980),[5] let us characterize moves which challenge the presuppositions of the preceding utterance as *challenging
moves*[6] (cf. Lakoff 1973; Labov and Fanshel 1977: 77).[7] A *challenging move* can occur after an initiating move as in (4), or after a
responding move. The head act of a challenging move is realized by
an initiating act.[8] Therefore, strictly speaking, a challenging move is
a kind of initiating move which challenges the presuppositions of
the preceding initiating move or responding move.

8.4 Three major subclasses of responding acts

Given the above criteria for identifying a responding move, we can
now decide whether an utterance realizes a responding act, since a
responding act is the head act of a responding move. Let us apply
the above criteria to the analysis of some data:

(5) [B:C:A:1:1]
    H: I was wondering if you could send me the um application
       forms
→ B: Yes um
    H: Would
    B: If you would like to give me the name and address.
    H: Oh that's it, I just gave you my address.

(6) [BCET:A:56]
    C has already offered B a cigarette once and B has declined.

    C: Are you sure you don't want a cigarette?
→ B: No, I couldn't take your last but one.

(7) [BCET:A:22]
    C: Could I stay at your place for a bit Rob?
→ B: um I don't know.

In (5), H's initial utterance is a request for action. Its illocutionary intent is to get B to send him the application forms. Its pragmatic presuppositions are:

a. B knows what application forms H is referring to;
b. H sincerely wants B to send him the application forms;
c. H believes that there is a need for B to send him the forms;
d. B may be able and willing to send H the application forms;[9]
e. it is not obvious that B will send him the application forms of her own accord.

In addition to the above presuppositions, there are also the presuppositions that B can hear and understand what H said. Since these presuppositions apply to all utterances, I shall only list and discuss those which are specific to an utterance in the ensuing discussion.

B, in saying 'yes', is fulfilling the illocutionary intent of H's utterance and also implying that the pragmatic presuppositions of H's utterance are supported. B's utterance therefore realizes a *fully fitting* response.

Consider now C's utterance in (6) which is an offer. Its illocutionary intent is to get B to accept his offer of a cigarette. Its pragmatic presuppositions are:

a. C sincerely wants B to accept the cigarette;
b. B may want to have the cigarette;
c. it is not obvious that B will take the cigarette of his own accord.

B, in saying 'no', is not fulfilling the illocutionary intent of C's offer. However, the utterance does not challenge the pragmatic presuppositions of the latter, because C does not assume that B will accept the cigarette—it gives B the option of refusal. Hence, B's utterance realizes a responding act of declining C's offer, but it is not a *fully fitting* one. We may refer to a *fully fitting* response as a *positive responding act* and one which is not *fully fitting* as a *negative responding act*. The former is 'preferred' and the latter 'dispreferred'. (This will be discussed in detail in section 8.6.)

C's utterance in (7) is a request for permission to stay at B's place. Its illocutionary intent is to get B to grant him the permission. Its pragmatic presuppositions are:

a. C sincerely wants to stay at B's place;
b. B may be able and willing to let C stay at his place;

c. it is not obvious that B will let C stay at his place of his own accord.

In saying 'I don't know', B is not fulfilling the illocutionary intent of C's requestive. But he is not challenging any of its pragmatic presuppositions either. It is, therefore, a responding act. Like B's utterance in (6) above, it is a 'dispreferred' response. However, it is not a negative responding act, because B is not refusing to grant the permission, but rather postponing the decision-making. We may refer to this kind of response as a *temporization*.[10]

We can say that there are three major subclasses of responding acts. Let us represent them as shown in Figure 8.1.

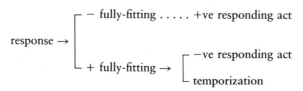

Figure 8.1: *Three major subclasses of responding acts*

II RESPONSES TO DIFFERENT INITIATIONS

In the first part of this chapter, we have identified three major subclasses of responding acts. In this second part, we shall see how they are realized in response to different initiating acts. We shall also examine how the initiating acts can be challenged.

8.5 Responses and challenges to elicitations

8.5.1 Elicit:inform

In section 8.3, we examined the illocutionary intent and pragmatic presuppositions of an *elicit:inform*. An utterance which provides the information that an elicit:inform seeks, whether directly or indirectly, is a *positive responding act*. An utterance in which the speaker expresses inability or reluctance to provide information realizes a *challenge*, because it challenges the presupposition that the addressee has the information. The following pieces of data are examples of challenges to elicit:informs:

(8) [B:E:A:3:1]

   X: I'm writing this paper here ah and ah Hong Kong being the most densely populated area on earth, is this still true?

→ **H:** Oh I don't know, there're a lot of dense people here, let me tell you ((*laughs*))

(9) [C:4:B:1:69]

   G: Is he here in Hong Kong?

→ **S:** Oh I don't want to talk about who he is.

   G: No, I wouldn't ask you but I just wondered if he worked here um.

In (8) and (9), the arrowed utterances are both challenges. In (8), the addressee challenges the presupposition that he is able to provide the information by declaring ignorance. In (9), S challenges the pre-supposition that she is willing to provide the information. Notice that the head act in (8), realized by 'Oh I don't know', can only be described as 'a declaration of inability to supply information', and the head act in (9) as 'a declaration of unwillingness to supply information'. There do not seem to be illocutionary verbs that can be used to capture their discourse function. Here, we have further examples of the lack of correspondence between verbs and acts, as pointed out in section 8.2.

Challenges are face-threatening and 'dispreferred'. However, some are more face-threatening than others. Challenging the presupposition that one is *able* to provide the requested information is less face-threatening than challenging the presupposition that one is *willing* to provide the requested information. As we can see, in (9), G, upon hearing S's challenge, immediately tries to repair the face damage by glossing the illocutionary force of his initial utterance as 'wonder', which does not demand an answer, rather than 'ask', which does. This is why interlocutors who are not willing to provide information often resort to declaration of ignorance, such as 'I don't know', which is less face-threatening. They would also use fillers, hesitations, or evasive answers to indicate their reluctance. The following is an example:

(10) [BCET:A:32]

C asked B how much he is earning a month.

C: So how much? I bet you're getting about three quid an hour, aren't you?

→ B: Well –

C: More?

B: Not –

C: Thirty-five hour week.

→ B: Not after tax.

C: No, not after tax, the actual rate.

B: Oh yeah.

C: Three-twenty? Three forty?

        [

B: I lost about a hundred in tax, which is a bit . . .

Notice that in the above stretch of discourse, B never flatly refused to supply the information, but he has not supplied the requested information either.

An utterance which challenges the speaker's right to ask for the information is even more face-threatening. For example, 'That's none of your business'. The following piece of data is another example:

(11) [BCET:D:28]

D was telling C about a novel that he has read which says that one thing Satan could not do is die.

C: How do you know the devil can't die?

→ D: Oh Jesus, I'm just TELLing you.

In (11), D is merely reporting what the novel said. Therefore, C's elicitation is considered unjustified and D challenges C's right to ask for an explanation. Again, the challenge here is much more face-threatening than that in (8).

8.5.2 Elicit:confirm

The illocutionary intent of an *elicit:confirm* is to get the addressee to confirm that the speaker's assumption is correct. It presupposes that:

a. the speaker believes that the expressed proposition is true, but

certain things in the context have led him to doubt his belief (see
Brazil 1985; Quirk *et al.* 1985);

b. the addressee is able to and will confirm that the speaker's
assumption is true.

Hence, an utterance which confirms the speaker's assumption realizes a *positive responding act* which fulfils the illocutionary intent
of an elicit:confirm. For example:

(12) [C:4:14]

　　　　　　　THINK you did that

　　S: //p I　　　　　　　　THIS year// r+ DIDn't you //

→ G: //p oh YEAH//

(13) [BCET:A:56]

　　C: //p so you're NOT COMing to the band tomorrow
　　　　then //

→ B: I don't think so, no.

　　C: You'd rather see Arthur.

　　B: Yeah.

An utterance which disconfirms the speaker's assumption challenges
the presuppositions of an elicit:confirm and is therefore not a
response, but rather a challenge. The following are some examples:

(14) [BCET:A:26]

　　B: //p it's not TOO late to apPLY now //r+ IS it//

　　　　　YEAH

→ C: //p　　　　 //p I THINK so //r+ they're ALL full up //

(15) [C:1:A:1:1]

　　H: Oh that's – oh what's that, oh what're you doing? Ah
　　　　you're putting – you want to give me a receipt?

　　　　　NO

→ S: //p　　　　 //

(16) [C:4:B:1:83]

　　*S has been talking about finding a school for her daughter in
　　Canada.*

　　G: You can't send her to the States.

→ S: Oh I CAN, but we have to pay a hundred per cent of
　　　　everything and we can't afford that.

In both (14) and (15), the disconfirmations are spoken in contrastive high key, indicating that they are contrary to the speaker's expectation (see Brazil *et al.* 1980). In (16), the disconfirmation is realized by making 'can' prominent, which marks its contrast to 'can't'. Disconfirmations are 'dispreferred', and this is why they are often presented in an indirect way. For example:

(17) [B:F:B:3:6]
   H and J are discussing the notion of ethnic ideological themes.

   H: Well I– I– this is Frank, oh this is Frank's notion.
   J: Yeah.
   H: //p OH //p THEN it's in your BOOK //r+ RIGHT //
→ J: Well, not that part of it, not that part of it.

J, instead of saying 'no' directly, 'softened' his response by saying 'not that part of it'.

An utterance in which the addressee indicates that he/she is unable to confirm the speaker's assumption is also a challenge. For example:

(18) [C:1:A:1]
   H: //p it's a HORrible town //r+ ISn't it//
          I don't KNOW
→ S: //p   // I – my parents live a couple hours
      away from Chicago, so – I don't know very much about it.

S's utterance 'I don't know' is also spoken in contrastive high key. Notice that a reason for her inability to confirm the speaker's assumption is also provided to reduce the face-threatening effect (see Tsui 1991a).

8.5.3 Elicit:agree

The illocutionary intent of an *elicit:agree* is to get the addressee to agree with the speaker's assumption that the expressed proposition is self-evidently true. It presupposes that:

a. the speaker believes that the expressed proposition is self-evidently true;
b. the addressee will agree with the speaker.

The following are all examples in which an elicit:agree is responded to by a fully-fitting positive responding act:

(19) [BCET:A:34]
    C: //r I supPOSE he's a bit SENile now //p ISn't he //
→ **B:** //p he LOOKS it //

(20) [BCET:47]
    C: //p well HARold was a GOOD one //p WASn't he //
→ **D:** Yeah, there was Harold and Callaghan.

(21) [BCET:44]
    B: //p I BET you're anti TRIdent missiles as WELL =
                                            [
→ **C:**   I'm CND, =
    B: = //p AREn't you //
      [
    C: = I mean, not officially.

A disagreement challenges presupposition (b), and is therefore a *challenge* rather than a *response*. For example:

(22) [BCET:A:6]
    A: //p we went QUITE late // p in the afterNOON //
        p on SUNday //p DIDn't we //
→ **C:** We went, um, what do you mean? we went we came
      back on the Monday, didn't we.

C's disagreement with A is delayed and is prefaced by fillers and false starts. Similarly, the disagreement in (23) below is prefaced by a token agreement, 'No', which serves to reduce the face-threatening effect of the subsequent disagreement (see Pomerantz 1978; Sacks 1987; Tsui 1991a):

(23) [BCET:A:2]
    C: //p IT's not THAT long really //p IS it //
→ **B:** No, but – the thing is I mean sometimes it won't turn up
      and you're late.
      [
    C: Yeah.

8.5.4 Elicit:commit

The illocutionary intent of an *elicit:commit* is to get the addressee to produce a verbal response which will commit him to the production of a further exchange(s) or a future action. It presupposes that:

a. the speaker sincerely wants the addressee to commit himself;
b. the addressee may be able and willing to commit himself.

Hence, a positive responding act is one in which the addressee commits himself. For example:

(24) [C:1:A:4:1]
      L: Can I talk to you?
→   S: Sure. =
        = Come in. Let's close the door. Have a seat.

(25) [B:C:A:5]
      R: Where shall I meet you?
→ H: Well ah I'll be finished with my class at five, it's =
                                           [
      R: uhuh
      H: = right in Tsimshatsui, so maybe we'll meet you at the
          Peninsula, between say five fifteen and five thirty?
      R: Okay, wonderful.

(26) [B:B:A:3:3]
      A: What time?
→ B: Let's say about seven.
      A: Seven o'clock huh, okay.

In (24), S commits herself to having a conversation with L, as can be seen from S's inviting L to sit down. In (25), H commits himself to meeting R at the Peninsula, and in (26) B commits himself to meeting A at seven o'clock. Since an elicit:commit does not assume that the speaker will commit him/herself, neither a refusal to commit nor a postponement of the decision to commit him/herself challenges its presuppositions. In (27) below, we have an elicit:commit responded to by a temporization:

(27) [C:2:A:7]
      S: it's just when you'll be around for us to look for you.
→ G: Oh that's um ((*pause*)) I don't know what John's

schedule is. I know we're out tonight and ah ((*pause*))
and ((*pause*)) I don't know about the rest of this week.
S: Or maybe tomorrow night?

An elicit:commit can also be responded to by a negative responding act as in (28) below:

(28) [Fieldnotes]
    A: Can I talk to you for a minute?
→ B: Well, um I'm pretty tied up at the moment. Can it wait?

In other words, similar to a requestive (see section 8.6), an elicit:commit can be responded to by all three subclasses of responses.

8.5.5 Elicit:repeat and elicit:clarify

Finally, the last two subclasses of elicitation which are meta-discursive are *elicit:repeat* and *elicit:clarify*. Positive responses to them would be, respectively, a *repetition* and a *clarification*. The following are examples of a repetition (29) and a clarification (30).

(29) [B:E:A:3:4]
    H: Oh and bring the Moser book, I'd like to see that.
    X: Oh I ah with the what?
→ H: With the book by Moser.

(30) [BCET:A:26]
    C: Do you get satisfaction though?
    B: Yes, I reckon you get more satisfaction as you go up the scale as well.
    C: ((*laughs*)) What – you mean the money scale.
→ B: No, the job, the job.

To summarize, we may say that for elicitations, the responding acts consist mainly of positive responses which fulfil their illocutionary intents. The exception is elicit:commit, which, in the sense that it commits the addressee to a future verbal or a non-verbal action, resembles requestives. Therefore, similar to requestives, all three sub-classes of responding acts are realized.

8.6 Responses and challenges to requestives

In section 8.4, we examined the illocutionary intents and pragmatic presuppositions of some requestives. In general, we can say that the illocutionary intent of a requestive is to get the addressee to comply and it presupposes that:

a. the speaker sincerely wants the action to be carried out and believes that the action needs to be carried out;
b. the addressee may be able and willing to carry out the action or to have the action carried out;
c. it is not obvious that the addressee will carry out the action of his/her own accord.

As pointed out before, because a requestive does not presuppose that the addressee is going to carry out the action or to have it carried out, a requestive can be responded to by a positive responding act and a negative responding act. The following are examples of positive responses to the five subclasses of requestives:

(31) (request for action)
   [B:C:A:2]
   J: um I wonder if you might give my apologies, I'm – not going to make it tomorrow
   [
   H: Okay. =
→   = Okay, Jack. Sure.

(32) (invitation)
   [Fieldnotes]
   A: Would you like to come and see the house? Why not come for lunch at say about twelve uh?
→ **B:** Mm, I'd love to.

(33) (proposal)
   [B:B:B:6:2]
   X: So why don't we arrange to get together maybe Sunday?
→ **H:** Okay, that'll be splendid, that'll be great.

(34) (offer)
    [B:G:B:4:3]
    X told H that she will be going to Canton.
    D: I'll see if I can find an old map of Canton that we had of
        the city, y'know, just as reference.
→ R: Oh Henry, that's very kind of you.
    D: I'll sen – I saw it in the book shop, but I have to, I'll
        search again, I'll put it in the mail box.
→ R: Ah, thank you very much.

(35) (request for permission)
    [C:2:A:4:1]
    T: Could I get some handouts?
→ S: Yeah, help yourself.

In all of the above exchanges, the addressees produce responses which fulfil the illocutionary intents of the requestives. The responses share a common characteristic: a commitment of some sort to a future action is involved after the addressee has produced the response. In (31), (32), and (33), the outcome of the exchange is such that the addressees have committed themselves to carrying out a future action. Although in (32) and (33) the future action involves the speaker as well, the illocutionary intent of addressee's compliance is basically to commit himself. In (34), once the offer is accepted, the speaker has committed himself to carrying out the proffered action. In (35), the addressee has committed herself to allowing the speaker to carry out the action. In other words, all positive responding acts to requestives involve compliance to the requested action.

Consider now the negative responses to requestives. The following are some examples:

(36) (request for action)
    [B:F:B:2:1]
    H: I'm going to pick it up tomorrow afternoon.
    J: Oh good.
    H: At ah at three o'clock, I don't know if you'd be free to
        come over because he said he'd like to give me about
        forty five minutes of training.
    J: Oh fine.

H: So, would you be would you be able to go?

→ J: Well, let's see, haha what time, three is impossible.

H: What?

J: Three o'clock is impossible, I have a meeting with the guy who's giving us money for the computer.

(37) (invitation)
[BCET:A:11]

C: Come down the local then.

→ B: Ah it's a bit rough for me down there.

(38) (proposal)
[B:D:B:2:2]

S: Or alternatively we could get together at five-fifteen when I'm finished.

→ J: No, I have to babysit. Actually, can I – 'cos Andrea's going to a Yoga class later.

(39) (offer)
[BCET:D:6]

C: Have you got – mu – I've got some paper if you want.

→ D: No, I've got tons of paper – stole it.

(40) (request for permission)
[Fieldnotes]

A: Can I use the telephone?

→ B: It's not working, sorry.

All of the above responses share a common characteristic: they do not fulfil the illocutionary intent of the requestives, and the outcome of the interaction is such that the addressee or the speaker, or both, are under no obligation to carry out a certain action.

Non-compliances to requestives are 'dispreferred', and they typically contain features like prefacing them with fillers such as 'well', 'let's see', and giving reasons for not complying.

A non-compliance to a requestive is to be distinguished from a challenge. While the former does not challenge the presuppositions of a requestive, the latter does. The following are examples of challenges to requestives:

(41) [B:C:A:1:1]

B: If you would like to give me the name and address.

175

→ **H:** Oh that's it, I just gave you my address.
    B: Oh that–

(42) [B:A:A:3:27]
    P: I got a book sitting in front of me called *The Human Factor* by Graham Greene and I'd like to

                              [

→ **H:**   Oh I read that, I like it.
    P: Oh you've read it.
    H: About this South African spy the girl he's married to Maluto, right? The the um

                [

    P: Yeah, yeah, right, right.
    H: I liked that one.
    P: Oh you've read it, okay, well, I can't give it to you now.

(43) [C:4:B:1:72]
    S and G are talking about their horoscopes and how one grows into one's horoscope.

    S: So now you've become that, can I read it and then I'll tell you if you're really like that

        [

    G: But one thing it wasn't –
→ **G:** I don't have it.

H's utterances in both (41) and (42) challenge the presupposition that there is a need for the action. The former is a challenge to a request for action, whereas the latter is a challenge to an upcoming offer. In (41), we can see that H's challenging move is responded to by an 'oh'-receipt token (Heritage 1984), which indicates that B now realizes that there is no need for the requestive. In (42), H's challenge is also responded to by an 'oh'-receipt token and the upcoming offer is aborted, as can be seen from the last line 'Oh you've read it, okay, well, I can't give it to you now'. Finally, in (43), S's request for permission to read G's horoscope presupposes that G has his own horoscope and this presupposition is challenged by G.

Requestives can also be responded to by temporizations in which the addressee neither complies nor refuses to comply. For example:

(44) (request for permission)
    [BCET:A:A:22]
    C: Could I stay at your place for a bit Rob?
→ B: um I don't know.

(45) (offer)
    [Fieldnotes]
    A: I can help you do the cooking if you want.
→ J: That's very sweet of you, I might take you up on that.

(46) (request for action)
    [Fieldnotes]
    A: Could you possibly give me some feedback on this draft
       by Thursday?
→ M: I'll try my best but I can't promise.

A temporization to a requestive is often a face-saving device. It avoids refusing a requestive outright. For example, the continuation of the conversation in (44) shows that B is, in fact, not very happy about C's staying at his place. Instead of refusing C's requestive, he resorts to a temporization.[11]

To summarize, in response to requestives, all three subclasses of responding acts are prospected responses, although a positive responding act is more strongly prospected than the other two.

8.7 Responses and challenges to directives

8.7.1 Mandatives

The illocutionary intent of a *mandative* is to get the addressee to perform a future action. It presupposes that:

a. the speaker wants the action carried out and that there is a need for the action to be carried out;
b. the speaker has the authority or the right to get the addressee to carry out the action;
c. the addressee is able and willing to carry out the action (see Searle 1969: 66);
d. it is not obvious that the addressee will carry out the action of his own accord.

Hence, a positive responding act is one in which the addressee complies with the mandative. For example:

(47) (instruction)
  [BCET:D:53]
  D: Leave me matches alone! I'm telling you a joke.
→ **C:** Right, what's that.

The above response commits the addressee to carrying out (or not carrying out) the action. Because a mandative gets the addressee to carry out the action by virtue of his/her authority or right, it does not give the addressee the option of not complying or temporizing. A refusal to comply is a challenge which can challenge any of the presuppositions given above. For example, D's utterance in (48) below challenges presupposition (d):

(48) [BCET:D:6]
  D is flipping through C's book.
  C: Don't for God's sake bend the spine.
→ **D:** I WON'T bend the spine.

Again, there is a cline along the dimension of face-threatening effect among challenges to mandatives. Challenging the presupposition that one is able to perform the action is least face-threatening, whereas challenging the authority or right of the speaker is most face-threatening—for example, 'Stop ordering me about', or 'Who do you think you are?'.

8.7.2 Advisives

The illocutionary intent of an *advisive* is also to get the addressee to carry out a future action. It presupposes that:

a. the speaker believes that there is a need for the advocated action;
b. the speaker believes that the advocated action is in the interest of the addressee;
c. the addressee is able and willing to carry out the action;
d. it is not obvious that the addressee will carry out the action of his/her own accord.

A positive response to an advisive is one in which the addressee agrees to carry out the advocated action. However, because an advisive does not presuppose that the speaker has the right or authority to get the addressee to carry out the action, and because the advocated action is in the interest of the addressee, whether the latter will *actually* carry it out is entirely up to him/her: there is no obligation on his/her part. The following are examples of compliances to advisives:

(49) (advice)
   [C:1:A:4:5]
   S: I think there are some things you can do, like, I I often
      write yes in the margin if I agree or I even put just an =
                                        [
   X: Okay.
   S: = exclamation point
   X: Or a question mark or
   S: Interesting or y'know, so that on every page there's =
                                                    [
   X: there's
   S: = evidence that I read it ((*laughs*))
                    [
→ X: that you've read it, yeah. Okay, alright,
      alright, I'll ah that'll help 'cos it just seems ah y'know
   S: TOO much work.

(50) (warning)
   [B:G:A:1:3]
   X: Well, you'll have to practise with him once or I mean
      really you can't just throw him in there and monkey =
                                        [
   H: No, no, I
   X: = around or he'll screw the subject and ruin the data.
                                  [
→ H: No I won't.

For (50), it should be noted that if the intonation and the context of situation make it clear that H's utterance means that he won't just let the assistant do the experiment without preparation even without X's warning, then it is challenging presupposition (d), hence realizing a challenge. An utterance in which the addressee refuses to

179

accept the advisive also realizes a challenge. Consider the following pieces of data:

(51) [B:C:B:3:3]

    H: Hey Don, if you have time tomorrow ah at the gymnasium, the English department is playing the ah the students or something, you might take a look at it, the gymnasium, right near your place.

→ X: You're joking, d'you know what I've got to do?

    H: Oh you've got to do –

    X: ((*laughs*)) It's a minor panic at the moment.

    H: Oh your dissertation.

    X: Right.

(52) [BCET:C:21]

    C has not been able to get a job since graduation.

    B: Teacher training's a good thing to be on.

→ C: Well, I don't want to be a teacher, or anything.

(53) [BCET:A:28]

    B: They have hostels in London.

→ C: I'm not staying in a bloody hostel.

In (51), X's utterance challenges presupposition (b). In (52), C's utterance challenges presupposition (c) and possibly presupposition (b) as well. In (53), B suggests to C that he can find cheap accommodation in London, like hostels. C's utterance challenges presupposition (c).

An utterance in which the addressee indicates that the advocated action has already been carried out challenges presupposition (d). For example:

(54) [B:B:B:2:1]

    X: Henry, ah I was running over a title for our book, I was wondering whether using English

    H: Alright, y'know, I look at these

                    [

    X: How does that grab you.

    H: It's ah it's we we can, y'know, that's alright. Y'know what I was thinking about doing is um take all these things like learning English, using English and then go to a thesaurus and see other words, it might, y'know, sometimes it rings a bell.

→ X: Well, that's what I did with a Roget's thesaurus.

(55) [B:A:A:3:24]

B: I think it would be nice if you have some data for Henry by the time he came

[

→ H: oh no, that's what we're doing, they're working on it already.

To summarize, a positive response to a directive is realized by a compliance. In the case of a mandative, the verbal compliance puts the addressee under the obligation to carry out the action, whereas in the case of an advisive, no such obligation is involved.

8.8 Responses and challenges to informatives

8.8.1 Reports

A *report* gives a factual account of events or states of affairs. Its illocutionary intent is to get the addressee to accept what the speaker has reported as a true representation of events or states of affairs. It presupposes that:

a. the speaker believes that the expressed proposition is true and that the expressed proposition is indeed true;
b. it is not obvious that the addressee knows about the event(s) or state(s) of affairs.

Hence, a positive responding act is realized by an acknowledgement of the report. As pointed out in the previous chapter, the acknowledgement can be in the form of a remark on the reported event or a message-received signal. The following are examples of positive responses to reports:

(56) [C:4:1]

S: John Fraser is a personal friend of ours, Michael went to school with him.

→ G: Oh really.

(57) [B:D:A:1:12]

    H: but did you hear what China said, they would be very happy the way Hong Kong handled everything, y'know, like, they'll they'll rush in if there's any law and order problem.

→ **J:** Oh will they, I didn't know that.

(58) [C:1:A:3:9]

    B: My spoken English students are going to take me to dinner and we can go–

→ **S:** That's nice.

    B: Yes.

(59) [B:A:A:3:7]

    K: But e– e– even ah Peter McCarthy told me who used to be pretty close to the VC says the VC's so busy he can't be bothered with the petty shit.

→ **X:** Oh I hope not.

In both (56) and (57), the report is responded to by an acknowledgement that the message is received, that there is a change of state of knowledge on the addressee's part. (Notice that both responses are prefaced with the change-of-state token 'oh'.) In (58) and (59), the addressees respond to the reports by doing something more than acknowledging receipt of the message; they make supportive remarks on the reported events.

An utterance in which the addressee queries or refuses to accept that the speaker has given a true account challenges presupposition (a). For example:

(60) [BCET:D:18]

    D: Well the women in this country go around kissing one another when they meet.

→ **C:** No they don't.

(61) [C:4:1:31]

    S has been telling G that she has been shot at for trespassing.

    S: Oh that's happened to me in Connecticut, it's happened to me in Indiana, it's happened to me in California.

→ **G:** You're kidding.
  S: Oh no.

It should be noted that in (61), 'You're kidding' can also be a positive response when the speaker intends it to be a supporting remark indicating his appreciation of the incredulous nature of the incident related. Again, intonation plays an important part in determining whether it is a challenge or a positive response.

An utterance in which the addressee indicates that the reported event(s) or state(s) of affairs are known to him/her already challenges presupposition (b). For example:

(62) [BCET:D:13]
  C: Those are computer books.
→ **D:** Yeah I know.

Because a report expresses what the speaker believes is a true account, it does not seem possible to respond to it by a temporization: the addressee either acknowledges it as true or challenges its presuppositions.

8.8.2 Assessments

An *assessment* asserts the speaker's judgement or evaluation of people, object(s), events, or state(s) of affairs. Its illocutionary intent is to get the addressee to agree with the speaker's judgement or evaluation. It presupposes that the speaker believes that his/her judgement or evaluation is an accurate representation of the evaluated referent. Theoretically, a positive responding act should be realized by an agreement with the speaker's evaluation or judgement. However, because four of the five subclasses of assessments involve evaluations directed at either the speaker or the addressee, the responses prospected are constrained by social considerations. As we saw in Chapter 7, different subclasses of assessments prospect different responses. In the following, we shall examine in further detail how responses are realized. Let us start with *assessing* first.

An *assessing* asserts the speaker's judgement or evaluation of a third party. It presupposes that the speaker believes that his/her judgement or evaluation is a true representation of the evaluated referent. Therefore, typically, a positive response to an assessing is realized by a second evaluation which agrees with the speaker's judgement. For example:

(63) [B:C:B:1:2]

> *H and X are talking about a British professor whom they have invited to Hong Kong.*

> H: I'm going to do something to make sure y'know well y'know when when Brown comes I thought originally that he's coming to see you, me and Jack, but I think Brown's too big just =

> [
> X: mhm

> H: = for us.

→ X: Yeah, I agree.

(64) [BCET:A:2]

> C: I suppose the cheaper fare's going to go up as well.

→ B: Yeah, I think they'll double.

(65) [BCET:D:16]

> D: Why do women stick up pictures of women all round the rooms and men stick up pictures of women? I think the men must get left out.

→ C: Yeah I know.

In (63), X makes a direct statement of agreement. In (64), B makes a second evaluation which is similar to C's evaluation. In (65), C's utterance realizes an agreement. (Cf. (60) above where 'Yeah, I know' in reply to a report realizes a challenge.)

An agreement is a prospected or 'preferred' response, whereas a disagreement challenges the presuppositions of an assessing. As pointed out before, the latter is often not given immediately, but delayed and prefaced with token agreement or acknowledgement, or contains hedges or fillers like 'well', 'uh', and so on, or is given in weak forms. For example:

(66) [B:A:A:3:28]

> 1 K: Did you read the one about the one about the
> 2   Geneva doctor so and so in Geneva?

>   [
> 3 X: No, I haven't.

    4 **K:** That's a good one, it's in the library.

→   5 **X:** Oh is it? I I I I kinda shy away from that. I read =

                                                        [

    6 **K:**   No

    7 **X:** = it, I I think it's too bizarre.

    8 **K:** No it was very good. He he he never disappoints ah

    9   Graham Greene.

→ 10 **X:** Yeah, that's true I must say. ((*laughs*))

X's contrary evaluation in line 5 is prefaced with a token acknowledgement, 'Oh is it?', and contains a faltering 'I I I I' and a hedge
'kinda'. As Sacks (1987) points out, the disagreement is 'pushed deep
into the turn' (see also Tsui 1991a). This contrasts with his agreement in line 10, which is not prefaced and does not contain any
hedges. The following are more examples:

(67) [B:E:B:1:4]

    H: Hey, it was very I I well I don't know I have my the
           faculty talk drives me bananas. It's to me it's the theatre
           of the absurd.

→ **M:** Some of them are, yeah, some of them I find interesting.

(68) [B:B:E:1:5]

    J: y'know I ah pulled out Giles's books yesterday,
          there're =

                                              [

    H: Oh.

    J: = two of them, ah one's called eh *Ethnicity of Language*,
           I wrote down the titles, I forgot where I put them.
           They're both edited editions, one of them has Fishman in
           there and the other one and I decided to look at it,
           y'know, it's it's interesting stuff, good stuff.

→ **H:** Yeah, sometimes a little heavy though, y'know um

                                            [

    J: Yeah, a
       little.

(69) [BCET:D:18]

    C: I thought those pictures were quite interesting.

→ **D:** I don't know, all art is useless.

In (67), M does not agree entirely with H. But we can see that the disagreement is prefaced with an agreement, 'some of them are, yeah'. In (68), H's second evaluation is prefaced with a token agreement 'yeah'. Notice that his evaluation is then immediately responded to by an agreement from J. In (69), D prefaces his disagreement with 'I don't know'. (For a detailed discussion of the function of 'I don't know', see Tsui 1991a.)

That agreement is a prospected response or a 'preferred' response can also be seen from the way the utterances are sequenced in the following piece of data:

(70) [B:A:A:3:4]

```
        1  K:  and I I got this impression with your Professor Lee,
        2      he's very easy-going, he's doing his own work with
        3      his computer, I mean, he's I don't think he's into all
        4      the ah pet- petty shit, y'know – which I think is =
                    [        [
        5  X:              No   No, no.
        6  K:  = wonderful, I think he's a y'know serious scholar,
        7      he's got his own little thing.
  →     8  X:  Yeah, he's he IS very scholarly.
        9  K:  Yeah, that, y'know I I wish people were like that
               here.
  →    10  X:  He's hard to flap actually, and ah works both ways,
       11      y'know, sometimes you would ah like him to flap a
       12      bit ((laughs)) over some things ((laughs)). On the
       13      other hand ah everything has its blessings.
```

In lines 1 to 6, K's assessing is a positive evaluation of several aspects of Professor Lee, which is responded to by an agreement first in line 8 in which X agrees with some of the aspects that K mentioned. The aspect which he disagrees with, Professor Lee's easy-going character, is delayed until line 10. Notice that the contrary second evaluation contains the features of a 'dispreferred' response, such as hedges like 'actually' and the qualification 'On the other hand, everything has its blessings'.

Because a contrary second evaluation is 'dispreferred', interlocutors often try to avoid or withhold it. This is why when an assessing is responded to by silence, the latter is often interpreted as an unstated contrary evaluation.

An assessing can also be responded to by a remark on the prior evaluation, which is usually given when the assessed person(s), object(s), or state(s) of affairs are not known to the addressee and, therefore, the latter is no position to agree. For example:

(71) [B:A:A:3:26–27]
    K: But I'm I'm very proud of the way they kept going through the literature, they work very hard.
→ **X:** Well, that's good.

(72) [B:C:B:1:9]
    E and F are talking about a linguistics book.

    E: But it's ah they're they're pretty good at explaining things.
→ **F:** Well, that's useful.

(73) [B:A:A:3:7]
    K: But I mean you have decisions, such high-level decisions like for couple hundred dollars.
→ **X:** Well, that's pathetic frankly.

Remarks in positive responses are usually supportive. A positive evaluation is responded to by a positive remark, as in (71) and (72), and a negative evaluation is responded to by a negative remark, as in (73).

A compliment asserts the speaker's positive evaluation of the addressee. To agree with a compliment implies a positive evaluation of oneself, and hence violates the norm of modesty. Therefore, typically, a response to a compliment is realized by downgrading the prior evaluation (see Chapter 7, examples (26) and (27)). Besides downgrading, there are also other ways of responding to a compliment. Pomerantz (1978) made a detailed study of the different ways of responding to a compliment, and observed that other than downgrading, the responses may be in the following forms:

(74) [Pomerantz 1978: 100]
    A: Good shot.
→ **B:** Not very solid though.

(75) [ibid.: 102]
    R: You're a good rower, Honey.
→ **J:** These are very easy to row. Very light.

(76) [ibid.: 105]
    E: Yer looking good.
→ **G:** Great. So'r you.

According to Pomerantz, (74) is a disagreement which proposes that the creditings within the prior assessment are exaggerated, and that lesser amounts of credit are justified; (75) is a reassignment of praise in which the recipient shifts the credit from himself to an other-than-self referent such as an object; (76) is a return compliment in which the recipient makes a similar compliment on the speaker. In addition to these three ways of responding, a positive response to a compliment can also be realized by thanking the speaker.

Similar to a compliment, an agreement with a self-denigration is socially unacceptable. An agreement implies a negative evaluation of the addressee and is very face-threatening. Hence, typically, a positive response makes an evaluation which is contrary to the speaker's negative evaluation of him/herself. An agreement with a self-denigration is a 'dispreferred' response, and seldom occurs except between interlocutors who know each other very well. For example:

(77) [Fieldnotes]
    Husband: I've put on a lot since you left.
→ **Wife:**   I know.

To say that one has put on weight is usually a negative evaluation, and is usually responded to by a disagreement like 'You haven't' or 'Not a bit'. The above response is permissible only because the interlocutors are husband and wife.

A positive response can also be in the form of mitigating the negative aspect of the self-denigration, as pointed out in Chapter 7, section 7.5. For example:

(78) [B:B:A:3]
    H: My God, ten years, I can't believe it. It doesn't seem that you were away that long. Maybe it just shows that I'm really getting old.

→ **X:** Eh listen, Henry, that's what's happening to all of us.
  H: Yeah.

(79) [Pomerantz 1984: 90]
  B: I have my desk full of trash.
→ **S:** Me too.

In (78), X's negative evaluation of himself as getting old is mitigated by H's saying that ageing is something that happens to 'all of us'. Similarly, in (79), B's denigration of himself as being untidy is mitigated by S's applying the same evaluation to herself.

That a disagreement is 'preferred' can be seen from the fact that while it is often given immediately, an agreement is often avoided or, if given at all, is delayed or given in a weak form. The following is an example from Pomerantz (1984):

(80) [Pomerantz 1984: 91–2][12]
  W: . . . Do you know what I was all that time?
  L: (no)
  W: Pavlov's dog.
→   (2.0)
  L: (I suppose.)
  W: D'you remember that story?
                 [
  L: Yes, I do.
  W: Yah. She, was brainwashing me Lila.
  L: Oh yes!
→   (0.7)
  L: 'N you were pickin' it up like mad.
    [
  W: And–

L's first response to W's self-denigration, which is an agreement, is delayed and is presented in a weak form. This weak agreement is later strengthened ('' 'N you were pickin' it up like mad'), and it is also delayed. This is why, in contrast to an assessing, when a self-denigration is responded to by silence or when no overt disagreement is given, the self-denigrating party is likely to interpret it as an agreement (see Pomerantz 1984: 93). Compare (80) with the following:

(81) [B:A:A:3:6]
    X has been telling K that his (K's) son is very cute.

  1 **X:** You ah you know, mix mix marriages produce some
  2   of the most beautiful kids, I think.
  3 **K:** Yeah.
→ 4 **X:** Well, I had to go and marry a white skin caucasian.
→ 5 **K:** No, somebody was saying Mary looks very pretty.
  6   Alice didn't recognize her. She's getting very tall, your
  7   kids are very tall.
→ 8 **X:** Yeah, she's going to be a pretty one.

K is American and his wife is Asian, whereas X and his wife are both American. By saying that he had to go and marry a white skin caucasian, X is implying that his kids are not pretty. X's negative evaluation of his kids, which is also a negative evaluation of himself, is immediately responded to by a disagreement.

A disagreement can be in the form of making a contrary evaluation, or it can be in the form of reclassifying the negative evaluation as a positive one. For example:

(82) [Pomerantz 1984: 87]
    R: .hh But I'm only getting a C on my report card in math.
→ **C:** Yeh but that's passing Ronald.

In (82), the addressee undermines the self-critical assessment of the speaker by favourably recategorizing or reformulating the grade 'C' that R has got in terms of *pass vs. fail* as opposed to *low grade vs. high grade*.

Because a disagreement is typically prospected by a self-denigration, a person who often self-denigrates may be accused of 'fishing for a compliment'. In (81), the fact that K's positive evaluation of X's daughter is agreed with by the latter in line 8 suggests that the latter could well be the response that X intends to solicit by his self-denigration.

In contrast to a compliment and a self-denigration, positive responses to a criticism and a self-commendation are realized by a second evaluation which agrees with or upgrades the prior evaluation (see Chapter 7, examples (28) to (31), (38), (40), and (41)). A criticism can also be responded to by an apology (see Chapter 7, examples (32) and (34); see also D'Amico-Reisner 1983: 105).

If a criticism prospects an agreement or an apology, how do we account for the following pieces of data?

(83) [B:D:B:1]

M has a bad cold and H couldn't recognize her voice.

H: You sound terrible, you sound like a man.
→ M: Thank you.

(84) [BCET:D:24]

D: um well was I telling you about you and Izzy – you know I had a funny thought about you two the other night, Laurel and Hardy.
→ C: Oh thanks a lot.

In both (83) and (84), the evaluations that the speakers make are clearly not complimentary. However, in both cases, the criticisms are responded to by thanking which is one form of positive response to compliments. Here, we have interesting examples of how language is manipulated to generate conversational implicature. By deliberately reclassifying a criticism as a compliment, the addressees in both cases are generating sarcasm (see Chapter 1, section 1.6.3).

A second evaluation which disagrees with or rejects a criticism or a self-commendation realizes a challenge which is usually avoided unless the interlocutors know each other very well, as in the following examples:

(85) [BCET:D:44]

D: You told them, oh you idiot. (criticism)
         NO
→ C: //p   // they were going to send me to court if I didn't explain.

(86) [Tannen 1984: 21]

John: You're making a big deal about nothing. (criticism)
→ Steve: YOU are

(87) [BCET:C:24]

B: I work hard. (self-commendation)
→ C: DO you ACTually work hard?

Challenges are often given in weak forms or contain features of 'dispreferred' responses. In (88) below, B's utterance, which rejects

C's criticism, contains the filler 'well', and is presented in a weak form of disagreement 'I don't know':

(88) [BCET:A:11]
    C: Come down the local then.
    B: Ah it's a bit rough for me down there.
    . . . . . .
    B: Well, 'cos ah we usually go into the – is it the Gun Barrels?
    C: Gun Barrels, yeah. Alright, go down there. Posh side presumably.
    B: Oh yeah.
→ C: You snob.
→ B: Well, I don't know.

In (89) following, D's criticism is not responded to at all. Instead, C changes the topic. Just as silence is a way of indicating disagreement with an assessing, a lack of response here indicates C's rejection of D's criticism. In other words, an overt rejection of a criticism is 'dispreferred', and this is why it is withheld:

(89) [BCET:D:15]
    D: You remind me of one of those French whores of the late nineteenth century that you see running around with Louis the fourteenth. It's sort of the hair, sort of =
                                             [
    C: .hhh
    D: = curls (like that) and goes straight into the air, you know, sort of
→ C: What was I saying? I was saying something.

8.8.3 Expressives

Expressives indicate the speaker's psychological state towards certain state(s) of affairs, person(s), or object(s). It presupposes that the psychological state expressed is true; that is, the speaker is sincere. Therefore, a positive responding act is one in which the addressee accepts that the expressed psychological state is true. Because expressives are often performed out of politeness, a positive responding act is often realized by a more enthusiastic response than a mere acceptance. For example, a positive responding act to an apology is often realized by accepting the apology as well as minimizing the debt the speaker has incurred, and the like. For example:

(90) [B:H:B:6:2]
    X: Well, hhh I'm sorry.
→ H: No, it's alright.

Generally speaking, we can say that a positive response to the three different types of expressives identified in the previous chapter can be realized as follows: those expressing empathy are responded to by thanking; those expressing the speaker's psychological state towards a debt incurred are responded to by acceptances and/or minimizations; and those expressing goodwill are either responded to by thanking or by returning the goodwill (see Chapter 7, section 7.6, for examples).

8.9 Concluding remarks

In this chapter, we have examined in detail the subclasses of responding acts and how they are realized in response to different initiations. In the light of our identification criteria for responses, let us look again at the exchange between Linus and Violet given as example (2) at the beginning of this chapter:

(91) [Labov 1972: 123]
    Linus: Do you want to play with me Violet?
    Violet: You're younger than me. (*shuts the door*)
    Linus: [*puzzled*] She hasn't answered my question.

Linus's elicitation is one which typically occurs prior to a requestive. Violet reclassifies the elicitation as a requestive and provides a reason for the implied non-compliance, which is, big girls don't play with little boys. Violet's utterance therefore constitutes a response, because although it does not fulfil the illocutionary intent of the requestive, it does not challenge its pragmatic presuppositions. It is a negative response which is 'dispreferred'. However, Linus insists (deliberately) on the discourse value of his initial utterance as an elicitation and fails (deliberately) to interpret Violet's utterance as a relevant piece of information. Violet's contribution is therefore (deliberately) treated as not an 'answer' to his 'question'.

9
Follow-up acts

9.1 Introduction

In Chapter 2, we examined the third element of an exchange, the
follow-up move, and argued that it is a very important element in
conversation. We also examined its functions and its relevance of
occurrence. We pointed out that it has the general function of
acknowledging the outcome of an exchange. In this chapter, we shall
try to identify subclasses of follow-up acts and examine how they
are realized.

9.2 The prospective nature of responses

While it is generally accepted that responses are prospected by
initiations, responses are seldom perceived as prospecting a further
utterance: they are often characterized as retrospective in focus (see
Coulthard and Brazil 1981; Stubbs 1981). It is true that the interpretation of a response is constrained by the preceding initiation.
However, this does not mean that responses are purely retrospective.
They are also prospective in the sense that different responding acts
prospect different follow-up acts. Take the following pieces of data,
for example:

(1) [B:C:A:5:1]
   I **X:** Where shall I meet you?
   R **H:** Well ah I'll be finished with my class at five, it's =
                                                      [
      X: uhuh
      H: = right in Tsimshatsui, so maybe we'll meet you at
          the Peninsula, between say five fifteen and five thirty?
→ F **X:** Okay, wonderful.

In (1), X's elicit:commit is followed by a positive response which commits H to meeting up with X at the Peninsula Hotel at a certain time. This response is further followed by X's enthusiastic acceptance of the positive outcome of the interaction. Compare this follow-up move with that in the following:

(2) [B:F:B:2:1]
   H told J that he is going to pick up a computer at three
   o'clock on the following day and asked J if he would be free
   at that time.
   I H: So would you be would you be able to go?
   R J: Well let's see haha what time, three is impossible.
   C H: What?
   R J: Three o'clock is impossible. I have a meeting with the
       guy who's giving us the money for the computer.
→ F H: Oh yeah, well anyways I'll go get it anyway.

Here, H's requestive that J go with him to get the computer is responded to by a negative response of not complying. As we can see, following J's reiteration of non-compliance, H produces a further utterance which accepts J's non-compliance. Although the follow-up moves in both (1) and (2) accept the outcome, there is an important difference between them. While that in (1) accepts a positive outcome, that in (2) accepts a negative outcome. This difference is reflected in the linguistic realizations of these two moves: the former is given immediately, the latter is prefaced with 'well' and 'anyways', indicating that the response is 'dispreferred'.

That these two follow-up moves are realized by different follow-up acts is supported by the fact that they cannot occur interchangeably. Consider the oddity in the following:

(3) [B:F:B:2:1]
   H told J that he is going to pick up a computer at three
   o'clock on the following day and asked J if he would be free
   at that time.
   I H: So would you be would you be able to go?
   R J: Well let's see haha what time, three is impossible.
   C H: What?

195

R J: Three o'clock is impossible. I have a meeting with the
       guy who's giving us the money for the computer.
? F H: Okay, wonderful.

The oddity can be easily explained: a negative outcome is not usually
responded to by an enthusiastic acceptance. The difference between
them can be seen from the fact that the follow-up move in (1) can
also be realized by 'Good', 'Great', 'Smashing', whereas that in (2)
can also be realized by expressions such as 'That's too bad', 'What
a shame', and so on, which register H's disappointment at J's not
being able to go, or by expressions like 'That's okay', 'Never mind',
and so on, which minimize the face-threatening effect of J's non-
compliance. We may say that the follow-up move in (1) is a kind of
endorsement of the positive outcome of the interaction, whereas that
in (2) is a kind of concession to accept the negative outcome.

In other words, a positive response prospects an endorsement of
the positive outcome, whereas a negative response prospects a concession to accept the negative outcome. This is further supported by
the following piece of data:

(4) [B:E:A:4:1]
     P called T who is a visiting professor at the university. P
     reminded T who he was and where they met.

     I P: And I'm just wondering, are y– ah you're going to be
           here till what date till th– will you be will you be here
           on on next Monday or you'll be gone?
     R T: Yes, we leave on Monday.
→ F P: Oh that's too bad.
     I T: What what what's it all about?
     R P: Well y'know we what I'd like you to do is I'd like you
           to talk to my Applied Linguistics students, about the
           about problems or the benefits of teaching literature
           English literature to non-native speakers of English.
           ((*pause*)) um ((*pause*)) your just y– y'know your
           experience there and then your background would be
           very good for the students to hear this. Now the the
           we only meet on Monday at 2:45.

Here, P's elicit:inform is responded to positively by T supplying a
piece of requested information. However, it is followed by a follow-

196

up move which typically follows a negative responding act. As can be seen from the rest of the discourse, T's elicitation is a 'pre-request' to check the time that T is leaving the territory. The information supplied, however, means that P has to abort the upcoming request to get T to speak to his students on Monday (see the last line). Therefore, he produces a follow-up move which typically follows a negative responding act.

The prospective nature of responses can be seen not only from the different follow-up acts that they prospect, but also from the way the subsequent development of the conversation is affected by the choice of different responses. In examples (5) to (9), we shall examine what is likely to occur when a follow-up move is not produced.

Let us look at the exchange subsequent to a positive responding act:

(5) [B:C:A:5:1–2]
```
      1 I   X: Eh, how about tomorrow night?
      2 R   H: Yeah, I'll oh I'm happy, yeah, okay.
  →   3 I   X: Where shall I meet you?
      4 R   H: Well, ah I'll be finished with my class at five. It's =
                                                    [
      5 bc  X:                                        uhuh
      6     H: = right in Tsimshatsui, so maybe we'll meet you
      7        at the Peninsula, between say five fifteen to five
      8        thirty.
      9 F   X: Okay, wonderful.
```

In the above exchange, X's proposal that he and H meet up the following evening (line 1) is followed by a positive response from H. This, in turn, is followed by an elicitation from X asking for the place of meeting, generating an exchange in which the place and time of meeting are agreed upon. This exchange (lines 3–9) advances the topic of talk. The following is a similar example:

(6) [B:C:A:1]
```
      I   H: I was wondering if you could send me the um
             application forms.
      R   B: Yes. um
     {I}  H: Would
  →   I   B: If you would like to give me the name and address.
```

Similar to (5), B's positive response to H's requestive to send him the application forms is followed by an initiating move in which B asks H to give her the name and address. Again, this move advances the topic of talk. Now compare (5) and (6) with the following piece of data:

(7) [BCET:A:56]
    I C: Are you sure you don't want a cigarette?
    R B: No, I couldn't take your last but one.
    I C: Well, the last one actually, that would be my last one.
    R B: No thanks.
→ I C: Go on have it Rob.
    R B: No no I'm not having it, I'd feel too bad.
    F C: Okay.

Here, B's negative response to C's offer is followed by C's making the offer again (see arrowed utterance). C's re-offer holds up the progress of the topic in the sense that C is trying to get B to accept an offer which has already been turned down twice in the preceding exchanges. This often happens when an invitation or an offer is declined or refused (see also Davidson 1984). In fact, in some cultures, for example the Chinese culture, a re-offer after a negative response is almost prospected: it is part of the politeness routine. It is only when an offer is refused again and again that the offerer will concede to accept the negative outcome. One who concedes immediately when his/her offer is refused is likely to be accused of being insincere in making the offer (see also Goffman 1971: 159).[1]

The development of the discourse subsequent to a temporization is similar to that subsequent to a negative responding act in its recursive nature. Take the following piece of data, for example:

(8) [BCET:A:27]
    I C: Could I stay at your place for a bit Rob?
    R B: um I don't know.
→ I C: I mean you personally wouldn't have any objections, I =
                                         [
    R B: I personally wouldn't =
        C: = know that Rob.
           [
        B: = but it depends on how long, you know, it doesn't bother me, shouldn't think it would bother Chalks.

198

→ I C: I could keep myself to myself, I wouldn't intrude.
   R B: No, but – no, except that you'd be in my room.
   I C: Well not necessarily . . .

Following B's temporization, C produces an initiation in which he tries to coax B into complying with his requestive. When B refuses to commit himself totally by hedging his response with 'but it depends on how long', B again produces an initiation in which he promises not to intrude on B's privacy. It is clear that what C is trying to do here is to get B to respond positively. The following is another example:

(9) [C:2:A:4:7]
   I G: In other words, why don't – when you think you –
           want to do it, why don't you just give us a call. I
           mean not tonight.
               [
   R S: Any time, we're we're ready any time. =
   I   = It's just when YOU'll be around for us to look look
        for you.
   R G: Oh that's um ((*pause*)) I don't know what John's
        schedule is. I know we're out tonight and ((*pause*)) ah
        and ((*pause*)) I don't know about the rest of this
        week.
→ I S: Or maybe tomorrow night?

In (9), G and S have been trying to arrange a time when S can go to G's house to borrow some tools. Following G's temporization, S produces an initiating move in which she tries to get G to commit herself to a definite time. Examples (5) to (9) above are all cases where, following a responding move, the next speaker chooses to produce an initiating move. However, we can see that the way the conversation unfolds is very much affected by the kind of responding act produced.

9.3 Subclasses of follow-up acts

9.3.1 Endorsement

In section 9.2, we saw examples of two types of follow-up acts. One of them enthusiastically endorses the positive outcome of the interaction. Let us identify this type of act as an *endorsement*. It is typically realized by a set of items like 'good', 'great', 'splendid', 'wonderful' (cf. Stubbs 1983: 190).[2] The following is a further example:

(10) [B:B:B:6:3]
    I H: How how how long will you be here till
    R X: un– until the next weekend.
→ F H: Oh great, great.

In informing exchanges which are initiated by assessments and responded to positively by agreements, endorsing follow-ups are typically realized by further agreements with the preceding agreements or upgrading the agreements (see also Pomerantz 1984: 68). The following are examples of agreeing with the preceding agreement:

(11) [C:4:7]
    I S: The problem is they get mosquitoes in here and they
            eat me alive.
    R G: Yeah, the mosquitoes are terrible.
→ F S: //p <u>ARE</u>n't they //

(12) [BCET:A:16]
    I B: Got to have a telephone.
    R C: Yes, I I feel that.
→ F B: //p   //
            you <u>NEED</u> it

(13) [BCET:A:15]
    I C: I've got a pipe upstairs. It's cleaning the bloody thing
            though.
    R B: Yeah, it's horrible.
→ F C: //p   //
            all that <u>GUNGE</u>

In (11), the negative polar interrogative spoken with proclaiming tone does not prospect a further contribution from G. It serves to reinforce G's agreement. In both (12) and (13), the follow-up utterances reformulate the preceding utterances and are spoken in low key. As Coulthard and Brazil point out, when a speaker reformulates the response in low key, he is indicating that he is not adding any new information but saying something which is situationally equivalent in meaning to the response (see Coulthard and Brazil 1981: 93).

In (14) and (15) below, we have endorsements realized by upgrading the agreement in the response:

(14) [B:A:A:3:9]
    I X: He's a cute looking little guy.
    R K: Yeah, yeah, he is he's a doll, he's he's

                            [
→ F X: Oh my god, that's
        for sure.

(15) [B:G:B:2:10]
    I H: Smart, smart, the the little one and the big one are so
        smart.
    R X: That's right.
→ F H: Very smart.

In requesting exchanges, an endorsement may be realized by an appreciation or expression of indebtedness. For example:

(16) [BCET:A:51]
    I C: Can I just use your lighter, I've run out of matches.
    R B: Oh aye ahhh (+NV)
→ F C: Ta

Similarly, in an eliciting exchange initiated by an elicit:inform, if the speaker considers the information provided by the addressee as a service rendered, an endorsement can also be realized by an appreciation for the service rendered. For example:

(17) [B:C:A:4]
    I T: Is it okay to call him at home?
    R W: Oh yeah sure.
→ F T: Okay, thank you.

Or, alternatively, an endorsement can be realized by the first speaker making a comment on the information provided. For example:

(18) [B:B:A:3:1]
    D has just returned to Hong Kong. He has been away for ten years.

    I **H:** So how do you feel to be back in the rain?
    R **D:** All kinds of strange things ((*laughs*))
                                     [
→ F **H:**   ((*laughs*)) I can just see the
         changes. =
    I   = So you're staying in Stanley.

That H's comment on D's response is a follow-up move rather than initiating another exchange can be seen from the fact that after the comment, H changes the topic of talk and elicits a confirmation from D that he is staying in Stanley. The following are some further examples:

(19) [B:D:A:1:16]
    I **H:** Have you been to Tiger Balm Garden?
    R **J:** Oh no, I've never been.
→ F **H:** Oh my God, that's unbelievable.

(20) [B:C:B:4:2]
    R promised Y to take part in a rehearsal. But later Y told R that it is an audition, not a rehearsal.

    I **R:** Oh this is an audition ((*laughs*)) not for doing it.
    R **Y:** No, I think it's a – this is what I'm pissed about too.
→ F **R:** Oh Jesus Christ.

Finally, in an eliciting exchange which is initiated by an elicitation to which the speaker already knows the answer (i.e. what can be referred to as a 'knowledge-checking' exchange), an endorsement is typically realized by an evaluation of the correctness of the response. An evaluation typically occurs in classroom exchanges, quiz exchanges, and mother–child exchanges. But it can also occur in exchanges in social discourse. For example:

(21) [Fieldnotes]
    I **A:** Guess how much I paid for this?

R B: A hundred and fifty?

→ F A: Very close, a hundred and twenty.

It is interesting to note that sometimes in this kind of exchange, an evaluative endorsement may be omitted when the addressee knows for sure that his response is right. For example:

(22) [BCET:D:44]
    C told D that she returned a long overdue book to the library.

    I C: And guess how much I had to pay?
    R D: Nothing. Cathy, you gave it away, you were too enthusiastic about it.
    F C: ∅

9.3.2 Concession

In (2) above, we have an example of a follow-up act which accepts a negative outcome. Let us identify it as a *concession*. Because a negative response does not fulfil the illocutionary intent of the preceding initiation, it is face-threatening. Hence, a concession is typically realized by minimizing the face-threatening effect, and (2) given above is an example. By saying 'I'll go get it anyway', H is trying to minimize the face-threatening effect of J's refusal of H's request to go and get the computer. The following are some further examples:

(23) [B:G:A:3:2]
    M has told J that he would not be able to teach a course for him.

    I   J: Even even on a once-a-week basis.
    R   M: Even once a week, 'cos I'm just so exhausted, I have late classes and then and then and then I have =
                                                                    [
    bc J: Yes
        M: = research I have to do which makes it, which complicates things. ((*laughs*))
    → F   J: Yeah, I understand.

203

(24) [B:A:A:4:3]
    I **P:** So so do you want me to pick you up, are you are
          you in your office now?
    R **X:** No, I'm I'm going to the h–, I'm at the Great Hall, I
          have to go to the head's office.
→ F **P:** Alright, maybe afterwards.

The follow-up in (23), 'Yeah I understand', not only indicates that
the speaker is willing to accept M's refusal, but also minimizes the
debt which has been incurred by M, hence saving M's face. In (24),
by saying 'maybe afterwards', P is trying to minimize the face-
threatening effect of his offer being turned down, hence saving his
own face.

A concession which occurs at the end of a sequence in which the
speaker has been attempting to achieve a positive outcome is often
realized by the speaker reluctantly accepting the negative outcome.
For example:

(25) [B:F:B:1:2]
    *X has invited H to lunch and he asks H to bring his wife
    along.*
    I **X:** Bring her along.
    R **H:** Yeah no.
    I **X:** Really.
    R **H:** Ah no two kids too ((*laughs*))
→ F **X:** Two kids, well – ((*laughs*))

(26) [B:D:B:4:3]
    *J asked B to give a speech at his institution on Friday and B
    told J that he would not be free on Friday.*
    I   **J:** I I can enquire whether they can have it another day,
           but Friday seems to be the =
    R **B:** = the set day. But it's very very difficult for me, I –
          it's ah because I um, y'know we have a a permanent
          booking for Saturday mornings and there's nothing I
          can do to change that. It's not in my hand, you see, =
                        [
    bc **J:**   mhm

B: = which means I have to be preparing them the the the afternoon and evening beforehand.

→ F₁   **J:** I see – oh that's too bad. It was a ((*pause*))

                                                    [

F₂ **B:**   Yeah.

In the follow-ups (arrowed) in (25) and (26), the speakers unwillingly accept the negative outcome, as can be seen from the fact that the concessions are marked by 'well' and 'that's too bad' which are indications of the speaker's reluctance in accepting the negative outcome.

9.3.3 Acknowledgement

Apart from endorsement and concession, there is another subclass of follow-up act which is typically realized by a closed set of items like 'okay', 'right', 'alright', 'yeah', 'oh I see', or a repetition of the preceding response in low key. It is a minimal acknowledgement that the response has been heard, understood, and accepted, and that the interaction has been felicitous. Let us identify this type of follow-up act as an *acknowledgement*. Acknowledgements can be considered a cross subclass which can realize the follow-up act pro-spected by any of the three subclasses of responding acts.

In the following, we shall examine how acknowledgements are realized. But before we do that, it must be pointed out that they are to be strictly distinguished from message-received signals in response to informatives, although they may have identical linguistic realiza-tions. Compare (27) and (28) in the following:

(27) [B:B:A:1:1]
H was telling G how to get in touch with a postgraduate student from China.

   I   **H:** She she's I think she's from Beijing but you can just call just to confirm that there might be ah another person also from from Beijing but I'm pretty sure she's she's from Beijing.

→ R **G:** Oh I see.

(28) [B:C:A:3:1]
   I   **B:** um oh what's happened to Terry Brown?

R A: Oh, he he's going to come to my class today at two
            forty five, he's with May right now.
→ F B: Oh I see.

'Oh I see' in (27) is a response indicating that the information has
been received and understood, whereas that in (28) not only indicates
that the response has been heard and received, but also acknowledges
it as an appropriate contribution to the preceding elicitation (see
Chapter 2, section 2.5).

An acknowledgement can be the follow-up act prospected by positive responses to all four subclasses of initiating act. The following
are some examples:

(29) [B:C:A:2] (requesting exchange)
      I   J: um I wonder if you might give my apologies, I'm –
              not going to make it tomorrow. =
                            [
   <R> K: Okay
      R   K: = Okay Jack. Sure.
→ F   J: Okay.

(30) [B:D:A:1:16] (eliciting exchange)
      I H: When's a good time to get you, maybe Sunday
             morning.
      R J: Well yeah because I don't play basketball any more on
             Sunday morning.
→ F H: Alright.

(31) [B:G:B:3:1] (directing exchange)
      I   A: Just make sure that y'know just make sure that you
              give students some work or something.
      R B: Mhm, mhm.
→ F   A: Yeah.

(32) [B:C:A:3:2] (informing exchange)
      I   A: I I still feel very embarrassed by the fact that you
              weren't introduced to him.
      R B: Mm well well no worry um that's that's the way =
                                [
         A: (   )
         B: = yeah.
→ F   A: = Alright.

The acknowledgements in the above examples are realized by a closed set of items, 'right', 'yeah', 'alright'. In the following, the acknowledgements are realized by a repetition of the response provided, spoken in low key:

(33) [B:H:B:1:1]
    I X: And who published it?
    R Y: Ah Collins.
→ F X: //p   //
             COLlins

(34) [B:D:A:1:6]
    I C: What're you playing, touch football or what?
    R D: It was ah basketball.
→ F C: //p   //
             BASket ball

(35) [B:B:B:2:2]
    I H: I mean we don't have to come to any conclusions that early, do we?
    R X: No, we don't, Henry.
→ F H: //p   //
             NO

As pointed out earlier, a low key, when co-selected with a repetition, indicates that the move is doing no more than acknowledging receipt of information (see Coulthard and Brazil 1981: 93).

It should be noted, however, that a repetition which is spoken in mid key does not realize a follow-up act since it is likely to be followed by another utterance. For example:

(36) [B:A:B:2:2]
    I X: Can I speak to Joe?
    R Y: Hold on please. ((*pause*)) Ah he's not in his room now.
→ I X: // p he's NOT in his ROOM //
→ R Y: No.

X's utterance (arrowed) is therefore an initiation in which X seeks confirmation from Y that he did hear Y say 'he's not in his room', and Y's utterance (arrowed) is a response expressing a confirmation. Sometimes, however, a speaker may reformulate or repeat the response in mid key without intending to solicit a confirmation: he is thinking aloud to himself. For example:

(37) [B:A:B:2:2]
    I X: Can I speak to Joe?
    R Y: Hold on please. ((*pause*)) Ah he's not in his room
          now.
→ F X: //p he's NOT in his <u>ROOM</u> //p   //
                                  <u>RIGHT</u>

Here, it is the item 'right' spoken in low key that acknowledges the outcome.

An acknowledgement can also be used as an alternative to a concession in accepting the negative outcome of the interaction. For example:

(38) [BCET:A:56]
    C: Are you sure you don't want a cigarette?
    B: No, I couldn't take your last but one.
    C: Well, the last one actually, that would be my last one.
    B: No thanks.
    C: Go on have it Rob.
    B: No no I'm not having it, I'd feel too bad.
→ C: Okay.

(39) [Davidson 1984: 127]
    A: You wan' me <u>bring</u> you anything?
       (0.4)
    B: <u>No</u>: no: <u>nothing</u>.
→ A: <u>AW</u>:kay.

In both (38) and (39), the negative outcomes of the exchanges are accepted with a minimal 'okay'.

Finally, acknowledgements can also realize the follow-up act prospected by temporizations. For example:

(40) [B:H:B:8:3]
    I D: Alright, well em what what what em what what time
          d'you what time would you like to do it.
    R H: I'll I'll let you know, let me see, let me see h– if I can
          get the thing done by the end of the week.

→ F D: Okay =
  I   = and then give me a ring and we we
                                          [
  R H: Alright then, okay then.
  F D: Yes. =
  I   = Well the as I say ah speed at this stage is of the
         essence because we can't get going until we brought =
                [[
  R H: Alright   alright
     D: = (   )
       [
     H: = no, that's alright. Alright, I'll get moving.

D's elicit:commit is responded to by a temporization from H in which he does not commit himself to a fixed date to discuss his work with D. It is then followed by a further utterance from D which accepts H's postponing the commitment. However, as we can see from the rest of the discourse, the subject is not closed: H is under the obligation to fix a date eventually.

Sometimes the follow-up act can be realized by not only accepting the temporization, but also minimizing the face-threatening effect of a potential negative outcome. This can occur when the exchange is initiated by a requestive. For example:

(41) [Fieldnotes]
     I A: Can you get me a bottle of Perrier water?
     R B: I'm not sure if they have it in the stores, but I'll try
              and get one.
→ F A: Okay, but it doesn't matter if you can't.

To summarize, we may say that there are basically three subclasses of follow-up acts: *endorsement*, which is prospected by positive responses; *concession*, which is prospected by negative responses; and *acknowledgement*, which is a cross subclass prospected by all three subclasses of response.

9.4 Turn-passing

As we pointed out in Chapter 2, a second follow-up move or follow-up moves subsequent to a first follow-up move in which items like 'yeah', 'okay', or 'alright' constitute the entire move functions as a 'turn-passing' signal. For example:

(42) [B:B:B:2:7–8]

I	X:	(I tell you what) I'm doing at present, I'm trying to make changes, a bit of change. Y'know, I'm just wondering, should we at this stage send them in any sample of a teacher's book or workbook. ((*pause*))
R	H:	Well, if you if you, like I don't want to do a lot of work for them in case they turn everything down, that's the trouble.
I	X:	What's that?
R	H:	I I don't want to do a lot of work for them if they if they're going to turn anything
F_1	X:	No, no, neither do I.
→ F_2	H:	Yeah.
F_3	X:	Em no. =
I		= Okay, we just leave it at that chapter and shoot it back to them and let them ( ) there.

According to the turn-taking rule of conversation (Sacks *et al.* 1974), after X has produced the first follow-up move, H has the floor and he is entitled to introduce a new topic, to carry on with the same topic, or even to terminate the conversation. But in the above excerpt, H is not doing any of the above in the arrowed utterance. Rather, he is indicating that he has no more to say and wishes to relinquish the floor. Hence, 'yeah' functions as a 'turn-passing signal'. That this is indeed its function is supported by the fact that X then takes the floor and produces a further follow-up move followed by a 'boundary marker' 'okay' and a concluding remark to terminate the sequence. Notice that if X did not continue to produce a 'boundary marker' after his further follow-up move, then the latter would realize another 'turn-passing' signal, indicating that he does not wish to take the floor either.

It should be noted that in polite formulaic exchanges, such as well-wishing, greeting, and so on, which typically consist of only two parts, the first follow-up move serves as a 'turn-passing' signal. For example:

(43) [B:B:A:3:5]
```
 1 I  H: So I'll so we look forward to seeing you at in ah
                                                     [
 2 R  X:                                              Yeah
 3         looking forward to Friday the fourth, Henry.
→ 4 F  H: Yeah.
 5 I  X: Good. How's everything going with you?
```

Because formulaic exchanges such as the above typically consist of only two parts, after X's response in lines 2–3, H is entitled to introduce a new topic or terminate the interaction. But he is doing neither of the above. He is passing the turn to X. This is supported by the fact that X then takes the floor, produces a 'boundary marker', realized by 'Good' spoken with a high fall, and introduces a new topic.

Although items like 'yeah' and 'okay' typically realize ackowledgements accepting the outcome of the preceding interaction, they do not realize this function when occurring in the second follow-up move slot. The following is yet another example:

(44) [B:A:B:3:3]
```
 I    S: Hey thank thanks again for the movie on ah I I =
                                                       [
 R    M:                                                Oh yeah
 I    S: = I'd like to read the story.
 R    M: Yeah, I'll try to get you a copy of the um of the story
         after this week is over.
 F₁   S: Okay.
→ F₂  M: Okay.
 I    S: Alright then, bye-bye then.
 R    M: Bye-bye.
```

As we can see, the second 'okay' realizes a different function from the first 'okay'. While the first one acknowledges the outcome of the exchange, the second one indicates that the speaker has no more to say. This is supported by the fact that S then takes the floor and initiates a 'closing exchange'. Let us identify the act in the second follow-up as a *turning-passing act*.

9.5 Concluding remarks

In this chapter, which is very much a sequel to Chapter 2, we have tried to identify more delicate subclasses of follow-up acts within the general function of acknowledging the outcome of the interaction in an exchange. Again, in the identification of these subclasses, we have to invent discourse act labels. There does not seem to be any speech act verb which can fully capture what is being done in these utterances. We have labelled them *endorsement, concession,* and *acknowledgement.* These three subclasses are identified on the basis of prospective classification. We pointed out that, contrary to common belief, responses are not merely retrospective, but also prospective. We supported this by showing that the choices of follow-up acts prospected by a positive response, a negative response, and a temporization are different. A positive response prospects either an *endorsement* or an *acknowledgement;* a negative response prospects either a *concession* or an *acknowledgement;* a temporization prospects only an *acknowledgement.* We may represent this as shown in Figure 9.1.

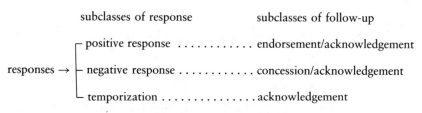

Figure 9.1: Subclasses of follow-up acts

Except for acknowledgements, there are a variety of linguistic realizations of the subclasses. For example, an endorsement can be realized by an appreciation or expression of indebtedness for a service rendered, an enthusiastic acceptance of the positive outcome, an agreement with or upgrading of the preceding agreement, or a comment on the information supplied. We could, if we wished, identify each of these as a more delicate subclass of endorsement and give them separate discourse act labels. And, as we go further down the scale of delicacy, we could further identify even more delicate subclasses. However, this would be the concern of another book.

Finally, we have looked at a much neglected element of interaction, the second follow-up move of an exchange. We have seen that sometimes when a speaker does not want to take the floor when he/she is entitled to a turn, he/she can, subsequent to a follow-up move, produce a further follow-up move to indicate that he/she wishes to relinquish the floor. This move is typically realized by a closed set of items like 'yeah', 'okay', 'alright', occupying the entire move. We have identified the act in this move as a *turn-passing act*.

PART FIVE

Further aspects of conversational description

10
Conversational processes and patterning

I CONVERSATIONAL PROCESSES

10.1 Introduction

In Chapter 2, we proposed that a basic unit of interaction is a three-move exchange with the structural elements *initiation, response,* and *follow-up.* In Chapters 4 to 9, we examined the subclasses of acts which realize the head acts of these moves. In other words, we have looked at the syntagmatic as well as the paradigmatic relations of the discourse acts. What we now need to account for is the actual patterning that is exhibited as the discourse unfolds.

As we have already pointed out in Chapter 1, conversation is a co-operative effort between at least two participants and there is no way that one participant can place absolute constraints on what the other can say. Yet this does not mean that one utterance can be followed by any other utterance and the conversation will still be coherent (see Tsui 1991c). At any one point in the conversation, there is a set of choices available to the speaker and each choice made opens up another set of choices to the next speaker. Halliday's concept of 'system' in grammar can be borrowed to describe discourse choices (see Chapter 1, section 1.7).

The aim of this chapter is to examine the *systems of choices* operating at various points in the discourse and demonstrate how the actual development in conversation is the realization of an ongoing process of choices made by speakers (see also Halliday 1984: 10). In describing the systems of choices and conversational processes, we shall be referring to the piece of data given in (1) for illustration. This will be followed by an application of the proposed descriptive framework to the analysis of this piece of data.

(1) [B:D:B:2:1–2]
    1 I   J: Hello, Sandy?[1]
    2 R S: Hi Hi Jef.
    3 F   J: Yes.
    4 I   S: Yeah, I just wanted to alert you of the fact that I
    5   AM back and I am free for the next fifteen
    6   minutes about and ah I wonder what your
    7   schedules are.
    8 R   J: Alright, I'll come down – w– I'm just talking with
    9   Rowena right now so I'll just come down.
                        [
   10 bc S: uhuh
   11 C S: Oh I'm not I'm at Sandy Bay, I'm not at the office =
                         [[
   12 R   J: Oh   Oh I
   13   see.
   14   S: = 'n I'm I'm going I'm going to the ah Yoga class
   15   at four fifteen, I'm boiling h–
                  [
   16 I   J: Why why don't you just – can you come up
   17   here for a minute? Or or you you want me to
   18   come down there?
   19 R S: No ah I was just I was just um I'm calling from
   20   the Sports Centre and I'm I'm going ah home in a
   21   minute. I just wanted to see how we can get in
   22   touch. =
   23 I   = Do you want to call me at home whenever
   24   you're finished with Rowena?
   25 R   J: Alright.
   26 I   S: I'll be there for the next um um twenty minutes
   27   or half an hour maybe.
   28 R   J: Alright. =
   29 I   = Just give me the number so I remember.
   30 R S: Five one.
   31 F   J: Five one.
   32 R S: Two nine.
   33 F   J: Two nine.
   34 R S: Eight two.
   35 F   J: Eight two.

36	F	S:	Yeah.
37	F	J:	Okay.
38	I	S:	Or alternatively we could get together at five
39			fifteen when I'm finished.
40	R	J:	No, I have to babysit. Actually, can I 'cos I think
41			Andrea's going to a Yoga class later.
42	I	S:	Yeah, there're three seem to be three classes um =

                                    [

43	R	J:	Yeah.
44		S:	= Yeah.
45		S:	Um
46	I	J:	So I'll I'll try and give you a call. If I don't I'll I'll
47			talk to you on Monday?
48	I	S:	Or tomorrow morning?
49	R	J:	Ah – tomorrow morning I have to go to the
50			British Council. ((*laughs*))
51	F	S:	Okay. Well it–
52	I	J:	I'll talk to you yyyyyeah, it it's–
53	I	S:	Try try to call me before four fifteen.
54	R	J:	Alright then. =
55	I		= Bye.
56	R	S:	Okay, bye.

10.2 Systems of choices at initiating move

In (1) above, lines 1 to 3 form an exchange which is typical of the opening routine for telephone conversations in which speakers greet and identify each other. The choices available are constrained by social conventions. (For a detailed description of possible telephone conversation openings, see Schegloff 1979: 28). Since it is not the concern here to describe choices which are specific to a particular conversational routine, we shall start with line 4.

In lines 4–7, after the identification/recognition routine, S produced an initiating move with an elicit:inform as the head act asking J about his schedule.

In producing an initiating move, the speaker has the choice of performing an elicitation, a requestive, a directive, or an informative. We can say that these four subclasses form a system of choices. If the speaker decides to perform a requestive, he has the further choice of performing any one of its five subclasses. These five subclasses form another system of choices. If he chooses to perform an elicitation, then he has the further choice of performing any one of the six subclasses of elicitations. These subclasses form yet another system of choices, and so on. We can represent the systems of choices available at the head of the initiating move as shown in Figure 10.1.

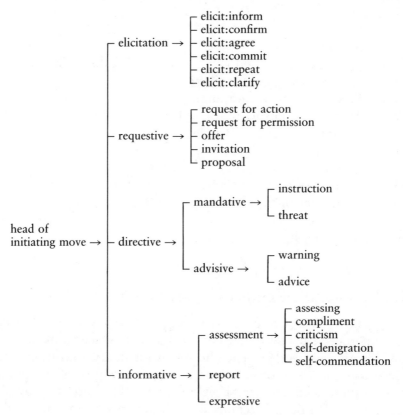

Figure 10.1: Systems of choices at the head of initiating move

Figure 10.1 shows that in producing an initiating move, the speaker has the choice of producing any one of the subclasses of discourse acts given. In lines 4–7 in (1) above, S makes the choice of producing an elicit:inform.

10.3 Discourse maintenance systems at Ti

Sacks *et al.* (1974), in looking at the organization of talk involving more than one person, observe that there is a turn-taking system in which speaker change occurs. In other words, after a speaker has produced an initiating move, there will be a change of speaker. The next speaker has a set of choices opened up to him/her. Consider the following example:

(2) [I]
    A: Have you got a pencil?
    B: (a) Yes, I have.
        (b) No, I haven't.
        (c) You know I don't use pencils.
        (d) Why do you ask?
        (e) Here you are. (+NV)
        (f) Where's yours?
        (g) What do you need a pencil for?

Utterances (a) to (g) are all possible choices for B after A has produced an elicitation, specifically an elicit:inform. B has the choice of maintaining or not maintaining the discourse framework (for the notion of 'discourse framework', see Chapter 8, note 5). If B makes the choice of maintaining the discourse framework (+ maintain), he produces the prospected response, as in (a) and (b), both of which supply the requested information. If he makes the choice of not maintaining the discourse framework (− maintain), then he can challenge the presuppositions of the elicit:inform (as in (c) in which he challenges the presupposition that A has the need to ask for the information (see Chapter 8, section 8.3)), or he can produce another initiation, as in (d). He can also reclassify A's utterance as a request for action, as in (e), (f), and (g). In doing so, he can choose to maintain the discourse framework and produce a compliance to the requestive (as in (e)), or he can choose not to maintain the discourse framework and challenge the presuppositions of the request for action (as in (f) in which he challenges the presupposition that there is a need for A to make the request, since B should have his own pencil. See Chapter 8, section 8.6). He can also produce another initiation, as in (g). In (1) above, J reclassifies S's elicitation as a requestive for him to go and meet her. And he maintains the discourse framework by producing a compliance which is a pro-spected response to a request for action.

Let us represent the system of discourse maintenance after an initiating move (symbolized as Ti) as shown in Figure 10.2.

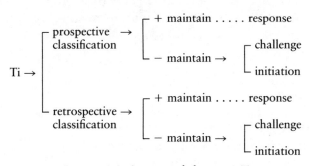

Figure 10.2: Systems of choices at Ti

10.4 Systems of choices at responding move

As I have pointed out before, the choice made in the initiating move will constrain the choices that are available to the next speaker. For example, the choice of a requestive will open up choices which are different from that opened up by a directive. In other words, there are different systems operating at the head of a responding move after the production of a different subclass of initiating act.

If the speaker chooses to produce an elicitation in the initiating move, and the next speaker wants to maintain the discourse frame-work, then the latter has only one choice, and that is to produce a positive responding act. He has to supply the missing information in response to elicit:inform; confirm the previous speaker's assumption in response to elicit:confirm; agree with the previous speaker's asserted proposition in response to elicit:agree; and clarify and repeat in response to elicit:clarify and elicit:repeat, respectively. The exception is elicit:commit in which all three subclasses of responding acts are available choices. These three choices form a system (see Chapter 8, section 8.5.4).

Inability or unwillingness to supply information in reply to elicit:inform, disconfirmation in reply to elicit:confirm, disagreement in reply to elicit:agree, failure to repeat and clarify in reply to elicit:

repeat and elicit:clarify, respectively, all challenge the presuppositions of elicitations. They are, therefore, not available choices in the responding move.

Similarly, following a directive or an informative, the next speaker has the only choice of producing a positive responding act if he wants to maintain the discourse framework. However, following a requestive, the next speaker has the choices of producing a positive response, a negative response, or a temporization. Let us represent the choices that are open to the speaker in the responding move as shown in Figure 10.3.

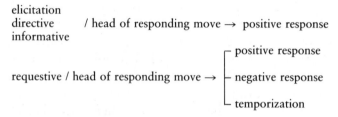

(Note: The symbol / stands for 'followed by'.)

Figure 10.3: Systems of choices at the head of responding move

10.5 Discourse maintenance systems at Tr

Following the responding move, there is again a set of choices opened up regarding turn-taking and discourse maintenance (symbolized as Tr). Consider the options available in the following example:

(3) [I]

I   A: Have you got a pencil?
Ti A → B
R   B: Yes I have.
Tr

            → (i)   I   B: Why, do you need one?   (B → B)
available → (ii) F_1 A: Good.   (B → A)
choices   → (iii) C A: What?   (B → A)
            → (iv) I   A: Can you pass it over?   (B → A)

After B has produced a responding move with a positive response as head act, he may continue to hold the floor (same speaker), or he may hand the floor over to A (change speaker). In other words, there is a system of speaker change in which there are two choices: 'same speaker' and 'change speaker'. If he chooses the former, the only choice available to him is to produce an initiating move (as in (i)). If he chooses to hand the floor over to A, then a system of discourse maintenance is opened up. A has the choice of either maintaining or not maintaining the discourse framework. If he makes the former choice, he produces a follow-up move (as in (ii)). If he makes the latter choice, then yet another system is opened up. He can either challenge the presuppositions of the preceding response (as in (iii), in which A challenges the presupposition that he can hear the response), or he can produce a new initiating move (as in (iv)).

In (1) above, after line 10, J hands the floor over to S who makes the choice of not maintaining the discourse framework. She challenges the presupposition that she is in her office which is conveyed by 'I'll come down ... I'll just come down'. (Their offices are at two ends of the corridor. 'Come down' refers to 'coming down the corridor'.) She informs J that she is not in her office. The challenge is, in turn, responded to by an 'oh'-receipt token, indicating a change of state of knowledge on J's part. The systems operating at Tr can be represented as in Figure 10.4.

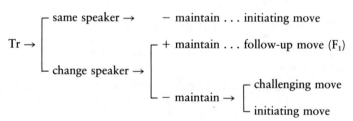

Figure 10.4: Systems of choices at Tr

10.6 Systems of choices at follow-up move

As pointed out in Chapter 9, the choice of a particular subclass of responding act constrains the choices that are available at the follow-up move, if the next speaker wishes to maintain the discourse framework. Following a positive response, two choices of follow-up acts are available: an endorsement and an acknowledgement; following a negative response, again two choices of follow-up acts are available: a concession and an acknowledgement. Finally, following a temporization, the only choice of follow-up act available is an acknowledgement. The systems of choices at F_1 can be briefly represented as in Figure 10.5.

$$+\text{ve response / follow-up} \rightarrow \left[\begin{array}{l} \text{endorsement} \\[6pt] \text{acknowledgement} \end{array} \right.$$

$$-\text{ve response / follow-up} \rightarrow \left[\begin{array}{l} \text{concession} \\[6pt] \text{acknowledgement} \end{array} \right.$$

$$\text{temporization} \rightarrow \text{acknowledgement}$$

Figure 10.5: Systems of choices at F_1

10.7 Discourse maintenance systems at Tf

Subsequent to a follow-up move, there is another set of choices opened up regarding turn-taking and discourse maintenance (symbolized as Tf). Consider the following example and the options that are available:[2]

(4) [based on Coulthard 1981: 19]

I	**D:**	But it's only the last three months that it's been making you feel ill
Ti	**D** $\rightarrow$ **P**	
R	**P:**	ill with it yes
Tr	**P** $\rightarrow$ **D**	
F_1	**D:**	YES YES
Tf		

available → (i) I   **D:** Do you feel nauseous?
choices → (ii) F_2 **P:** Yes doctor.
        → (iii) I   **P:** And sometimes I feel so ill that I don't feel like eating.

As we can see, similar to the systems at F_1, there is also a system of speaker change here. The speaker may continue to hold the floor (same speaker), or hand the floor over (change speaker). If he chooses the former, he can only produce an initiating move (as in (i)). If he chooses the latter, then a system of discourse maintenance is opened up. The next speaker has the choice of maintaining or not maintaining the discourse framework. If he chooses to maintain it, he produces a second follow-up move, usually with a turn-passing act as head (as in (ii)) (see Chapter 9, section 9.4). If he chooses not to maintain it, he produces an initiating move (as in (iii)). The system operating at Tf can be represented as in Figure 10.6.

Tf →
- same speaker → − maintain . . . initiating move
- change speaker →
  - + maintain . . . follow-up move (F_2)
  - − maintain . . . initiating move

Figure 10.6: Systems of choices at Tf

Theoretically, there can be an infinite number of follow-up moves after the first follow-up move. But, as Coulthard and Brazil (1981) point out, exchanges with more than three follow-up moves seldom occur. In any case, the systems of discourse maintenance following any subsequent follow-up move would be the same as those operating at Tf.

The systems operating at Tf do not take into consideration cases where a follow-up move is followed by neither a follow-up move nor an initiating move, but rather a responding move, as in lines 30–35 in (1). Sinclair and Coulthard (1975), in observing that a follow-up move can be followed by a responding move (instead of by an initiating move) when the teacher withholds the initiating move, propose that a 'bound exchange' can consist of only a responding move and a follow-up move, resulting in a sequence consisting of IRF(Ib)RF. For example:

(5) [Sinclair and Coulthard 1975: 54]
    I T: This I think is a super one. Isobel. Can you think what it means?
    R S: Does it mean that there has been an accident further down the road?
    F T: No.

R S: Does it mean a double bend ahead?
F T: No.

Here, the last two utterances constitute an exchange, consisting of only the elements 'R' and 'F', which are bound to the preceding exchange.

In the case of lines 30 to 35 in (1) above, we have a sequence consisting of two 'bound exchanges'. 'Bound exchanges' usually occur when the response given in the preceding exchange is incomplete. In this sense, we can say that the production of a 'bound' responding move supports the presuppositions and interactional expectation set up by the initiating move in the preceding exchange. Taking into consideration the possibility of a follow-up move followed by a responding move in a 'bound exchange', we may say that at speaker change, if the next speaker wishes to maintain the discourse framework, he has the choices of producing a second follow-up move or a 'bound' responding move. Therefore, the systems operating at Tf should be revised as shown in Figure 10.7.

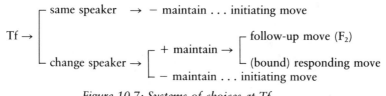

Figure 10.7: Systems of choices at Tf

In the above discussion, we have seen how the concept of system accounts for conversation as an interactive process during which each choice made by an interlocutor affects the subsequent development of the conversation, and that the actual conversational patterning is the realization of the choices made.

10.8 Analysis of data

In the following, I shall demonstrate how the entire descriptive framework can be applied to the analysis of the telephone conversation given in (1). This will be followed by a discussion of aspects of conversational patterning that have yet to be accounted for.

Key to abbreviations in data analysis

T.T. and D.M	= Turn-taking and discourse maintenance	S.S.	= Same speaker
+ main	= Maintaining the discourse framework	Ch.S.	= Change of speaker
− main	= Not maintaining the discourse framework	Req	= Requestive
Ele	= Element of structure	Dir	= Directive
I	= Initiating move	Inf	= Informative
R	= Responding move	Eli	= Elicitation
F_1	= First follow-up move	Exp	= Expressive
F_2	= Second follow-up move		
C	= Challenging move		
B.R.	= Bound responding move		
P.C.	= Prospective classification		
R.C.	= Retrospective classification		
+ve R	= Positive responding act		
−ve R	= Negative responding act		
T	= Temporization		

Note that at Tr, change of speaker is automatic.

Data analysis

T.T. D.M.	Ele	Systems of choices	Actual choice	Subclass	Linguistic realization
	I	I → [Eli / Req / Dir / Inf]	Inf	Exp: greeting	**J:** Hello, Sandy?
Ti		Ti → [P.C. → [+ main .... R / − main → [C / I]] ; R.C. → [+ main .... R / − main → [C / I]]]	P.C. + main R		
	R	Inf .... +ve R	+ve R		**S:** Hi, hi, Jef.
Tr		Tr → [S.S. → − main .... I ; Ch.S. → [+ main .... F_1 / − main → [C / I]]]	+ main F_1		
	F_1	+ve R .... F_1	F_1		**J:** Yes.

Conversational processes and patterning

T.T. D.M.	Ele	Systems of choices	Actual choice	Subclass	Linguistic realization
Tf		Tf → [S.S. → − main .... I ; Ch.S. → [+ main → [F_2 ; B.R.] ; − main .... I]]	− main I		
	I	I → [Eli ; Req ; Dir ; Inf]	Eli	Elicit: inform	**S:** Yeah, I just wanted to alert you of the fact that I AM back and I am free for the next fifteen minutes about and ah I wonder what your schedules are?
Ti		Ti → [P.C. → [+ main .... R ; − main → [C ; I]] ; R.C. → [+ main .... R ; − main → [C ; I]]]	R.C. + main R		
	R	Req → [+ve R ; −ve R ; Temp]	+ve R to req for action		**J:** Alright, I'll come down – w– I'm just talking with Rowena right now so, I'll just come down.
Tr		Tr → [S.S. → − main .... I ; Ch.S. → [+ main .... F_1 ; − main → [C ; I]]]	Ch.S. − main C		

229

T.T. D.M.	Ele	Systems of choices	Actual choice	Subclass	Linguistic realization
	C	I → ⎡ Eli / Req / Dir / Inf ⎤	Inf	Report	**S:** Oh I'm not I'm at Sandy Bay, I'm not at the office 'n I'm I'm going I'm going to the ah Yoga class at four fifteen, I'm boiling h–
Ti		Ti → ⎡ P.C. → ⎡ + main .... R / − main → ⎡ C / I ⎤ ⎤ / R.C. → ⎡ + main .... R / − main → ⎡ C / I ⎤ ⎤ ⎤	P.C. + main R		
	R	Inf .... +ve R	+ve R		**J:** Oh, Oh I see.
Tr		Tr → ⎡ S.S. → − main .... I / Ch.S. → ⎡ + main .... F₁ / − main → ⎡ C / I ⎤ ⎤ ⎤	Ch.S.* − main I		
	I	I → ⎡ Eli / Req / Dir / Inf ⎤	Req	Offer	**J:** Why why don't you just – can you come up here for a a minute? Or or you you want me to come down there?

---

* Because J's response 'Oh, oh I see.' overlaps with S's report, and S carries on speaking after J has finished, J's following initiation is considered to be a change of speaker.

T.T. D.M.	Ele	Systems of choices	Actual choice	Subclass	Linguistic realization
Ti		Ti → P.C. → [+ main .... R / − main → [C / I]] ; R.C. → [+ main .... R / − main → [C / I]]	P.C. + main R		
	R	Req → [+ve R / −ve R / Temp]	−ve R		**S:** No ah I was just I was just um I'm calling from the Sports Centre and I'm I'm going ah home in a minute. I just wanted to see how we can get in touch. =
Tr		Tr → S.S. → − main .... I ; Ch.S. → [+ main .... F₁ / − main → [C / I]]	S.S. − main I		
	I	I → [Eli / Req / Dir / Inf]	Req	Req for action	**S:** = Do you want to call me at home whenever you're finished with Rowena?
Ti		Ti → P.C. → [+ main .... R / − main → [C / I]] ; R.C. → [+ main .... R / − main → [C / I]]	P.C. + main R		

T.T. D.M.	Ele	Systems of choices	Actual choice	Subclass	Linguistic realization

| | R | Req → ⎡ +ve R / −ve R / Temp ⎤ | +ve R | | **J:** Alright |

| Tr | | Tr → ⎡ S.S. → − main .... I / Ch.S. → ⎡ + main .... F₁ / − main → ⎡ C / I ⎤ ⎤ ⎤ | Ch.S. − main I | | |

| | I | I → ⎡ Eli / Req / Dir / Inf ⎤ | Inf | Report | **S:** I'll be there for the next um um twenty minutes or half an hour maybe. |

| Ti | | Ti → ⎡ P.C. → ⎡ + main .... R / − main → ⎡ C / I ⎤ ⎤ / R.C. → ⎡ + main .... R / − main → ⎡ C / I ⎤ ⎤ ⎤ | P.C. + main R | | |

| | R | Inf .... +ve R | +ve R | | **J:** Alright. = |

| Tr | | Tr → ⎡ S.S. → − main .... I / Ch.S. → ⎡ + main .... F₁ / − main → ⎡ C / I ⎤ ⎤ ⎤ | S.S. − main I | | |

| | I | I → ⎡ Eli / Req / Dir / Inf ⎤ | Dir | Mandative: instruction | **J:** = Just give me the number so I remember. |

232

T.T. D.M.	Ele	Systems of choices	Actual choice	Subclass	Linguistic realization

Ti

$$Ti \rightarrow \begin{cases} P.C. \rightarrow \begin{cases} + \text{main} .... R \\ - \text{main} \rightarrow \begin{cases} C \\ I \end{cases} \end{cases} \\ R.C. \rightarrow \begin{cases} + \text{main} .... R \\ - \text{main} \rightarrow \begin{cases} C \\ I \end{cases} \end{cases} \end{cases}$$

P.C.
+ main
R

R Dir .... +ve R +ve R **S:** Five one

Tr

$$Tr \rightarrow \begin{cases} S.S. \rightarrow - \text{main} .... I \\ Ch.S. \rightarrow \begin{cases} + \text{main} .... F_1 \\ - \text{main} \rightarrow \begin{cases} C \\ I \end{cases} \end{cases} \end{cases}$$

Ch.S.
+ main
F_1

F_1 +ve R .... F_1 F_1 Endorsement **J:** Five one

Tf

$$Tf \rightarrow \begin{cases} S.S. \rightarrow - \text{main} .... I \\ Ch.S. \rightarrow \begin{cases} + \text{main} \rightarrow \begin{cases} F_2 \\ B.R. \end{cases} \\ - \text{main} .... I \end{cases} \end{cases}$$

Ch.S.
+ main
B.R.

B.R. Dir .... +ve R +ve R **S:** Two nine.

Tr

$$Tr \rightarrow \begin{cases} S.S. \rightarrow - \text{main} .... I \\ Ch.S. \rightarrow \begin{cases} + \text{main} .... F_1 \\ - \text{main} \rightarrow \begin{cases} C \\ I \end{cases} \end{cases} \end{cases}$$

Ch.S.
+ main
F_1

F_1 +ve R .... F_1 F_1 Endorsement **J:** Two nine.

T.T. D.M.	Ele	Systems of choices	Actual choice	Subclass	Linguistic realization
Tf		Tf → ⌈ S.S. → − main .... I ⌊ Ch.S. → ⌈ + main → ⌈ F_2 ⌊ B.R. ⌊ − main I	Ch.S. + main B.R.		
	B.R.	Dir .... +ve R	+ve R		**S:** Eight two.
Tr		Tr → ⌈ S.S. → − main .... I ⌊ Ch.S. → ⌈ + main .... F_1 ⌊ − main → ⌈ C ⌊ I	Ch.S. + main F_1		
	F_1	+ve R .... F_1	F_1	Endorsement	**J:** Eight two.
Tf		Tf → ⌈ S.S. → − main .... I ⌊ Ch.S. → ⌈ + main → ⌈ F_2 ⌊ B.R. ⌊ − main I	Ch.S. + main F_2		
	F_2**	F_1 .... F_2	F_2	Turn-passing	**S:** Yeah.
Tf		Tf → ⌈ S.S. → − main .... I ⌊ Ch.S. → ⌈ + main → ⌈ F_3 ⌊ B.R. ⌊ − main I	Ch.S. + main F_3		
	F_3	F_2 .... F_3	F_3	Turn-passing	**J:** Okay.

** For the analysis of this utterance and the following as turn-passing follow-up moves, see the discussion in section 10.7.

Conversational processes and patterning

T.T. D.M.	Ele	Systems of choices	Actual choice	Subclass	Linguistic realization
Tf		Tf → ⎡ S.S. → − main .... I ⎣ Ch.S. → ⎡ + main → ⎡ F₄ ⎣ B.R. ⎣ − main I	Ch.S. − main I		
	I	I → ⎡ Eli ⎢ Req ⎢ Dir ⎣ Inf	Req	Proposal	**S:** Or alternatively we could get together at five fifteen when I'm finished.
Ti		Ti → ⎡ P.C. → ⎡ + main .... R ⎢ ⎣ − main → ⎡ C ⎢ ⎣ I ⎣ R.C. → ⎡ + main .... R ⎣ − main → ⎡ C ⎣ I	P.C. − main R		
R		Req → ⎡ +ve R ⎢ −ve R ⎣ Temp	−ve R		**J:** No I have to babysit. Actually, can I 'cos I think Andrea's going to a Yoga class later.
Tr		Tr → ⎡ S.S. → − main .... I ⎣ Ch.S. → ⎡ + main .... F₁ ⎣ − main → ⎡ C ⎣ I	Ch.S. − main I		
	I	I → ⎡ Eli ⎢ Req ⎢ Dir ⎣ Inf	Inf	Report	**S:** Yeah, there're three seem to be three classes um

T.T. D.M.	Ele	Systems of choices	Actual choice	Subclass	Linguistic realization
Ti		Ti → ⎡ P.C. → ⎡ + main .... R ⎣ − main → ⎡ C ⎣ I ⎣ R.C. → ⎡ + main .... R ⎣ − main → ⎡ C ⎣ I	P.C. + main R		
	R	Inf .... +ve R	+ve R		**J:** Yeah. Yeah.
Tr		Tr → ⎡ S.S. → − main .... I ⎣ Ch.S. → ⎡ + main .... F₁ ⎣ − main → ⎡ C ⎣ I	S.S. − main I		
	I	I → ⎡ Eli ⎣ Req ⎣ Dir ⎣ Inf	Req	Offer	**J:** So I'll I'll try and give you a call. If I don't I'll I'll talk to you on Monday?
Ti		Ti → ⎡ P.C. → ⎡ + main .... R ⎣ − main → ⎡ C ⎣ I ⎣ R.C. → ⎡ + main ... R ⎣ − main → ⎡ C ⎣ I	P.C. − main I		
	I	I → ⎡ Eli ⎣ Req ⎣ Dir ⎣ Inf	Req	Req for action	**S:** Or tomorrow morning?

T.T. D.M.	Ele	Systems of choices	Actual choice	Subclass	Linguistic realization
Ti		$Ti \rightarrow$ P.C. $\rightarrow$ [+ main .... R / − main → [C / I]] ; R.C. $\rightarrow$ [+ main .... R / − main → [C / I]]	P.C. + main R		
	R	Req $\rightarrow$ [+ve R / −ve R / Temp]	−ve R		**J:** Ah − tomorrow morning I have to go to the British Council. ((*laughs*))
Tr		$Tr \rightarrow$ S.S. $\rightarrow$ − main .... I ; Ch.S. $\rightarrow$ [+ main .... F_1 / − main → [C / I]]	Ch.S. + main F_1		
	F_1	−ve R .... F_1	F_1	Concession	**S:** Okay. Well it−
Tf		$Tf \rightarrow$ S.S. $\rightarrow$ − main .... I ; Ch.S. $\rightarrow$ [+ main → [F_2 / B.R.] / − main .... I]	Ch.S. − main I		
	I	$I \rightarrow$ [Eli / Req / Dir / Inf]	Req	Offer	**J:** I'll talk to you yyyyyeah, it it's−

T.T. D.M.	Ele	Systems of choices	Actual choice	Subclass	Linguistic realization

Ti

Systems of choices:

```
         ┌ P.C. → ┌ + main .... R
         │        └ − main → ┌ C
Ti →     │                   └ I
         │
         └ R.C. → ┌ + main .... R
                  └ − main → ┌ C
                             └ I
```

Actual choice: P.C. + main R

I

```
      ┌ Eli
      ├ Req
I →   ├ Dir
      └ Inf
```

Actual choice: Dir
Subclass: Mandative: instruction
Linguistic realization: **S:** Try try to call me before four fifteen.

Ti

```
         ┌ P.C. → ┌ + main .... R
         │        └ − main → ┌ C
Ti →     │                   └ I
         │
         └ R.C. → ┌ + main .... R
                  └ − main → ┌ C
                             └ I
```

Actual choice: P.C. + main R

R Dir .... +ve R

Actual choice: +ve R
Linguistic realization: **J:** Alright then. =

Tr

```
         ┌ S.S. → − main .... I
         │
Tr →     │        ┌ + main .... F₁
         └ Ch.S. →
                  └ − main → ┌ C
                             └ I
```

Actual choice: S.S. − main I

I

```
      ┌ Eli
      ├ Req
I →   ├ Dir
      └ Inf
```

Actual choice: Inf
Subclass: Exp: farewell
Linguistic realization: **J:** = Bye.

238

T.T. D.M.	Ele	Systems of choices	Actual choice	Subclass	Linguistic realization
Ti					

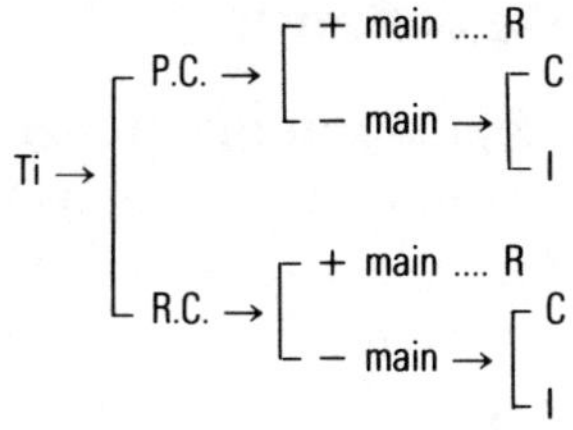

$$\text{Ti} \rightarrow \begin{cases} \text{P.C.} \rightarrow \begin{cases} + \text{ main } .... \text{ R} \\ - \text{ main } \rightarrow \begin{cases} \text{C} \\ \text{I} \end{cases} \end{cases} \\ \text{R.C.} \rightarrow \begin{cases} + \text{ main } .... \text{ R} \\ - \text{ main } \rightarrow \begin{cases} \text{C} \\ \text{I} \end{cases} \end{cases} \end{cases}$$

Actual choice (Ti row):
P.C.
+ main
R

T.T. D.M.	Ele	Systems of choices	Actual choice	Subclass	Linguistic realization
	R	Inf .... +ve R	+ve R		**S:** Okay, Bye.

II CONVERSATIONAL PATTERNING

10.9 Patterning beyond the exchange

The characterization of utterances proposed in the present descriptive framework is confined to the discourse functions of utterances at the level of the exchange. It does not account for the structural functions of utterances in relation to the entire conversation, which can only be adequately described if we look beyond the exchange.

10.9.1 Pre-closings

Consider B's utterances in lines 19 and 32 below:

(6) [C:2:A:1]
 A passes by B's office.

  1 **A:** Hi, would you like a piece of apple cake?
  2 **B:** Have you got some?
  3 **A:** I've got some next door. =
  4   = I'll just get it.
      ((*A goes back to her office next door to get the apple cake and B waits for her in the office*))
      ((*pause*))
  5 **A:** What a week it was – first you get classes and now
  6   the taxi strike.
  7 **B:** Yeah.
  8 **A:** ((*to herself*)) Your piece of cake ((*cutting up cake*))
  9 **B:** You must make that pretty often huh?
10 **A:** Yeah, my husband loves it.
11   ((*A gives B a piece of cake*))
12 **B:** Mmmm, thank you.
13 **A:** This is to ensure that he doesn't eat the whole cake
14   ((*laughs*))
      [
15 **B:**   ((*laughs*)) That's not very nice.
16 **A:** He shouldn't eat the whole cake, just half of it is
17   enough for him.
        [
18 **B:**   ((*laughs*))

→ 19 **B:** Thanks very much.
 20 **A:** You're welcome. =
 21   = Stay home this weekend?
     . . . . . .
→ 32 **B:** Thanks very much for the apple cake.
 33 **A:** You're welcome.

In the proposed descriptive framework, they will be characterized as *expressives*. While it is true that they are expressives in which B thanks A for the apple cake, their function in relation to the entire conversation is an attempt to bring the conversation to a close. This structural function only becomes apparent if we look at the preceding exchanges. The fact that in line 12, B has already thanked A for the apple cake suggests that her thanking in line 19 is likely to be a 'pre-closing' initiation (Schegloff and Sacks 1973). And when A thanks B for the third time in line 32, we can be quite sure that its structural function is to bring the conversation to a close.

Utterances which realize the structural function of bringing a conversation to a close occur frequently (ibid.). They may be realized by thanking the other party again for favours done, as in (6) above; by apologizing once again when in the preceding exchanges the speaker has failed to comply with a request, as in (7) below; by reiterating an arrangement made, as in (8) below; by making a concluding remark; and so on.

(7) [B:F:B:2:5]
→ **X:** Sorry, I c– I'd love to join you and I'd love to get the the
     basic disc training, but ah as as the donor is here
     ((*laughs*))   (   )
                  [
     H: Okay. Well, good luck good luck with the
     meeting tomorrow then.
 X: Huh?
 H: Good luck with the meeting.
 X: Yeah, we've got to butter him up. ((*laughs*))
 H: ((*laughs*))
 X: Okay, Henry.
 H: Alright. Bye-bye.
 X: Thanks. Bye-bye.

241

(8) [B:A:A:2]
→ H: Alright, so I'll see you at twelve-thirty. I'll I'll ah I'll
   meander down to um to well I I can meet you at the
   steps of the ah of the Science Centre.
   X: Okay, yeah, let's do that, that's that's easier, yeah =
                                                          [
   H: half past =
   X: = (   ) half past, half past twelve.
       [
   H: = twelve.
   H: Okay then.
   X: Okay good.
   H: Bye-bye.
   X: See you, bye.

The arrowed utterance in (7) occurs near the end of a conversation
in which X has turned down H's request to attend a training session
with him. The arrowed utterance in (8) occurs near the end of a
conversation in which X and H have already agreed to meet up at the
specified time. These utterances initiate exchanges which typically
precede what Schegloff and Sacks (1973) call the 'closing section' of
a conversation.

   The problem of characterizing utterances such as the above is even
more acute when we encounter data like the following:

(9) [Schegloff and Sacks 1973: 313]
   B has called to invite C but has been told C is going out to
   dinner.

→ B: Yeah, well get on your clothes and get out and collect
   some of that free food and we'll make it some other time
   Judy then.
   C: Okay then Jack.
   B: Bye-bye.
   C: Bye-bye.

(10) [B:A:A:3:8–9]
   X and Y have been talking about people in their institution
   not doing any work.

→ X: Well, let's you and I stay working as long as we can. =
   [

K: Yeah.
X: = Okay, I read two things by you recently.

In both (9) and (10), the arrowed utterances cannot be characterized as realizing any of the subclasses of initiating act. As Schegloff and Sacks (ibid.) point out, they are neither directives nor requestives, although they have certain imperative aspects in their language forms. To characterize them as such would be to miss their conversational functions, which are to invite the other party to close the conversation for (9), and to close the topic for (10).

In order to account for the structural function of this kind of utterance, we need to look at the structure of the unit above the exchange, possibly a sequence.[3] If a sequence has as its elements of structure, 'opening exchange(s)', 'main exchanges', 'pre-closing exchange(s)', and 'closing exchange(s)', then an utterance which realizes the initiating move in a 'pre-closing exchange' would function as a signal to close the conversation, and one which realizes the responding move in that exchange would function as an agreement to close the conversation. However, a lot of work has yet to be done on the macro-structure of conversation and other spoken discourse genres before a structural statement of this kind can be made.

10.9.2 Insertion sequence

Another aspect of conversational patterning that needs to be accounted for is what Schegloff (1972) refers to as an 'insertion sequence'. Take the following piece of data, for example:

(11) [C:1:A:2]
    I   1 H: Do you get the *TESOL Quarterly*?
    R   2 S: Yeah.
    I   Q1 3 H: Did you get this issue?
    I   Q2 4 S: What – month is it?
    R   A2 5 H: um number two, June eighty-three.
→   ?   A1 6 S: Yeah, I think I probably did.

In the proposed descriptive framework, S's utterance (arrowed) can only be either an initiating or a follow-up move. It cannot be a responding move because of the structural constraint of an exchange: a responding move cannot be followed by another responding move. To consider it a follow-up move is unsatisfactory, because its function is clearly not to acknowledge the outcome of the exchange initiated by S in line 4. The only alternative is to characterize it as an initiating move. But, as we can see, the utterance contains the item 'yeah' which is typical of a responding move or a follow-up move, and it is clearly related to the initiating move in line 3 as well as the preceding exchange in lines 4 and 5.

According to Schegloff (ibid.), lines 4 and 5 would be an exchange which is embedded within the adjacency pair consisting of the question in line 3 and the answer in line 6. This kind of analysis is attractive in that it does account for the 'answerhood' (Levinson 1983: 293) of S's utterance in line 6—that is, the feature 'yeah' which is typical of a response. However, this kind of analysis is not without problems. It assumes that the second pair part to the first pair part will occur after the 'insertion sequence'. But very often we find that the answer does not occur at all. Take lines 1 to 4 in (6) above:

Q1 1 **A:** Would you like a piece of apple cake?
Q2 2 **B:** Have you got some?
A2 3 **A:** I've got some next door. =
? 4   = I'll just get it. (*goes next door to get the cake*)

Here, we find that B's response to A's offer does not occur after the exchange in lines 2–3. Rather, B's elicitation is taken by A as implying that her offer is accepted. In cases like this, it is doubtful that the latter should still be considered 'inserted'.

10.9.3 Sequence-final follow-up moves

In the present descriptive framework, the functions of the follow-up move are characterized at the level of organization of an exchange. The inadequacy of this characterization is thrown into relief when we try to describe conversational patterning such as that given in lines 30 to 35 in (1), in which S gives J her telephone number. In our analysis of data, they are considered 'bound exchanges' consisting of only responding and follow-up moves which are related to the initiating move in line 29 'Just give me the number so I remember'. This description satisfactorily accounts for the fact that lines 30, 32, and 34 are responses to the directive in line 29, and lines 31, 33, and 35 are follow-up moves indicating that the information has been received and is appropriate. However, this leaves us no choice but to describe line 36 as a turn-passing follow-up move since the head act of a second follow-up move is usually a turn-passing act. But the function of line 36 is not so much to hand the floor over to J, but rather to acknowledge the outcome of the entire sequence in which S gives J her telephone number. It indicates that the interaction has been felicitous. The function of this follow-up move is to acknowledge the outcome of the entire sequence.

This kind of sequence-final follow-up move is frequently found in conversation (see Tsui 1989). The following is another example:

(12) [B:F:B:2:5]

H called X to ask if they could both go and get a donated computer and some disc training. X could not go because he had to meet the donor of the computer. He agreed to go on his own. They then talked about where they should put the computer when H has got it.

I H: Alright, so when when I when I get it um where should I put it?

R X: Well, I'll tell um Hunston to move out today then.

I H: Oh I'll tell him, I'll tell him right now, so ah he's right there, he's right

             [

R X: oh he's – okay. =

I   = Yeah, tell him we're going to get one tomorrow and so he should ah get some help to get out.

R H: Okay.

→ F X: //p   //

      oKAY =

I   = Sorry, I c– I'd love to join you and I'd love to get the the basic disc training but ah as as the donor is here ((*laughs*))

R H: Okay.

Here, the follow-up move acknowledges the outcome of the interaction of not only the preceding exchange but the entire sequence. In other words, it marks the end of the sequence, and interlocutors can now either move on to a new topic of talk or bring the conversation to a close. This can be seen from the fact that X's 'Okay' is spoken in low key.[4] It can also be seen from the fact that it is followed by

X apologizing for turning down H's requestive which is an attempt to bring the conversation to a close (see Schegloff and Sacks 1973: 317).

The following is yet another example:

(13) [B:E:A:2:2]
   H and S are making arrangements to go out for a meal. H
   suggested a restaurant called the Spring Deer.

   I   H: And what what time shall we meet there?
   R   X: um ((*pause*)) Spring Deer, Okay.[5]
   I   H: Seven?
   R   X: What time um
   I   H: Seven thirty?
   R   X: Yeah, I guess that's a good time.
   I   H: Between seven and seven thirty then.
   R   X: Alright, between seven and seven thirty.
   I   H: Or or you're going to make it definite, say seven th-
          y'know seven th – or seven o'clock or or seven fifteen.
   R   X: Alright seven fifteen.
   → F H: //p   //
               alRIGHT =
   I   = But you better call 'cos it is hard to get
             reservations.

Here, the follow-up move occurs when a time agreeable to both has been reached. Prior to that—that is, when H and X are still negotiating the time—the exchanges consist of only two parts. The occurrence of the follow-up move marks the end of a sequence. He then moves on to the topic of making reservations. Similar to (12), the final 'Alright' is spoken in low key.

The function of signalling the end of the sequence and acknowledging the outcome of an exchange may be realized separately or simultaneously. For example:

(14) [B:C:A:3:1]
   I   B: Where where is he staying?
   R   A: He's staying at the ah Chung Chi Guest House.
   → F B: //p OH //r I see //

(15) Coulthard and Brazil 1981: 95]
   I   A: Have you got the time?

R B: It's three o'clock.

→ F A: //p   //
        THANKS

In (14), B's follow-up move 'I see' is spoken in mid key and with a referring tone which indicate that it is not sequence-final. Hence, its function is only to acknowledge the outcome of the preceding interaction. In (15), A's follow-up move is spoken in low key and with a proclaiming tone. As Coulthard and Brazil (1981: 95) point out, given that the exchange occurs between strangers in the street, the follow-up move terminates the entire encounter. In other words, its function is not only to acknowledge the outcome, but to signal the end of the encounter as well. It is when the two functions are realized separately that problems of description are created. This again suggests that we need to look at the structure of conversational units which are larger than an exchange, and at how structural location within this larger unit assigns meaning to utterances. Studies in discourse analysis are beginning to look at the macro-structures of discourse genres such as service encounters (see Ventola 1987).

10.10 Concluding remarks

In this volume, I have tried to make a linguistic description of English conversation, using a corpus of naturally-occurring conversational data. I have focused on four areas in this framework. Firstly, the descriptive units of conversational interaction. Following Sinclair and Coulthard (1975), I have proposed a hierarchical rank scale of *act*, *move*, and *exchange*, with *act* being the smallest unit. Secondly, the criteria for characterizing the functions of utterances. I have put forth two criteria: the structural location of the utterance within the exchange and the response that it prospects. I have also pointed out that conversation is a co-operative effort between participants and that an addressee can always retrospectively classify the function of an utterance. Hence, the discourse value of an utterance is determined by both the speaker and the addressee. Thirdly, the structure of conversational organization. I have demonstrated that an 'adjacency pair', which is widely accepted as a unit of conversational organization, fails to account for some conversational data. I have proposed, instead, a 'three-part exchange' which is more powerful as well as theoretically motivated. Fourthly, conversational processes. I have pointed out that conversational participants do not, in fact, have the absolute freedom of saying whatever they like. There are constraints governing what can occur if the conversation is to remain coherent. The concept of systems has been adopted to describe the choices that are available to the speaker and how each choice that he/she makes constrains the choices that are available to the next speaker.

In constructing the descriptive framework, I have constantly shunted back and forth between linguistic concepts and conversational data. The former provides the theoretical motivation for the framework and the latter tests out the power of the concepts and provides the insights and bases for revision of the framework.

In this final chapter, I have applied the descriptive framework to a piece of conversation and have pointed out some aspects of conversational patterning that the framework cannot adequately account for. The aspects outlined are only some of the obvious ones. I am sure more will become apparent as the framework is applied to a larger quantity and variety of conversational data. It is obvious, even by looking at the present corpus, that there are certain limitations in confining the description of utterances to the level of exchange. However, this study is not an attempt to answer all questions in conversational description, but rather an attempt to formalize some of the observations of functions of conversational utterances, processes, and organization.

Some maintain that conversation is such a complex process that any attempt to formalize conversational descriptions in discrete categorial terms is not only futile but misguided. I certainly do not share this view. I find the process that I have gone through in trying to formalize my observations of conversational data very useful in that I have gained insights into the nature of conversation. I hope that by the time you, the reader, have reached this part of the volume, you will agree with me.

Glossary

Chapter 1

Conversational implicature

A term introduced by Grice (1975) to refer to the implications that can be deduced from what has actually been said, based on the assumption that interlocutors are observing the general principle of conversation which states that they are to co-operate with each other and try to be truthful, informative, relevant, and clear.

Elements of structure

A technical term in grammatical description which refers to the component parts which make up the structure of a particular unit. The elements of structure of the grammatical unit 'sentence': 'Mary closed the door quietly' are S (subject) realized by 'Mary', P (predicator) realized by 'closed', C (complement) realized by 'the door', and A (adjunct) realized by 'quietly'. The elements of structure of the discourse unit 'exchange' are IRF which stands for *initiation, response,* and *follow-up.*

Marked form

A linguistic form which is less basic than its counterpart. For example, the noun 'boy' in English. The singular form is more basic than the plural form 'boys'. It also has less material than the latter since it does not have an 's'. The singular is the 'unmarked form' and the plural is the 'marked form'. Let us take another example of 'order' in English. The more basic form of an 'order' is an imperative. For example, 'Report to me at nine tomorrow morning'. However, 'orders' can also be in interrogative form if the context of situation makes it clear that the addressee does not have the option of not complying. The interrogative form is the 'marked form' and the imperative is the 'unmarked form'.

It should be noted that there are other interpretations of 'marked-ness'. Some interpret it as pertaining to frequency of occurrence, so that the more frequently found forms are the 'unmarked forms', and the less frequently found ones are the 'marked forms'. Some interpret it as pertaining to specificity. For example, 'bitch' is sex-specific, whereas 'dog' is not. The former is therefore 'marked', whereas the latter is 'unmarked'.

Place

'Place' is a technical term in grammatical description. For example, the sentence, 'Mary closed the door quietly' can be analysed as follows:

Mary / closed / the door / quietly.
S (subject) P (predicator) C (complement) A (adjunct)

We say that it has a structure which consists of four 'places'. Filling these four 'places' are four elements of structure: S (subject), P (predicator), C (complement), and A (adjunct). The sentence 'Hurriedly he left' can be analysed as follows:

Hurriedly / he / left
A (adjunct) S (subject) P (predicator)

We say that it has a structure which consists of three places. Filling these three places are three elements of structure: A (adjunct), S (subject), and P (predicator). Notice here that all three elements fill a different place from those in the previous sentence (see Halliday 1961; see also Berry 1977: 62–71 for detailed explanation and exemplification).

Hence, a three-part exchange has a structure which consists of three 'places'. Filling these three places are the elements of structure I (initiation), R (response), F (follow-up).

Rank scale

A relation among units of grammar in which, going from top (largest) to bottom (smallest), each consists of one or more of the unit next below. For example, a sentence consists of clauses, which in turn consist of groups, which in turn consist of words, which in turn consist of morphemes.

Speech act theory

A theory proposed by a philosopher, J. L. Austin, which analyses utterances as performing actions. It looks at the meaning of an utterance as conveyed by the words and structures, the intention of the speaker in making an utterance, and the effect of the utterance on the addressee.

Chapter 2

Ritual interchanges

A term proposed by Goffman (1967) to describe exchanges whose production are governed by constraints regarding how an individual should handle him/herself in relation to others. For example, in asking somebody to do something, the speaker presents the utterance as a mere request that can be turned down. The request is, in turn, granted with good spirit. Or, if the request is turned down, a reason for turning down the request is given. Hence, no matter what the outcome of the request is, the one who makes the request is let off the hook and a good relationship with the other is maintained (see Goffman 1967: 19–22).

Primary knower

A notion proposed by Berry (1987) to describe an interlocutor who has the missing information in an exchange initiated by a question. For example:

A: What's the time please?
B: Three fifteen.
A: Thank you.

B is the 'primary knower', because he knows the time. A is described as the 'secondary knower' by Berry. However, in the following exchange, the teacher is the 'primary knower', because he already knows the answer to the question:

T: What is the capital of France?
P: Paris.
T: Well done.

Chapter 3

Class

A linguistic term for groupings of linguistic items which are more likely to represent certain elements of structure than to represent others. For example, the items 'open', 'has gone off', 'sang', 'has taken over', are all more likely to represent the element of structure P (predicator) than any other elements. On this basis, they are grouped together with other similar items to form a class, called 'verbal group'.

Similarly, the items 'quickly', 'last year', 'in their bath', 'by chance', are more likely to represent the element A (adjunct) and they are considered to belong to a class called 'adverbial group'.

In spoken discourse, there are groupings of acts which are more likely to represent one element of structure than others. For example, elicitations and requests are more likely to represent initiations than responses. They therefore belong to the same class.

Illocutionary act

A term in speech act theory which refers to the speech action that is performed in saying something. For example, if at the dinner table, A says to B 'Can you reach the salt?', intending to get B to pass the salt, then A is performing the illocutionary act of 'requesting' B to pass the salt.

Realization

The physical expression (either in speech or in writing) of an abstract linguistic unit. For example, the speech act 'request' is an abstract unit. It can be expressed in a variety of forms. For example, 'Will you close the door?', 'Close the door, please', and 'Would you mind closing the door?', are all linguistic realizations of the act of 'requesting' the hearer to close the door. It is used interchangeably with actualization, exponence, and representation.

Chapter 4

AB-event

The term 'AB-event' is used by Labov and Fanshel (1977) to refer to an event or any piece of information that both participants know that they both have knowledge of.

Assertive and non-assertive forms

Examples of assertive forms are some, somebody, something, sometimes, already. Examples of non-assertive forms are any, anybody, anything, ever. According to Quirk *et al.* (1985), assertive forms are usually associated with positive statements, whereas non-assertive forms are usually associated with questions. For example:

(1) Have you sent *any* letters off?
(2) Yes, I have sent *some* off *already*.

(2) asserts that something is true, whereas (1) does not. This is why an assertive form is used in the former, whereas a non-assertive form is used in the latter.

Key and termination

'Key' refers to the pitch level of a tone unit. According to Brazil *et al.* (1980: 24), in English, no matter how wide a speaker's pitch range is, he uses only three pitch contrasts: low, mid, and high. Brazil *et al.* refer to them as 'keys'.

The pitch of the tonic syllable is referred to as 'termination'. In Brazil's system, there are three significant contrasts in the system of termination: low, mid, and high. For example:

key	termination
high	<u>GO</u> //
mid // p he's GOing to	
low	

The tonic syllable in the above utterance is 'go'. It is spoken in mid key with high termination.

Prominence

The degree to which a sound or a syllable stands out from others. According to Brazil *et al.*, making any word prominent by putting stress on it is a meaningful choice. For example, in saying 'JOHNny IS coming', the speaker is making 'is' prominent. By doing so, he is conveying the information that Johnny *is* coming, as opposed to the assumption that Johnny *is not* coming (see Brazil *et al.* 1980: 41).

Referring and proclaiming tone

Brazil *et al.* (1980) distinguish five tones on the basis of how each contributes to the communicative value of an act of speech:

(1) fall-rise, referred to as 'referring tone' (r)
(2) fall, referred to as 'proclaiming tone' (p)
(3) rising, referred to as 'referring tone' (r+)
(4) rise-fall, referred to as 'proclaiming tone' (p+)
(5) level (o)

The major distinction is between referring tone (r) and proclaiming tone (p); r+ and p+ are variants of r tone and p tone, respectively. According to Brazil *et al.*, in choosing r tone for a particular part of an utterance, the speaker is marking it as shared knowledge between himself and the addressee. In choosing p tone, he is marking it as something new. For example (Brazil *et al.* 1980: 16):

(1) //r he'll be TWENty // p in AUGust //

(2) //p he'll be TWENty // r in AUGust //

In (1), the speaker is telling the addressee *when* a mutual acquaintance will have his twentieth birthday. In (2), however, he is telling the addressee *how old* the acquaintance will be in August. In other words, the shared knowledge in (1) is the age (twenty) and the new information is the time (August). In (2), the shared knowledge is the time (August) and the new information is the age (twenty).

Both r+ tone and r tone are used to indicate shared knowledge. The choice of one over the other is determined by role relationship. r+ is used by the dominant speaker, or one who wants to *claim* dominance (see ibid.: 54).

Both p+ tone and p tone are used to indicate new information. The p+ tone is used when the speaker wants to signal that the information provided is not only new to the addressee but to him/herself as well. For example:

//p+ it's <u>RAIN</u>ing//

In using the p+ tone, the speaker indicates that he also did not know that it was raining. There is often an emotional element associated with the p+ tone, such as surprise, delight, disappointment, and so on.

Finally, the level tone is used in oblique discourse; that is, discourse in which the speaker is orientated towards the language, when the tone group boundary is not a potential completion. An example would be when the following is read aloud from print.

//o in <u>AUG</u>ust // p he'll be <u>TWEN</u>ty//

Chapter 5

Face-threatening act

According to Brown and Levinson (1987), intrinsically face-threatening acts are acts which by their nature run contrary to the face wants of the addressee and/or of the speaker. Their notion of 'face', which is adopted from Goffman (1967), refers to the public image that every member of society wants to preserve for himself. It is something which is emotionally invested and can be lost, maintained, or enhanced. Therefore, it is something which must be constantly attended to in interaction.

Brown and Levinson suggest that there are two kinds of face: negative face, which is the want of every adult person that his/her actions be unimpeded by others, and positive face, which is the want of every adult person that his/her wants be desirable to others as well. A face-threatening act is an act which threatens either the positive or negative face of the other party. For example, in asking somebody to do something for you (that is, in making a request), you are putting pressure on him/her to do it. Hence, you are threatening his/her negative face by impeding his/her freedom of action. In criticizing somebody, you are threatening his/her positive face, by showing that you do not care about his/her wants. Therefore, 'requests' and 'criticisms' are both face-threatening acts.

Precondition

Conditions that must be satisfied before a speech act can be effectively performed. For example, one of the preconditions for making a request is that the addressee is able to perform the action. This is why before a request is made, the speaker checks to see if the addressee is able to perform the action. For example, before making a request for a cup of Turkish coffee, the speaker may ask, 'Do you have Turkish coffee?'.

Chapter 6

Exercitives

'Exercitives' is one of the five categories of speech acts in Austin's taxonomy. It is defined as 'the exercise of powers, rights, or influence' (1962: 150). Some of the examples provided by Austin are: appointing, voting, ordering, advising, and warning.

Commissives

'Commissives' is another one of the five categories of speech acts in Austin's taxonomy. They are speech acts which commit the speaker to a certain course of action. Some of the examples given by Austin are: promise, agree, vow, oppose, favour, consent, undertake, contract.

Why-impositives

According to Sadock (1974), 'impositives' are speech acts by which the speaker imposes his/her desire or will upon the addressee. They cover 'order', 'demand', 'request', and 'suggestion'. Why-impositives are impositives which are realized by why-questions. For example, 'Why don't you ...?' and 'Why not ...?'.

Chapter 7

Maxim of modesty

One of the 'maxims of politeness' proposed by Leech (1983) which states that one is to (1) minimize praise of self, and (2) maximize dispraise of self. Leech observes that to violate this maxim is to boast, which is socially unacceptable.

Maxim of sympathy

One of the 'maxims of politeness' proposed by Leech (1983) which states that one is to (1) minimize antipathy between self and others, and (2) maximize sympathy between self and others. This maxim explains why the utterance 'I'm terribly sorry to hear about your cat' is automatically interpreted as a condolence which is an expression of sympathy for misfortune, and the utterance 'I'm delighted to hear about your cat' is automatically interpreted as a congratulation (see Leech 1983: 138–9).

Chapter 8

Contrastive high key

According to Brazil's intonation system, by choosing high key, the speaker is marking the content conveyed in a tone unit as contrastive to whatever has been assumed to be true or whatever has been said before. For example:

```
high                             WIFE
mid    // p this is eLIZabeth // p peter's        //
low
```

Here, a possible contextualization of this utterance is when A asks B if the woman next to Peter is his mistress, B replies by saying that the woman is Elizabeth, who is Peter's wife. The word 'wife' is spoken in high key to indicate that it is contrastive to 'mistress' (see Brazil *et al.* 1980: 28).

Illocutionary intent

The speaker's intention in performing an illocutionary act. For example, in performing an act of asking a question, such as 'What is the time please?', the speaker's intention is to get the hearer to tell the time.

Illocutionary force

A term in speech act theory which refers to the interpretation of the function of an utterance in a given context of situation. For example, the utterance 'Daddy will be home soon' issued by a mother to her child may have the illocutionary force of assertion, prediction, or warning, depending on the context of situation.

Illocutionary verb

A verb which can be used in the formula 'I + verb (+ that) X' to form an utterance in which an illocutionary act is performed (referred to as an explicit performative). For example, 'promise' and 'assert' are illocutionary verbs, because they can be used in the performative formulae 'I promise that I'll be there at six' and 'I assert that the earth is flat' to perform, respectively, the act of 'promising' and 'asserting'. Verbs like 'feel' and 'think' are not illocutionary verbs, because they cannot be used to form explicit performatives. For example, 'I feel that he is not telling the truth' and 'I think he is lying' are not explicit performatives.

Pragmatic presuppositions

There are various definitions of pragmatic presuppositions. However, the following two features are common to all: they are firstly what the speaker assumes to be true in saying something and secondly what the speaker assumes to be shared knowledge between him/herself and the addressee. For example, if the speaker says to the addressee, 'Could you open the door?', he assumes that it is true that the door is closed, that B is able to close the door, and that there is shared knowledge with regard to which door he is referring to. For the various interpretations of the notion of presupposition, see Levinson (1983: Chapter 4).

Proposition

The basic unit of meaning that a sentence expresses. A proposition consists of something that is named (entity) and an expression of a state or action (predicate) associated with the entity. For example, the sentence 'That pretty girl next door is my colleague' expresses the propositions that 'the girl is pretty', 'the girl lives next door', and 'the girl is my colleague'.

Chapter 9

Delicacy

A technical term in grammatical description. It is a scale of differentiation. For example, in an analysis of the mood of clauses, we may identify two types of mood: 'indicative' and 'imperative'. In a more detailed analysis of these two types of mood, we may further classify 'indicative' into 'declarative' and 'interrogative', and 'imperative' into 'inclusive imperative' and 'exclusive imperative'. 'Declarative' and 'interrogative' are more delicate categories than 'indicative'. 'Inclusive imperative' and 'exclusive imperative' are more delicate categories than 'imperative'.

Boundary markers

A group of linguistic items such as 'Okay', 'Now', 'Right', 'Good', 'Listen', and so on, usually spoken with falling intonation. Their function is to mark boundaries in conversation. They can be used to mark the end of a topic, the beginning of a topic, or both.

Chapter 10

Syntagmatic and paradigmatic relations

The sequential relationship between linguistic units in a linear order is called syntagmatic relations. The relationship that a linguistic unit has with other linguistic units, given a specific linguistic environment, is called paradigmatic relations. For example:

The cat sat on the mat.
                    floor.
                    bed.

The relationships between 'the', 'cat', 'sat', 'on', 'the', and 'mat' are syntagmatic. The relationships between 'mat', 'floor', and 'bed' are paradigmatic.

Notes

Chapter 1

1 By this, I mean taking the utterance out of the discourse context. A major criticism of speech act theory is that utterances are taken in isolation and the speech acts they perform are determined by introspecting as to whether they satisfy the conditions laid down (known as felicity conditions). (See Austin (1962) and Searle (1969) for the felicity conditions for various speech acts.) This overlooks the fact that what speech act is performed cannot be determined by the linguistic form alone. A lot depends on the context of situation as well as what precedes and follows in the discourse.

2 The term *utterance* as used by Sinclair and Coulthard is a technical term referring to everything said by one speaker before he/she stops speaking and another speaker starts to speak (except in cases of overlap of speech). It is equivalent to a turn. In the discussion in this volume, the word 'utterance' is used to refer to the issuance of a sentence, or a sentence-fragment in a particular context of situation (see Levinson 1983: 18).

3 Sinclair and Coulthard's concept of move structure is borrowed from the structure of the grammatical unit *group*. Consider the sentences below:

(1) *The man next door* is my father's colleague.
(2) *That pretty girl* is my niece.

The *nominal groups* 'the man next door' and 'that pretty girl' have structures as follows:

modifier	modifier	headword	qualifier
	the	man	next door
that	pretty	girl	

The *headword* is obligatory, and the *modifiers* and *qualifiers* are optional. For example, it is possible to have 'The man is my father's colleague.' and 'That girl is my niece.', but not 'The next door is my father's colleague.', and 'That pretty is my niece.'.

4 If there is only one act in the move, then that particular act is the head act. For example, if A says, 'Why are you standing?' and if the context of situation makes it clear that A intends to get the addressee to sit down, then the utterance realizes the act of an invitation to sit down.

5 It should be noted that despite the fact that Sinclair and Coulthard proposed these two criteria for classification, their own taxonomy of acts is not based rigorously on them. Some of the acts are identified in terms of content rather than discourse function. Moreover, the classification, though adequate for classroom discourse, is far too general for other discourse types (see Coulthard 1985: 126; Turner 1987: 66). For example, within the category that solicits a non-verbal response, which is a directive, there is no attempt to distinguish between 'request', 'offer', and 'order'.

Chapter 2

1 Another interpretation could be that Linus does understand Violet's response. However, by pretending not to see the relevance of Violet's response, Linus is implying that he does not share Violet's view that big girls don't play with little boys and therefore does not find her response acceptable. In either interpretation, the effect of Linus's utterance is to indicate the interaction has not been felicitous.

2 The data are recordings from an English lesson in a Hong Kong secondary school. I myself observed the lesson. Details of the lesson have been reported in Tsui (1985).

Chapter 3

1 The term 'class' is borrowed from the linguistic concept of 'class'. See the Glossary.

2 In speech act terminology, we can say that we may perform an illocutionary act in order to achieve a multitude of perlocutionary effects.

3 Austin (1962: Chapters VIII and IX) points out that it is important to distinguish between 'in saying it I was warning him' from 'by saying it I convinced him, or surprised him, or got him to stop'. The former is an illocutionary act, whereas the latter are perlocutionary acts.

4 This precondition is supported by an episode in Lewis Carroll's *Alice's Adventures in Wonderland* (p. 71).

> 'Have some wine,' the March Hare said in an encouraging tone.
> Alice looked all round the table, but there was nothing on it but tea. 'I don't see any wine,' she remarked.
> 'There isn't any,' said the March Hare.
> 'Then it wasn't very civil of you to offer it,' said Alice angrily.

5 In fact, it is better described as a pre-invitation rather than a pre-offer.

6 Halliday (1984: 28) makes a similar distinction between utterances which demand information and those which demand goods and services.

7 Edmondson (1981) refers to a request in which the action cannot be carried out immediately after the utterance of the request as a 'Then-request'.

8 For an interesting discussion of 'say' as a general reporting speech act verb, see Caldas-Coulthard (1987: 153). In her data, 'said' is used to report elicitations, directives, informatives, replies, and acceptances.

9 It should be noted, however, that sometimes the distinction between the reports of requestives and elicitations is not so neat and tidy. Both can be, and often are, reported by *asked if*. For example, ' "Would you like another drink?" she asked' can be reported as 'She *asked* me *if* I would like another drink.'; and ' "Do you speak French?" she asked' can also be reported as 'She *asked* me *if* I spoke French.' The important distinction between requestives and

elicitations is that while requestives can be reported by *asked to* and *asked if*, elicitations cannot be reported by *asked to*.

10 The technical term 'challenging move' is different from the term 'a challenge' as defined by Labov and Fanshel (1977: 77) who state that 'a challenge is a speech act that asserts or implies a state of affairs that, if true, would weaken a person's claim to be competent in filling the role associated with a valued status'.

11 Taylor and Cameron assert that 'preference' cannot be a purely structural concept which has nothing to do with the psychological or functional sense. They argue that the formal differences between 'preferred' and 'dispreferred' seconds may be motivated by preserving the 'face' of interlocutors, which is the psychological or functional basis for 'preference' organization.

12 The term 'temporization' is borrowed from Garvey (1975). However, the characterization of temporizing acts here is different from Garvey's. To him, 'temporizing acknowledgements' cover utterances in which the addressee would comply but the compliance is postponed and those in which the addressee queries the reason for the request. Here, the latter would be characterized as challenges.

Chapter 4

1 The analysis of questions in Quirk *et al.* (1985) is basically the same as that in Quirk *et al.* (1972).

2 Similar observations have been made by Davies (1988: 42) in her analysis of English questions. The question 'Are the activities of the City of London good for the British economy?' addressed to the Chairman of the Stock Exchange by a radio interviewer does not really seek merely a 'yes' or 'no' answer, but rather the reasons for giving a 'yes' or 'no' answer.

3 For example:

(i) [Portuguese]
  A: Queres café? (Do you want coffee?)
  B: Quero (I want)

(ii) [Mandarin Chinese]
    A: nā dìen yǐng hǎu kàn má? (Is that film good?)
    B: (a) hǎu kàn (good)
       (b) bù hǎu kàn (not good)

Indeed, in Mandarin Chinese, yes–no questions are often presented in alternative form. It is lingua-centric and even misleading to call these questions 'yes–no questions'. For example, (ii) would often occur as 'nā diěn yǐng hǎu bù hǎu kàn?' (Is that film good or not good?). The expected answers to both forms are the same: 'hǎu kàn' (good) or 'bù hǎu kàn' (not good).

4 In Tsui (1987b) I labelled this subclass *elicit:supply*. The label is here changed to *elicit:inform* to bring it into line with the labels for the other subclasses of elicitation in which the second part of the label signifies the response prospected.

5 I am grateful to David Brazil for pointing this out.

Chapter 5

1 The data are recordings of an English lesson in a English-medium primary school in Hong Kong. I wish to thank the principal for her kind assistance and the teacher for allowing me to observe and record the lesson.

2 Although Leech (1983: 216–19) puts 'command' and 'request' into the same category of 'directives', he does note that one of the crucial differences between the two is that a 'command' has the feature 'unconditional', meaning S assumes that H will comply, whereas a 'request' has the feature 'conditional', meaning S assumes that the 'directive' will only take effect if H agrees.

Similarly, although Lyons (1977: 745–9) subsumes 'commands' and 'requests' under the general term 'mands' which are a subclass of 'directives', he notes that the crucial difference between a 'request' and a 'command' is that the former leaves to the addressee the option of refusing to comply with the 'mand', whereas the latter does not.

Butler (1988: 133) suggests that forms which appear to refuse the addressee any options and/or represent the speaker's imposition of authority and will are classified as 'orders', whereas those which explicitly give the addressee options are classified as 'requests'.

3 The term 'unmarked form' refers to the linguistic concept of markedness (see 'marked form' in the Glossary entry for Chapter 1).

4 Halliday (1984) observes that no matter how rarely we may actually use an imperative in giving orders, we have a feeling that it is in some sense the unmarked way of doing so.

5 Churchill (1978: 66) proposes that there are two parts to all 'requests': the first addresses the addressee's right to agree or refuse to comply, and the second states what act the speaker would like the addressee to perform.

6 Gordon and Lakoff (1975: 85–6) assert that the utterance 'I want you to take this garbage out' conveys a 'request'. They argue that because one of the felicity conditions of a 'request' is 'S wants H to do A', then if the speaker S sincerely requests that addressee H do A, then S wants H to do A. They call this speaker-based sincerity condition and propose that one can convey a 'request' by asserting this speaker-based sincerity condition. This kind of analysis overlooks the fact that when the speaker of the above utterance does not give the addressee the option of non-compliance by virtue of his right or power/authority over the latter, it can hardly be characterized as a 'request'.

7 Leech gives the following example: if a passenger asks a driver to stop the bus at the bus-stop, very little politeness is required, because it is the driver's duty to let passengers off at bus-stops. However, if a passenger asks a driver to stop the bus at a place where there is no bus-stop, then a great deal of politeness accompanied with apologies and accounts will be necessary, because the driver has no obligation to do so.

Mitchell-Kernan and Kernan (1977) in their study of directives from role-playing data discover that those which took the form of statement of personal desire, i.e. needs and wants, are characterized by a clear expectancy of compliance by the addressee.

8 One could argue that in inviting someone for supper, the person who invites is also committing himself to the action of preparing the supper. However, as far as the utterance is concerned, the speaker is trying to get the addressee to commit himself to coming for supper. It is on this basis that I consider it an addressee action.

9 In the actual data, J chooses to apologize for not being able to go to the meeting instead of thanking K for the favour done. This is because K is going to the meeting as well and J is taking his inability to go to the meeting as a debt owed to K as well.

10 Hancher (1979) asserts that certain speech acts combine directive with commissive illocutionary force and he calls them 'hybrid speech acts'. According to him, speech acts like 'offer' have hybrid nature because to offer something to somebody is both to direct that person's action and also to commit oneself to a corresponding course of action.

11 Here, we can see that when performative verbs are used, they do not necessarily perform the named action.

12 Lakoff (1977) introduced rules of politeness, one of which is to give the addressee options. She points out that very often this form of politeness is conventional rather than real. In certain circumstances, the speaker knows that the addressee does not really have a choice and yet he has to behave as though the latter does, for the sake of politeness.

13 According to Leech (1983), utterances like 'Can you answer the telephone?' can be considered preliminary to a request. He suggests that (1) can be considered a compression of a more elaborate dialogue in (2):

(1) **A:** Can you answer the phone?
    B: OK.

(2) **A:** Can you answer the phone?
    B: Yes.
    A: In that case, please answer it.
    B: OK.

Chapter 6

1 Prospecting a non-verbal action refers to both getting the addressee to do something and *not* to do something. For example, the non-verbal action prospected in (1) is to stop playing with the matches.

2 This does not mean that an 'order' and an advisory 'directive' are

necessarily realized by an imperative and a why-impositive, respectively. An 'order' can be realized by a why-impositive, as in 'Why don't you shut up' just as an advisory 'directive' can be realized by an imperative as in 'Don't try to exchange your money at a bank', as in (2).

3 Green (1975) suggests that the maker of a 'suggestion', which is characterized as an *advisive* here, does not care quite as much whether the action he suggests is carried out or not as does the giver of an 'order' or a 'request'.

4 Green (1975: 124) suggests that 'warnings' are made in the interest of the addressee, not the speaker. She also points out that the giver of a warning assumes that some ill will befall the addressee if he does not listen to it.

5 Katz (1977), in classifying performative types, points out that if the basis of classification is differences in the purpose of communication, then semantic differences among 'advise', 'counsel', and 'recommend' should not be the basis for recognizing them as new subtypes under *advisive*.

6 Leech (1983) claims that the verb 'advise' can be either assertive or directive. For example, in 'She advised us that there had been a mistake', the verb 'advise' is used in an assertive sense, whereas in 'She advised us to arrive early', it is used in a directive sense. However, the verb 'warn' is simultaneously assertive and directive. For example, 'They warned us that the food was expensive' and 'They warned us to take enough money'. According to Leech, although these two sentences have different syntactic constructions, the illocutionary meaning of 'warn' is, in each case, simultaneously assertive (warning H that something will happen if . . .) and directive (warning H to do something about it).

7 This is similar to a notice in public areas which says 'Thank you for not smoking' which is a *directive* to prohibit smoking.

8 In fact, the example that Sadock gives does not have a reading of 'warning', even when the speaker is talking about his reflex action. It is a kind of 'condition' imperative which shows an if–then sequence (see Bolinger 1977).

9 The very fact that the utterance is considered ambiguous by Sadock undermines his point about 'warning' and 'threaten' not being separate illocutionary acts. By pointing out that the utterance is a 'warning' at one reading and 'threaten' at another, he is, in fact, saying that they are separate illocutionary acts.

Chapter 7

1 Informatives include many of the acts which have been identified as 'verdictives' and 'expositives' by Austin (1962), or 'assertives' by Searle (1979), such as 'state', 'inform', 'predict', 'report', 'criticize', 'praise', etc., as well as those which have been identified as 'behabitives' (Austin 1962) or 'expressives' (Searle 1979), such as 'thank', 'apologize', 'congratulate', etc.

2 Goffman (1974: 503) observes that in ordinary informal talk, the recounting of a personal experience by a participant is often interposed with signals of understanding, approval, sympathy, etc. Stubbs (1981), however, maintains that an 'informing' act does not prospect a response.

3 Here, *report* includes what Goffman (1974: 504) refers to as 'a replay of personal experience'. According to Goffman, a 'replay' is more than merely reporting. It is something that the listener can empathize with.

4 Drew (1984) characterizes reportings as giving detailed accounts of some activities or circumstances without explicitly stating the implications of the reportings.

5 Heritage (1984) points out that a free-standing 'oh' in response to an 'informing' is not frequently found in his data. Very often an 'oh' is followed by an assessment of the good or bad news delivered (see Heritage 1984: 302; see also the ensuing discussion in this chapter).

6 Heritage observes that 'yes' is regularly associated with responses that assert prior knowledge of the information delivered in the previous turn.

7 The terms 'upgrade' and 'downgrade' are borrowed from Pomerantz (1978, 1984).

8 Leech (1983: 136) points out that while it is perfectly acceptable to agree with a commendation of other people, it is socially unacceptable to agree with a commendation of oneself. For example:

A: They were so kind to us.
B: Yes they were, weren't they.

A: You were so kind to us.
*B: Yes I was, wasn't I.

9 Manes and Wolfson (1981) point out that 'compliments' are almost always addressed to the person who owns the object being complimented or who is himself being complimented.

10 In Pomerantz (1984: 90), this kind of response is considered an agreement with the prior negative evaluation. However, she adds a caveat that it is a weak agreement, because it also undermines the negative evaluation by proposing that the negative attribute is less negative than the prior speaker had proposed. Here, I argue that it is a downgrading rather than an agreement.

11 Pomerantz (1978: 88) refers to this kind of assessment as 'self-praise'.

12 Pomerantz (1978: 88) points out that there is a system of constraints governing how interlocutors may praise themselves. The constraints may be enforced by others, so that a speaker who praises himself may be criticized by others, either to his face or behind his back. They can also be enforced by the speaker himself by adding a disclaimer or a qualification when he self-praises.

13 Goffman (1971: 79) refers to 'greetings' and 'farewells' as 'access rituals' which mark a change in the accessibility of the interlocutors.

Chapter 8

1 Bach and Harnish (1979) propose a subcategory of 'responsives' under the general category of 'constatives'. But their responsives are restricted to responses to questions.

2 Searle formulates a set of conditions under which a 'promise' is considered to be successfully performed. The first condition is 'that normal input and output conditions obtain'. By 'output', he means the conditions for intelligible speaking, and by 'input', he means the conditions of understanding. These conditions include such things as both the speaker and the addressee know how to speak the language; both are conscious of what they are doing; both have no physical impediment to communication; and so on.

Keenan and Schieffelin (1983) propose four prerequisites for a speaker to make a discourse topic known to the listener. They are:

(1) the speaker must secure the attention of the listener;
(2) the speaker must articulate his utterance clearly;
(3) the speaker must provide sufficient information for the listener to identify objects, etc., included in the discourse topic;
(4) the speaker must provide sufficient information for the listener to construct the semantic relations obtaining between the referents in the discourse topic.

Keenan and Schieffelin point out that (1) and (2) are general requirements of any successful communication and (3) and (4) are specific requirements of topic establishment. These four prerequisites correspond to presuppositions (e) and (f) proposed here.

3 The term 'challenge' is used in opposition to 'supporting' the assumption or pragmatic presuppositions of the preceding utterance. It does not have the connotation of aggressiveness. See Burton (1980: 142ff.) where the term originates. See also note 5 below.

4 It should be noted that elicitations which are prefaced by 'Do you know' do not presuppose that the addressee has the information. Hence, a declaration of ignorance does not challenge its presuppositions.

Katz (1972) points out that a declaration of ignorance is not a possible answer, because it is not responding to the content of the question, but rather to the speaker's presumption that the addressee has the answer to the question. He further points out that in declaring ignorance, the addressee is saying that the speaker's presumption is false.

5 Burton introduces the notion of 'discourse framework' which pertains to the presuppositions of the initiating move and the interactional expectation set up by that move. She proposes that any move which maintains the framework set up by a preceding initiating move

is a 'supporting move'. A 'supporting move' facilitates the progress of the topic presented in the preceding utterance. Any move which breaks up the discourse framework and holds up the progress of the topic is a 'challenging move'.

6 The technical term 'challenging move' is different from the term 'challenge' as defined by Labov and Fanshel (1977: 77) who state:

> A challenge is a speech act that asserts or implies a state of affairs that, if true, would weaken a person's claim to be competent in filling the role associated with a valued status.

7 According to Lakoff, a question like 'What's the time please?' has the underlying structure 'I request that you supply the information necessary for us to know what time it is'. Utterances like those in (a) and (b) given in (4) respond to the complement of the question and are considered to be 'answers', whereas utterances like those in (c) to (i) respond to the verb of questioning itself and are considered to be 'replies'. She considers them all appropriate responses, although some of them do not satisfy the questioner (see Lakoff 1973: 460–1). In the present description, (c) and (i) are characterized as challenging moves.

8 The following is an example of a challenging move occurring after a responding move:

[BCET:A:1]
I 1 C: Do you get the bus?
R 2 B: Yeah.
→ C 3 C: The bus?
R 4 B: And – the tube.
I 5 C: How long's it take?
R 6 B: It's quicker.
→ C 7 C: Quicker?
R 8 B: And cheaper.

C's utterances in lines 3 and 7 challenge the presupposition that B has, on both occasions, provided an appropriate piece of information. They are both challenging moves, with elicit:confirm as the head acts.

9 I say 'may be able and willing to' because in saying 'I was won-

dering if you could send me the application forms', the speaker is *not* assuming that *X is able and willing to*, but rather assuming that *there is a possibility that X is able and willing to* (cf. Searle 1969: 66).

10 The term 'temporization' is borrowed from Garvey (1975). However, the characterization of temporizing acts here is different from Garvey's. In his characterization, 'temporizing acknowledgements' cover utterances in which the addressee would comply but the compliance is postponed, and those in which the addressee queries the reason for the request. According to the characterization here, the latter would be characterized as a challenge.

11 The following is a continuation of (44):

[BCET:A:A:22]
C: Could I stay at your place for a bit Rob?
B: um I don't know.
C: I mean you personally wouldn't have any objections, I =
                                            [
→ B: I personally wouldn't but =
C: = know that Rob.
    [
B: = it depends on how long, you know, it doesn't bother me, shouldn't think it would bother Chalks.
C: I could keep myself to myself, I wouldn't intrude.
→ B: No, but – no, except that you'd be in my room.
C: Well not necessarily . . .
    . . . . . .
B: They have hostels in London.
C: I'm not staying in a bloody hostel.
B: It's not as bad as that. I know it sounds as if it's all tramps, but it's not. They're not, they're about two-fifty a night.
C: Yeah, well, seven nights a week you're talking of fourteen, what is it seventeen quid a week.
B: Yeah, yeah I suppose it's a lot isn't it? Especially when you can live at our place for nought.
C: Yeah, well, you don't mind that surely.
B: I don't mind.

Later on in the conversation, B kept suggesting places where C could get accommodation.

12 According to Pomerantz's transcription notation, the words in single parentheses are in doubt, and the figures stand for the duration of silence timed in tenths of a second.

Chapter 9

1 Goffman (1971) points out that when offers are declined, it is not only possible to re-offer, but in some cases it is part of the ritual to do so.

2 Stubbs proposes a category called 'endorse' and defines it as explicitly supporting the preceding utterances. It 'backs up, adds weight to, approves, upholds, chimes in with, ratifies, or recognizes as relevant previous talk' (Stubbs 1983: 190). The category *endorsement* proposed here is very close in nature to it, except that in Stubbs' description, 'endorse' is a response, whereas an *endorsement* is a follow-up.

Chapter 10

1 Usually in telephone conversations, the identification/recognition sequence starts in the second move, as pointed out by Schegloff (1979: 28). However, in this instance, Jef has already been told that the caller is Sandy. This is why we have Jef identifying Sandy in the first move.

2 The example is taken from Coulthard (1981: 19). The available options, however, are my own additions.

3 In Chapter 2, we pointed out that the unit 'sequence' had been proposed as the possible unit above the exchange (see Coulthard and Brazil 1981). However, because the structure of a 'sequence' has yet to be identified, it was not proposed as a unit above the exchange in the hierarchical rank scale (see Chapter 2, note 3).

4 As Coulthard and Brazil (1981: 95) point out, a low termination marks the point at which prospective constraints stop; that is, the move no longer expects a further response.

5 X's utterance is not responding to the immediately preceding question, but to H's suggestion of going to the Spring Deer, which is not shown in the text.

Suggestions for further reading

Chapter 1

1 For a concise and succinct introduction to Conversation Analysis, Speech Act Theory, and Discourse Analysis, read Coulthard (1985) *An Introduction to Discourse Analysis*, Chapters 2, 4, and 6. For more recent developments in Conversation Analysis, read Heritage (1989) 'Current developments in conversational analysis'.

2 For a detailed introduction to the methodology and basic findings of Conversation Analysis, read Levinson (1983) *Pragmatics*, Chapter 6.

3 For a discussion of the concerns of Conversation Analysis and how they differ from those of linguistics, read Lee (1987) 'Prologue: Talking organisation', and Sharrock and Anderson (1987) 'Epilogue. The definition of alternatives: Some sources of confusion in interdisciplinary discussion', both in Button and Lee (eds.) (1987) *Talk and Social Organization*.

4 For an explanation of the conception of the Sinclair and Coulthard descriptive system, read Coulthard (1981) 'Developing the description' in Coulthard and Montgomery (eds.) (1981) *Studies in Discourse Analysis*.

5 To understand better the Sinclair and Coulthard descriptive system and the system proposed in this book, read Halliday (1961) 'Categories of the theory of grammar'. The article first appeared in *Word* 17/3: 241–92. It is reprinted in Kress (ed.) (1976) *Halliday: System and Function in Language*, with the last section deleted. The full version is better because in the last section, Halliday draws an analogy between the categories and the meals in a day which makes it easier to understand the categories.

6 Berry (1977) *An Introduction to Systemic Linguistics*, Vols. I and II, gives a very clear, readable, and detailed explanation of the basic concepts in systemic grammar. For the purpose of understanding the Sinclair and Coulthard system and the systemic terminologies used in this book, read Vol. I, particularly Chapters 5 to 9.

7 Sinclair and Coulthard (1975) *Towards an Analysis of Discourse*, Chapter 3, presents the entire system of analysis and Chapter 4 applies the system to two pieces of classroom discourse data. Chapter 5 contains a report on the problems encountered in applying the system to other situations such as doctor–patient interviews, media discussions, and committee meetings. (A more detailed discussion of the findings of these applications is found in Coulthard and Montgomery (1981).) This chapter also contains an interesting discussion of their theoretical justification of their proposal of discourse as a separate level of linguistic patterning. This is a very important chapter which helps us to see that the Sinclair and Coulthard descriptive system is not just one of the many descriptive tools for analysing classroom language, but rather a theoretical model of linguistic description.

8 For Searle's own exposition of 'indirect speech act', read Searle (1979), Chapter 2. Read also Coulthard (1985: 26–30) and Levinson (1983: 263–75). For a critical discussion of the concept of 'indirect speech act', read Levinson (1983), Chapter 5: 5.5, where he discusses in detail the theories put forward to explain indirection in speech acts—'idiom theory' (Sadock 1974), (Green 1975), and 'inference theory' (Gordon and Lakoff 1975). Read also Coulthard (1985: 26–30).

Chapter 2

1 For a thorough discussion of 'supportive interchanges' and 'remedial interchanges', read Goffman (1971) *Relations in Public*, Chapters 3 and 4. Read also Owen (1983: 49–103) *Apologies and Remedial Interchanges*.

2 The most detailed exposition of the notion of 'adjacency pair' is

found in Schegloff and Sacks (1973) 'Opening up closings'. There is also a discussion of the sequential constraints governing 'adjacency pairs' in Schegloff (1968) 'Sequencing in conversational openings'. In this article, Schegloff examines Summons–Answers sequences and the concept of an item being 'officially absent'. Read also Sacks (1972) 'On analyzability of stories by children', in Gumperz and Hymes (eds.) 1972: 325–45.

3 For an excellent discussion of how 'adjacency pairs' fail to account for conversational organization, read Goffman (1981) *Forms of Talk*, Chapter 1.

Chapter 3

1 Levinson's detailed criticism of the discourse analysis approach is contained in his book *Pragmatics* (1983), Chapter 6.

2 For an excellent discussion of the issue of ambiguity in linguistic communication, read Schegloff (1978) 'On some questions and ambiguities in conversation'. This article also contains discussions and examples of the importance of sequential location in utterance description, particularly in pages 81–8.

3 Readers who are interested in important taxonomies of acts proposed in the speech act and linguistic literature should read Austin (1962), Chapter XII; Searle (1979), Chapter 1; Bach and Harnish (1979); Schiffer (1972); Fraser (1974).

4 For a more detailed argument against the position that it is impossible to characterize utterances in terms of action categories and to formulate sequencing rules in conversation, read Tsui (1991d) 'The description of utterances in conversation'.

Chapter 4

1 For Quirk *et al.*'s exposition of the different classes of 'questions', read Quirk *et al.* (1985) *A Comprehensive Grammar of the English Language*, pp. 806–26.

2 For Lyons' detailed analysis of 'questions', read Lyons (1977) *Semantics*, Vol. 2, pp. 753–68. It contains his arguments against the analysis of 'questions' as subtypes of 'mands', which is a general term covering commands, demands, requests, entreaties, and so on. It also contains a very interesting discussion of the various kinds of questions and their presuppositions. The question of what constitutes a valid answer to a question is also dealt with.

3 For a detailed discussion of the intonation of 'questions', read Brazil (1985) *The Communicative Value of Intonation in English*, Chapter 6. It contains an interesting and insightful discussion of how the use of tone and the level of termination—together with the context of interaction, which includes dimensions like who knows what about whose intention—determine the kind of 'question' that an utterance realizes. The kinds of 'questions' dealt with are: declarative questions, yes–no questions, information questions, and social elicitations which are for phatic purposes.

4 For a detailed treatment of the intonation of tag questions and its communicative value, read Brazil (1984) 'Tag questions'.

5 To gain a better understanding of Brazil's intonation system, read Brazil *et al.* (1980) *Discourse Analysis and Language Teaching*, Chapters 1 to 5. There is an audio-tape to go with the examples given in the text and the exercises at the end of each chapter.

6 For a pragmatic analysis of questions, read Hudson (1975) 'The meaning of questions'. In this article, Hudson isolates the various components which together make up the illocutionary meaning of questions. He makes a distinction between illocutionary forces generated by all the components of specific situations and the inherent properties of sentences which are one of these components. Hudson's main concern is the latter. The types of questions dealt with are full polar interrogatives, tags on declaratives, and tags on non-declaratives.

7 For a transformational approach to the analysis of questions, read Katz and Postal (1964) *An Integrated Theory of Linguistic Description*, pp. 70–120. Katz and Postal deal with, in particular, the underlying structures of yes–no questions and wh-questions. They also deal with the analysis of question as a kind of request, the way in which yes–no questions are also wh-questions, and the presuppositions of questions.

Chapter 5

1 For discussions of the differences between 'requests' and 'commands', read Lyons (1977) *Semantics*, Vol. II, Chapter 16: 16.2; Leech (1983) *Principles of Pragmatics*, Chapter 9: 9.2.

2 For an excellent discussion of the different linguistic realizations of 'directives' (which is used by Ervin-Tripp to refer to illocutionary acts which attempt to get the addressee to do something) in different social contexts, read Ervin-Tripp (1976) 'Is Sybil there? The structure of some American English directives'. She presents ample data to demonstrate that there is a systematic relation between the syntactic forms of 'directive' and social features such as familiarity, rank, location, difficulty of task, and whether or not compliance is expected. Read also her article 'Wait for me, Roller Skate!' (1977) which discusses the linguistic realizations of 'directives' used by children and their comprehension of directive intent. Mitchell-Kernan and Kernan (1977) 'Pragmatics of directive choice among children' use the classification scheme proposed by Ervin-Tripp (1976) to examine the social distribution of directive types used by children.

3 Brown and Levinson (1987) *Politeness*, Chapter 5, discusses in great detail how politeness strategies are realized in language. Diagrammatic summaries of the derivation of the strategies can be found on pp. 102, 131, 214. They are based on the basic concepts of 'positive politeness' which attends to the positive self-image that the addressee wants to claim for him/herself, 'negative politeness' which attends to the addressee's want to be 'unimpeded', and going 'off record' in which the speaker's intent is not stated explicitly so that the meaning is negotiable.

Leech (1983: Chapters 5 and 6) lists a number of maxims of politeness which govern the choice of linguistic forms. The maxims are formulated on the scales of cost–benefit, praise–dispraise, agreement–disagreement, antipathy–sympathy; and the relationship between self and other.

Edmondson (1979) 'Illocutionary verb, illocutionary acts and conversational behaviour' proposes the H-Support Maxim and its relation to the notion of politeness.

4 Studies done on 'indirect speech acts' are far too many to list here.

Some of the important ones are as follows. Searle (1979) *Expression and Meaning*, Chapter 2. Levinson (1983) *Pragmatics*, Chapter 5: 5.5–5.7, contains an excellent review of the various theories put forward to account for indirection in speech. Chapter 6: 6.4.3 puts forward a re-analysis of the problems of 'indirect speech act' in the tradition of Conversation Analysis. For some of the theories put forward to account for the interpretation of 'indirect speech acts', read Gordon and Lakoff (1975) 'Conversational postulates' in which they propose a set of postulates that can be used to derive illocutionary force from surface meaning. Their proposal has been criticized by Green (1975) 'How to get people to do things with words' and by Morgan (1977) 'Conversational postulates revisited'. Sadock (1974) *Towards a Linguistic Theory of Speech Acts*, Chapters 4 and 5, proposes that the disparity between force and form arises when a frequently associated use (or idiomatic use) becomes encoded in semantic form. Labov and Fanshel in their work *Therapeutic Discourse* (1977: 71–103), formulate a set of rules for the interpretation of indirect speech acts.

5 Merritt (1976) 'On questions following questions in service encounters' contains a very interesting discussion of the interpretation of customer-request as request for information and request for service. The discussion is exemplified by ample data.

6 Goffman (1971) *Relations in Public*, Chapter 4, contains a very interesting discussion of requests. Goffman perceives requests as a form of remedial work in which the 'requester' asks permission from the 'requestee' to intrude into the latter's territory.

Owen (1983) *Apologies and Remedial Interchanges* makes a close study of Goffman's notion of remedial interchanges, illustrated with ample empirical data.

Chapter 6

1 For a detailed discussion of how true imperatives can be distinguished from 'pseudo-imperatives', read Schreiber (1972) 'Style disjuncts and the performative analysis', pp. 339–45. Schreiber proposes that the acid test is whether style disjuncts such as 'frankly, honestly' can co-occur with the imperative in question.

2 For a detailed discussion of 'whimperatives', read Green (1975) 'How to get people to do things with words'. In this article, Green examines the different approaches to the analysis of whimperatives. Sadock, in *Towards a Linguistic Theory of Speech Acts* (1974: Chapter 6), discusses the formal properties of whimperatives and how they differ from imperative requests. He also discusses, in the same chapter, the formal properties of why-impositives and how they differ from whimperatives.

3 Katz, in *Propositional Structure and Illocutionary Force* (1977: Chapter 6), gives an analysis of the semantic structure of advisives and the justifications for identifying two subtypes of advisives.

4 Leech, in *Principles of Pragmatics* (1983: Chapter 9), discusses the importance of not confusing speech act behaviours with the verbs that are used to describe them. He also makes a classification of illocutionary verbs on the basis of their semantic features.

5 For a detailed treatment of 'warning' and 'threatening', read Fraser (1975a) 'Warning and threatening'. Read also Sadock (1974: Chapter 6). Katz (1977: Chapter 6) contains an interesting discussion of why the verb 'threaten' cannot be used performatively. For a detailed discussion of why certain illocutionary verbs cannot be used performatively, read Vendler (1976) 'Illocutionary suicide'.

6 For the distinction between illocutionary verbs and acts, read Tsui (1987c) 'Aspects of the classification of illocutionary acts and the notion of a perlocutionary act'. In this article, I demonstrate how taxonomies of illocutionary acts are often classifications of speech act verbs rather than speech acts.

Chapter 7

1 For a detailed discussion of back-channel cues, read Goffman (1974) *Frame Analysis*, especially Chapter 13. Here, Goffman makes an interesting comparison between face-to-face informal talk and stage performance.

2 Heritage (1984) 'A change-of-state token and aspects of its sequential placement', in Atkinson and Heritage (eds.) (1984) *Structures of Social Action*, contains ample data on the use of 'oh' in

response to informings. It also contains an interesting discussion of the occurrences of 'oh' in other conversational sequences.

3 Drew (1984) 'Speakers' reportings in invitation sequences' contains an interesting discussion of the properties of reportings. Drew also demonstrates how reportings of activities or circumstances are used to extend and decline invitations.

4 Pomerantz (1978) 'Compliment responses: Notes on the co-operation of multiple constraints', in Schenkein (ed.) 1978: *Studies in the Organization of Conversational Interaction*, and Pomerantz (1984) 'Agreeing and disagreeing with assessments: Some features of preferred/dispreferred turn shapes', in Atkinson and Heritage (eds.) 1984: *Structures of Social Action*, contain very detailed discussion of responses to assessments, compliments, and self-deprecation, exemplified by ample data.

5 Leech (1983) *Principles of Pragmatics*, Chapter 6, contains a brief discussion of the various maxims of politeness, among which the 'approbation maxim' and the 'modesty maxim' are particularly relevant to the discussion of assessments in this chapter.

6 Goffman (1971) *Relations in Public*, Chapters 3 and 4, contains detailed and fascinating discussions of supportive and remedial interchanges. He points out that these interchanges, which have been treated traditionally as empty and trivial, penetrate into almost all encounters between individuals.

Chapter 8

1 For the notion of 'preference organization', read Sacks (1987) 'On the preferences for agreement and contiguity in sequences in conversations'. This is Sacks's public lecture given in 1973 and edited by Schegloff from a tape-recording. It appears in Button and Lee (eds.) (1987: 54–69). Read also Pomerantz (1978) 'Compliment responses: Notes on the co-operation of multiple constraints', in Schenkein (ed.) (1978: 79–112) *Studies in the Organization of Conversational Interaction*; and Pomerantz (1984) 'Agreeing and disagreeing with assessments: Some features of preferred/dispreferred turn shapes', in Atkinson and Heritage (eds.) 1984: *Structures of Social Action*, pp. 57–101. The last two articles also contain a detailed

discussion of compliments, self-deprecation, and their responses, exemplified by ample data.

2 Wolfson and Judd (eds.) (1983) *Sociolinguistics and Language Acquisition* contains a very good selection of articles which discuss a variety of speech acts based on data analysis. Of relevance to this chapter are the following articles:

(a) Nessa Wolfson, 'An empirically based analysis of complimenting in American English'. It discusses the functions of compliments to create or maintain solidarity, to soften criticism, to replace greeting routines, to open conversations, and so on; the topic of compliments; the relationship between the status and sex of the interlocutors and the kinds of compliment given. The discussion is based on about one thousand examples of compliments that occur in her data.

(b) Joan Manes, 'Compliments: a mirror of cultural values'. It discusses how compliments and their responses express cultural values.

(c) Lynne D'Amico-Reisner, 'An analysis of the surface structure of disapproval exchanges'. The term 'disapproval' as used in this article roughly corresponds to making a negative evaluation of the addressee. The data presented are interesting.

(d) Joan Rubin, 'How to tell when someone is saying "No" revisited', on how to recognize negative responses, how to respond negatively, and the social parameters involved.

3 For the notion of 'face', read Goffman (1967) *Interaction Ritual: Essays on Face-to-Face Behaviour*. For the application of this notion to the analysis of speech acts, read Brown and Levinson (1987) *Politeness: Some Universals in Language Usage*, Chapter 3.

Chapter 9

For the subsequent development of conversation after a negative response, read Davidson (1984) 'Subsequent versions of invitations, offers, requests, and proposals dealing with potential or actual rejection', in Heritage and Atkinson (eds.) 1984: *Structures of Social Action*.

Chapter 10

1 For the concept of 'system', read Halliday (1961) 'Categories of the theory of grammar'. Read also Berry (1977), Vol. I, Chapter 8, for detailed explanation and exemplification of this concept.

2 For a thorough discussion of how conversation is brought to a close and the functions of utterances occurring in the 'closing section' of a conversation, read Schegloff and Sacks (1973) 'Opening up closings'.

3 For the notion of an 'insertion sequence', read Schegloff (1972) 'Notes on a conversational practice: Formulating place', in Sudnow (ed.) 1972: *Studies in Social Interaction.*

Bibliography

Atkinson, J. and **J. Heritage.** 1984. *Structures of Social Action.* Cambridge: Cambridge University Press.
Austin, J. L. 1962. *How To Do Things With Words.* Oxford: Clarendon Press.

Bach, K. and **R. M. Harnish.** 1979. *Linguistic Communication and Speech Acts.* Cambridge, Mass.: MIT Press.
Benson, J., M. Cummings, and **W. Greaves.** (eds.) 1988. *Linguistics in a Systemic Perspective.* North Holland: John Benjamins.
Berry, M. 1977. *An Introduction to Systemic Linguistics,* Vols. I and II. London: Batsford.
Berry M. 1981. 'Systemic linguistics and discourse analysis: A multi-layered approach to exchange structure', in Coulthard and Montgomery (eds.) 1981.
Berry M. 1982. Review article: M. A. K. Halliday (1978) *Language as Social Semiotic: The Social Interpretation of Language and Meaning* in *Nottingham Linguistic Circular.* 1: 64–94.
Berry M. 1987. 'Is teacher an unanalyzed concept?', in Halliday and Fawcett (eds.), Vol. I, 1987.
Bolinger, D. L. 1967. 'The imperative in English', in *To Honor Roman Jakobson I.* The Hague: Mouton.
Bolinger, D. L. 1977. *Meaning and Form.* London: Longman.
Brazil, D. 1984. 'Tag questions', in *Ilha Do Desterro—a Bilingual Journal of Language and Literature.* No. 11.
Brazil, D. 1985. *The Communicative Value of Intonation in English. Discourse Analysis Monograph,* No. 8. English Language Research, University of Birmingham.
Brazil, D., M. Coulthard, and **C. Johns.** 1980. *Discourse Analysis and Language Teaching.* London: Longman.
Brown, P. and **S. Levinson.** 1987. *Politeness: Some Universals in Language Usage.* Cambridge: Cambridge University Press.
Burton, D. 1980. *Dialogue and Discourse.* London: Routledge and Kegan Paul.
Burton, D. 1981. 'Analyzing spoken discourse', in Coulthard and Montgomery (eds.) 1981.
Butler, C. S. 1988. 'Politeness and semantics of modalised directives', in Benson, Cummings, and Greaves (eds.) 1988.
Button, G. and **J. R. E. Lee.** (eds.) 1987. *Talk and Social Organization.* Philadelphia: Multilingual Matters.

Caldas-Coulthard, C. R. 1987. 'Reporting speech', in Coulthard (ed.) 1987.

Churchill, L. 1978. *Questioning Strategies in Sociolinguistics*. Rowley, Mass.: Newbury House.

Cole, P. and **J. Morgan.** (eds.) 1975. *Syntax and Semantics Vol. 3: Speech Acts*. New York: Academic Press.

Coulmas, F. (ed.) *Conversational Routine: Explorations in Standardized Communication Situation and Prepatterned Speech*. The Hague: Mouton.

Coulthard, M. 1981. 'Developing the description', in Coulthard and Montgomery (eds.) 1981.

Coulthard M. 1985. *An Introduction to Discourse Analysis*. London: Longman.

Coulthard, M. 1987a. 'Intonation in discourse', in Coulthard (ed.) 1987.

Coulthard, M. (ed.) 1987b. *Discussing Discourse*. English Language Research Monographs. University of Birmingham.

Coulthard, M. (ed.) 1992. *Advances in Spoken Discourse Analysis*. London: Routledge.

Coulthard, M. and **M. Ashby.** 1976. 'A linguistic description of doctor–patient interviews', in Wadsworth and Robinson (eds.) 1976. *Studies in Everyday Medical Life*. London: Robertson.

Coulthard, M. and **D. Brazil.** 1981. 'Exchange structure', in Coulthard and Montgomery (eds.) 1981.

Coulthard, M. and **M. Montgomery.** (eds.) 1981. *Studies in Discourse Analysis*. London: Routledge and Kegan Paul.

D'Amico-Reisner, L. 1983. 'An analysis of the surface structure of disapproval exchanges', in Wolfson and Judd (eds.) 1983.

Davidson, J. 1984. 'Subsequent versions of initiations, offers, requests and proposals dealing with potential or actual rejection', in Atkinson and Heritage (eds.) 1984.

Davies, E. 1988. 'English questions: a "significance-generating device" for building in context', in Steiner and Veltman (eds.) 1988.

Dressler, W. (ed.) 1978. *Current Trends in Text Linguistics*. Berlin: de Gruyter.

Drew, P. 1984. 'Speakers' reportings in invitation sequences', in Atkinson and Heritage (eds.) 1984.

Edmondson, W. 1979. 'Harris on performatives'. *Journal of Linguistics* 15: 331–4.

Edmonson, W. 1981. *Spoken Discourse – A Model for Analysis*. London: Longman.

Ervin-Tripp, S. 1976. 'Is Sybil there? The structure of American English directives'. *Language in Society* 5: 25–66.

Ervin-Tripp, S. 1977. 'Wait for me, Roller Skate', in Ervin-Tripp and Mitchell-Kernan (eds.) 1977.

Ervin-Tripp, S. and **C. Mitchell-Kernan.** (eds.) 1977. *Child Discourse*. New York: Academic Press.

Fawcett, R., M. A. K. Halliday, S. Lamb, and **A. Makkai.** (eds.) 1984. *The Semiotics of Language and Culture*, Vol. I. London: Frances Pinter.

Firth, J. R. 1935. 'The technique of semantics', in Firth, J. R. (ed.) 1957.

Firth, J. R. 1957. *Papers in Linguistics 1934–1951*. London: Oxford University Press.

Franck, D. 1981. 'Seven sins of pragmatics: Theses about speech and theory, conversational analysis, linguistics and rhetoric', in Parret, Sbisa, and Verschueren (eds.) 1981.

Fraser, B. 1974. 'An analysis of vernacular performative verbs', in Shuy and Bailey (eds.) 1974.

Fraser, B. 1975a. 'Warning and threatening'. *Centrum* 3/2, Fall 1975: 169–80.
Fraser, B. 1975b. 'Hedged performatives', in Cole and Morgan (eds.) 1975.
Fries, C. C. 1952. *The Structure of English*. New York: Harcourt Brace.

Garvey, C. 1975. 'Requests and responses in children's speech'. *Journal of Child Language* 2: 41–63.
Goffman, E. 1967. *Interaction Ritual: Essays on Face-to-Face Behaviour*. New York: Anchor Books.
Goffman, E. 1971. *Relations in Public*. New York: Harper and Row.
Goffman, E. 1974. *Frame Analysis*. New York: Harper and Row.
Goffman, E. 1976. 'Replies and responses'. *Language in Society* 5: 257–313.
Goffman, E. 1981. *Forms of Talk*. Oxford: Blackwell.
Gordon, D. and G. Lakoff. 1975. 'Conversational postulates', in Cole and Morgan (eds.) 1975.
Green, G. M. 1975. 'How to get people to do things with words', in Cole and Morgan (eds.) 1975.
Grice, H. P. 1975. 'Logic and conversation', in Cole and Morgan (eds.) 1975.
Gumperz, J. J. and D. Hymes. (eds.) 1972. *Directions in Sociolinguistics*. New York: Holt, Rinehart, and Winston.

Halliday, M. A. K. 1961. 'Categories of the theory of grammar'. *Word* 17/3: 241–92. Reprinted in Kress, G. (ed.) 1976.
Halliday, M. A. K. 1963. 'Class in relation to the axis of chain and choice in language'. *Linguistics* 2: 5–15.
Halliday, M. A. K. 1984. 'Language as code and language as behaviour: a systemic functional interpretation of the nature and ontogenesis of dialogue', in Fawcett, Halliday, Lamb, and Makkai (eds.), Vol. I, 1984.
Halliday, M. A. K. and R. P. Fawcett. (eds.) 1987. *New Developments in Systemic Linguistics*, Vol. I. London: Frances Pinter.
Hancher, M. 1979. 'The classification of co-operative illocutionary acts'. *Language in Society* 8: 1–14.
Harris, S. 1980. *Language Interaction in Magistrates' Courts*. Unpublished PhD thesis, University of Nottingham.
Heritage, J. C. 1984. 'A change-of-state-token and aspects of its sequential placement', in Atkinson and Heritage (eds.) 1984.
Heritage, J. C. 1989. 'Current developments in conversation analysis', in Roger and Bull (eds.) 1989.
Heritage, J. C. and J. Atkinson. 1984. 'Introduction', in Atkinson and Heritage (eds.) 1984.
Hewings, M. 1987. 'Intonation and feedback in the EFL classroom', in Coulthard (ed.) 1987.
Huddleston, R. D. 1984. *Introduction to the Grammar of English*. Cambridge: Cambridge University Press.
Hudson, R. A. 1975. 'The meaning of questions'. *Language* 51: 1–31.

Jefferson, G. 1972. 'Side sequences', in Sudnow (ed.) 1972.
Jespersen, O. 1933. *Essentials of English Grammar*. London: Allen and Unwin.

Kachru, B. B. and H. F. W. Stahlke. (eds.) 1972. *Current Trends in Stylistics*. Edmonton, Alberta: Linguistic Research.

Kachru, B. B. *et al.* (eds.) 1973. *Issues in Linguistics: Papers in Honour of Henry and Renee Kahane.* Urbana: University of Illinois Press.

Katz, J. J. 1972. *Semantic Theory.* New York: Harper and Row.

Katz, J. J. 1977. *Propositional Structure and Illocutionary Force.* New York: Crowell.

Katz, J. J. and P. M. Postal. 1964. *An Integrated Theory of Linguistic Description.* Cambridge, Mass.: MIT Press.

Keenan, E. O. 1983. 'Conversational competence in children', in Ochs and Schieffelin (eds.) 1983. First appeared in *Journal of Child Language* I/2: 163–83.

Keenan, E. O. and B. Schieffelin. 1983. 'Topic as a discourse notion: A study of topic in the conversation of children and adults', in Ochs and Schieffelin (eds.) 1983. First appeared in C. Li (ed.) 1976: *Subject and Topic.* New York: Academic Press.

Kress, G. (ed.) 1976. *Halliday: System and Function in Language.* London: Oxford University Press.

Labov, W. 1972. *Sociolinguistic Patterns.* Philadelphia: University of Pennsylvania Press.

Labov, W. and D. Fanshel. 1977. *Therapeutic Discourse.* New York: Academic Press.

Lakoff, R. 1973. 'Questionable answers and answerable questions', in B. B. Kachru *et al.* (eds.) 1973.

Lakoff, R. 1977. 'Politeness, pragmatics and performatives', in Rogers, Wall, and Murphy (eds.) 1977.

Lee, J. R. E. 1987. 'Prologue: Talking organisation', in Button and Lee (eds.) 1987.

Leech, G. 1983. *Principles of Pragmatics.* London: Longman.

Leech, G. and J. Svartvik. 1975. *A Communicative Grammar of English.* London: Longman.

Levinson, S. 1981. 'The essential inadequacies of speech act models of dialogue', in Parret, Sbisa, and Verschueren (eds.) 1981.

Levinson, S. 1983. *Pragmatics.* Cambridge: Cambridge University Press.

Lyons, J. 1977. *Semantics I and II.* Cambridge: Cambridge University Press.

Lyons, J. 1981. *Language and Linguistics.* Cambridge: Cambridge University Press.

Mackay, A. and D. Merill (eds.) 1976. *Issues in the Philosophy of Language: Proceedings of the 1972 Oberlin Colloquium in Philosophy.* Yale: Yale University Press.

Manes, J. 1983. 'Compliments: a mirror of cultural values', in Wolfson and Judd (eds.) 1983.

Manes J. and N. Wolfson. 1981. 'The compliment formula', in Coulmas (ed.) 1981.

McCawley, J. D. 1977. 'Remarks on the lexicography of performative verbs', in Rogers, Wall, and Murphy (eds.) 1977.

Mehan, H. 1979. *Learning Lessons—Social Organization in the Classroom.* Cambridge, Mass.: Harvard University Press.

Merritt, M. 1976. 'On questions following questions in service encounters'. *Language in Society* 5: 315–57.

Mishler, E. G. 1975. 'Studies in dialogue and discourse: an exponential law of successive questioning'. *Language in Society* 4: 31–51.

Mitchell-Kernan, C. and K. T. Kernan. 1977. 'Pragmatics of directive choice among children', in Ervin-Tripp and Mitchell-Kernan (eds.) 1977.

Morgan, J. L. 1977. 'Conversational postulates revisted'. *Language* 53/2: 277–84.

Ochs, E. and B. Schieffelin. (eds.) 1983. *Acquiring Conversational Competence*. London: Routledge and Kegan Paul.
Ohmann, R. 1972. 'Instrumental style: Notes on the theory of speech as actions', in Kachru and Stahlke (eds.) 1972.
Owen, M. 1983. *Apologies and Remedial Interchanges*. The Hague: Mouton.

Parret, H., M. Sbisa, and J. Verschueren. (eds.) 1981. *Possibilities and Limitations of Pragmatics: Proceedings of the Conference on Pragmatics*, Urbino, July 8–14, 1979. Amsterdam: Benjamins.
Pomerantz, A. 1978. 'Compliment responses: Notes on the co-operation of multiple constraints', in Schenkein (ed.) 1978.
Pomerantz, A. 1984. 'Agreeing and disagreeing with assessments: Some features of preferred/dispreferred turn shapes', in Atkinson and Heritage (eds.) 1984.
Psathas, G. (ed.) 1979 *Everyday Language: Studies in Ethnomethodology*. New York: Irvington.

Quirk, R., S. Greenbaum, G. Leech, and J. Svartvik. 1972. *A Grammar of Contemporary English*. London: Longman.
Quirk, R., S. Greenbaum, G. Leech, and J. Svartvik. 1985. *A Comprehensive Grammar of the English Language*. London: Longman.

Roger, D. and P. Bull. 1989. *Conversation*. Philadelphia: Multilingual Matters.
Rogers, A., B. Wall, and J. Murphy. (eds.) 1977. *Proceedings of the Texas Conference on Performatives, Presuppositions and Implicatures*. Washington: Centre for Applied Linguistics.
Rubin, J. 1983. 'How to tell when someone is saying "No" revisited', in Wolfson and Judd (eds.) 1983.

Sacks, H. 1972. 'On analyzability of stories by children', in Gumperz and Hymes (eds.) 1972.
Sacks, H. 1987. 'On the preferences for agreement and contiguity in sequences in conversations', in Button and Lee (eds.) 1987.
Sacks, H., E. Schegloff, and G. Jefferson. 1974. 'A simplest systematics for the organization of turn-taking for conversation'. *Language* 50/4: 696–753.
Sadock, J. M. 1974. *Towards a Linguistic Theory of Speech Acts*. New York: Academic Press.
Schegloff, E. 1968. 'Sequencing in conversational openings'. *American Anthropologist* 70/6: 1075–95. Also in Gumperz and Hymes (eds.) 1972.
Schegloff, E. 1972. 'Notes on a conversational practice: Formulating place', in Sudnow (ed.) 1972.
Schegloff, E. 1978. 'On some questions and ambiguities in conversation', in Dressler (ed.) 1978.
Schegloff, E. 1979. 'Identification and recognition in telephone conversation openings' in Psathas (ed.) 1979.
Schegloff, E. 1988. 'Presequences and indirection'. *Journal of Pragmatics* 12: 55–62.
Schegloff, E., G. Jefferson, and H. Sacks. 1977. 'The preference for self-correction in the organization of repair in conversation'. *Language* 53/2: 361–82.

Bibliography

Schegloff, E. and H. Sacks. 1973. 'Opening up closings'. *Semiotica* 7/4: 289–327.

Schenkein, J. (ed.) 1978. *Studies in the Organization of Conversational Interaction.* New York: Academic Press.

Schiffer, S. 1972. *Meaning.* Oxford: Clarendon Press.

Schreiber, P. A. 1972. 'Style disjuncts and the performative analysis'. *Linguistic Inquiry* 3: 321–47.

Searle, J. 1969. *Speech Acts.* Cambridge: Cambridge University Press.

Searle, J. 1979. *Expression and Meaning.* Cambridge: Cambridge University Press.

Searle, J. and D. Venderveken. 1985. *Foundations of Illocutionary Logic.* Cambridge: Cambridge University Press.

Sharrock, W. and B. Anderson. 1987. 'Epilogue. The definition of alternatives: Some sources of confusion in interdiscipinary discussion', in Button and Lee (eds.) 1987.

Shuy, R. and C. J. Bailey. (eds.) 1974. *Towards Tomorrow's Linguistics.* Georgetown: Georgetown University Press.

Sinclair, J. M. and M. Coulthard. 1975. *Towards an Analysis of Discourse.* London: Oxford University Press.

Stalnaker, R. C. 1977. 'Pragmatic presuppositions', in Rogers, Wall, and Murphy (eds.) 1977.

Steiner, E. H. and R. Veltman. (eds.) 1988. *Pragmatics, Discourse and Text.* London: Frances Pinter.

Stenström, A. 1984. *Questions and Answers in English Conversation.* Lund Studies in English, Malmo: Liber Forlag.

Stubbs, M. 1981. 'Motivating analysis of exchange structure', in Coulthard and Montgomery (eds.) 1981.

Stubbs, M. 1983. *Discourse Analysis—The Sociolinguistic Analysis of Natural Language.* Oxford: Blackwell.

Sudnow, D. (ed.) 1972. *Studies in Social Interaction.* New York: Free Press.

Tannen, D. 1984. *Conversational Style.* Norwood, N.J.: Ablex.

Taylor, T. J. and D. Cameron. 1987. *Analyzing Conversation.* Oxford: Pergamon Press.

Tsui, A. B. M. 1985. 'Analyzing input and interaction in second language classrooms'. *RELC Journal* 16/1: 8–32.

Tsui, A. B. M. 1987a. 'Analyzing different types of interaction in ESL classrooms'. *International Review of Applied Linguistics in Language Teaching* (IRAL) XXV/4: 336–53.

Tsui, A. B. M. 1987b. 'On elicitations', in Coulthard (ed.) 1987.

Tsui, A. B. M. 1987c. 'Aspects of the classification of illocutionary acts and the notion of a perlocutionary act'. *Semiotica* 66/4: 359–77.

Tsui, A. B. M. 1989. 'Beyond the "adjacency pair"'. *Language in Society* 18/4: 545–64.

Tsui, A. B. M. 1991a. 'The pragmatic functions of "I don't know"'. *TEXT*, 11/4: 607–22.

Tsui, A. B. M. 1991b. 'The interpenetration of language as code and language as behaviour', in Ventola (ed.) 1991.

Tsui, A. B. M. 1991c. 'Sequencing rules and coherence in discourse'. *Journal of Pragmatics* 15: 111–29.

Tsui, A. B. M. 1991d. 'The description of utterances in conversation', in Verschueren (ed.) 1991.

Tsui, A. B. M. 1992. 'A functional description of questions', in Coulthard (ed.) 1992.

Turner, G. J. 1987. 'Sociosemantic networks and discourse structure', in Halliday and Fawcett (eds.), Vol. I, 1987.

Van Dijk, T. A. 1981. *Studies in the Pragmatics of Discourse.* The Hague: Mouton.

Vendler, Z. 1972. *Res Cogitans.* Ithaca, N.Y.: Cornell University Press.

Vendler, Z. 1976. 'Illocutionary suicide', in Mackay and Merill (eds.) 1976.

Ventola, E. 1987. *The Structure of Social Interaction.* London: Frances Pinter.

Ventola, E. (ed.) 1991. *Recent Systemic and Other Functional Views on Language.* Berlin, New York: Mouton de Gruyter.

Verschueren, J. (ed.) 1991. *Pragmatics at Issue,* Vol. I. Amsterdam/Philadelphia: John Benjamins.

Willis, J. 1981. *Spoken Discourse in the E.L.T. Classroom: A System of Analysis and Description.* Unpublished MA thesis, University of Birmingham.

Wolfson, N. 1983. 'An empirically based analysis of complimenting in American English', in Wolfson and Judd (eds.) 1983.

Wolfson, N. and **E. Judd.** (eds.) 1983. *Sociolinguistics and Language Acquisition.* Rowley, Mass.: Newbury House.

Index

Entries relate to Chapters 1 to 10, the glossary, and the notes. References to the glossary are indicated by 'g' and to the notes by 'n'.

293

Index